THEORIES OF MODERNITY AND POSTMODERNITY

Theory, Culture & Society

Theory, Culture & Society caters for the resurgence of interest in culture within contemporary social science and the humanities. Building on the heritage of classical social theory, the book : eries examines ways in which this tradition has been reshaped by a new generation of theorists. It will also publish theoretically informed analyses of everyday life, popular culture, and new intellectual movements.

EDITOR: Mike Featherstone, *Teesside Polytechnic*

SERIES EDITORIAL BOARD
Roy Boyne, *Newcastle upon Tyne Polytechnic*
Mike Hepworth, *University of Aberdeen*
Scott Lash, *University of Lancaster*
Roland Robertson, *University of Pittsburgh*
Bryan S. Turner, *University of Essex*

Also in this series

Reproduction in Education, Society and Culture
Revised edition
Pierre Bourdieu and Jean-Claude Passeron

The Tourist Gaze
Leisure and Travel in Contemporary Societies
John Urry

Global Culture
Nationalism, Globalization and Modernity
edited by Mike Featherstone

Theories of Modernity and Postmodernity

EDITED BY
BRYAN S. TURNER

SAGE Publications
London • Newbury Park • New Delhi

First published 1990
Reprinted 1991

 SAGE Publications Ltd
28 Banner Street
London EC1Y 8QE

SAGE Publications Inc
2111 West Hillcrest Drive
Newbury Park, California 91320

SAGE Publications India Pvt Ltd
32, M-Block Market
Greater Kailash – I
New Delhi 110 048

British Library Cataloguing in Publication data

Theories of modernity and postmodernity. – (Theory, culture
    and society).
    1. Culture. Postmodernism
    I. Turner, Bryan S. (Bryan Stanley), *1945–*   II. Series
306

    ISBN 0–8039–8370–0
    ISBN 0–8039–8371–9 pbk

Library of Congress catalog card number 90–61357

Typeset by Fakenham Photosetting Ltd, Fakenham, Norfolk
Printed in Great Britain by Billing and Sons Ltd, Worcester

CONTENTS

CONTRIBUTORS

David Ashley, Department of Sociology, University of Wyoming, Laramie, USA. He has published various articles on sociological theory in *Sociological Perspectives*, *Symbolic Interaction*, and *Current Perspectives in Social Theory,* among other journals and anthologies.

Ayşegül Baykan, Department of Sociology, Washington and Jefferson College, Pittsburgh, USA. Her doctoral dissertation from the University of Pittsburgh (1988) was on 'The Transition from the Ottoman Empire to Turkish Republic'.

Norman K. Denzin, Department of Sociology, University of Illinois at Urbana-Champaign, USA. His most recent publications include *On Understanding Emotion* and *The Alcoholic Self*. Professor Denzin is the editor of *Studies in Symbolic Interaction*.

Scott Lash, Department of Sociology, Lancaster University, UK. He is author of *Sociology of Postmodernism* and the co-author (with John Urry) of *The End of Organized Capitalism*. He edited (with Sam Whimster) *Max Weber, Rationality and Modernity*.

Roland Robertson, Department of Sociology, University of Pittsburgh, USA. He has written many books and articles on sociological theory, sociology of religion and globality, including *Meaning and Change*, *The Sociological Interpretation of Religion*, and (with Peter Nettl) *International Systems and the Modernization of Societies*.

Adam B. Seligman, Department of Sociology, University of California, Los Angeles, USA. He has published *Order and Transcendence: The Role of Utopias and the Dynamics of Civilizations*, and (with S.N. Eistenstadt and L. Roniger) *Centre Formation Protest Movements and Class Structure in Europe and the United States*.

Barry Smart, Department of Sociology, University of Auckland, New Zealand. He has published a number of studies on sociological theory including *Sociology, Phenomenology and Marxian Analysis*, *Foucault, Marxism and Critique* and *Michel Foucault*. He is the editor of *Social Futures* for Routledge.

Lieteke van Vucht Tijssen, Faculty of Social Sciences, University of Utrecht, The Netherlands. She has published a number of studies of Max Weber, Max Scheler, relativism, and sociological theory. Her research interests include the study of women intellectuals in Weimar Germany.

Bryan S. Turner, Department of Sociology, University of Essex, UK. He has published a number of volumes on sociology of religion, sociological theory and medical sociology, including *The Body and Society*, *Religion and Social Theory*, *Medical Power and Social Knowledge*, and (with Georg Stauth) *Nietzsche's Dance*.

Charles Turner, Department of Sociology, Goldsmiths' College, University of London, UK. His doctoral dissertation was on 'Modernity and Politics in the work of Max Weber', and he has published a number of articles on sociological theory.

Deena Weinstein, Department of Sociology, De Paul University, Chicago, Illinois, USA. She is the author of *Bureaucratic Opposition* and *Serious Rock*. She translated (with Michael Weinstein) Georg Simmel's *Schopenhauer and Nietzsche*.

Michael Weinstein, Department of Political Science, Purdue University, West Lafayette, Indiana, USA. He has published a number of works on political science, philosophy, sociology and criticism, including *Culture Critique* and *Finite Perfection: Reflections on Virtue*.

Philip Wexler, Graduate School of Education and Human Development, University of Rochester, New York, USA. He is the author of *Social Analysis of Education: After the New Sociology*, *Critical Social Psychology* and *The Sociology of Education: Beyond Equality*. He is the editor of *Critical Theory Now* (in press) and of the journal, *Sociology of Education*.

PART ONE

INTRODUCTION: DEFINING POSTMODERNITY

1

PERIODIZATION AND POLITICS IN THE POSTMODERN

Bryan S. Turner

Modernity and postmodernity

In this introductory comment I address three major issues. The first task is to establish some parameters of meaning for the use of the principal concepts in the chapters which follow. In this discussion, the objective is to establish the irredeemably contested nature of the two major concepts: modernity and postmodernity. It is not possible to impose, by a definitional fiat, an agreed set of terms for debate, precisely because these issues are essentially contested. There are no agreed terms of reference, which would be binding on the contestants and which could bring about some practical outcome. Postmodernism in sociology rules out any such simplistic agreement. Secondly, my introduction raises the great difficulty of finding an adequate periodization of modernity and postmodernity. In particular, if postmodernity is an effect of a deep *fin-de-siècle* crisis, then it is interesting to compare other historical periods that experienced major and traumatic crises, especially in western Europe. There is, for example, an increasing focus on the legacy of the Baroque crisis in contemporary historical sociology, art history and social theory. This parallel interest in Baroque and postmodernity is not an accident. Finally, I sketch an outline of the complicated relationship between postmodernism and radical politics. Although postmodernism has often been associated with neo-conservatism, partly as a consequence of Jürgen Habermas's view of modernity as an incomplete project (Habermas, 1981), I conclude that there can be an important alliance between progressive politics (in gender issues, multicultural alternatives to racism, in ecology movements and cultural criticism) and postmodernism. However, much of the misunderstanding about the political nature of postmodernism is an effect of different politico-cultural contexts as between America and Germany. These differences are the long-term consequences of different wartime and post-war experiences, especially in relation to the legacy of fascism. Within a broader context, it is necessary to raise again the problem of the relationship between modernity, rationality and the Holocaust (Bauman, 1989). Thus, whether or not postmodernism is reactionary or progressive will depend a great deal on whether we view postmodernism as anti-modernism or beyond modernism.

Although the notion of postmodernism in art history and aesthetic theory is relatively well established, it is only in the last decade that there has been any significant or general interest in postmodernism in the social sciences (Featherstone, 1988). However, it is clearly the case that postmodernism as an issue is much older than the current fashion in sociology might suggest. For example, it is now common to refer to Arnold Toynbee's *Study in History* (vol. 8) as one location of the notion of a postmodern era emerging with the growing importance of multiculturalism as a consequence of Europe's expanding penetration of other (increasingly subordinate) cultures (Owens, 1985). Furthermore, as Jürgen Habermas (1987) has noted, the very intensity of the debate in sociology, especially in the works of Max Weber, over the nature of the process of modernization eventually laid the foundations for a debate as to what might follow modernity. Indeed, I shall argue later that Weber's ambiguity about modernization as rationalization pre-dated the contemporary question mark over the modern (Holton and Turner, 1989). The importance of Weber's notions about the autonomy of the various spheres of social and cultural institutions is also analysed in this volume by Charles Turner, but the Weberian version of differentiation is not a bland pluralism, but a vision of endless value conflicts and antagonisms. The secular problem of antagonistic value conflicts means that a 'grand narrative' of personal meaning is not available in later modernism, apart from the minimalist redemption made possible by a 'calling' in science or politics.

We should identify one further precursor of the contemporary debate in sociology over postmodernity, namely Daniel Bell's development of the idea of the post-industrial society (1973) and the inevitability of cultural contradictions inside capitalism (1976). Indeed, it is ironic that, given the pounding which the concept of 'post-industrialism' received in the 1970s, the theory of post-industrial society has returned with a vengeance. It is probably important to stress that, until recently, Bell's contribution to the postmodern debate had been seriously neglected (O'Neill, 1988). The relationship between post-industrial and postmodern societies has yet to be fully explored (Turner, 1989), but Bell's view of the centrality of knowledge and information to post-industrialism is an important ingredient for the foundations of postmodern theory, especially in J.-F. Lyotard's *The Postmodern Condition* (1984). This claim is not to suggest, of course, that the *whole* of Lyotard's view of postmodernism is indebted to Bell's view of the relationship between the new technologies of communication and postindustrialism. Lyotard not only draws on a far wider range of sources, but his work is far more concerned than is the case for Bell, with the consequences of post-structuralist semiotics and deconstructionism for western systems of rationalism (Benjamin, 1989; Lyotard, 1988). However, Bell's contribution to the debate is not confined simply to an analysis of the information revolution and its consequences for production, authority and politics. His critical attack on the assumptions of unity and coherence of social systems, which he claims are analytical flaws in structuralism from Comte to Parsons, permitted him to develop the idea of contradictory principles between culture, society and politics (Bell, 1982). This critique of social systems integration was an important step in the development of the rejection of structuralism.

Thus, while it is possible to identify a number of important streams of social theory leading into the contemporary fascination with the postmodern, there is little agreement about the meaning of the concepts. Various contributions to this collection succinctly outline a number of possibilities. Following Habermas (1987), Barry Smart points out that the term 'modern' can be traced back to the fifth-century Latin term *modernus* to differentiate the Christian from the pagan era. He also notes that the contemporary use of the term has its roots in Kant's conception of a universal history, which would be a distinctive break with the past. Unfortunately, we now have a proliferation of terms: modernity, modernism, modernization and modern. In his contribution, Scott Lash argues that we should follow Weber and Habermas in regarding modernization as a process of cultural differentiation and social autonomization (Lash, 1987), thereby defining modernism as the late nineteenth-century effect of the process of differentiation. David Ashley in this collection has also identified this notion of differentiation in the work of Habermas as an important defining characteristic of the process of modernization. In the art world, this cultural differentiation and autonomy gave rise to a new aestheticism under the slogan 'art for art's sake'. The result was to place Baudelaire's *Les fleurs du mal* at the centre of the modern/postmodern debate, which was prefigured in Nietzsche's fascination with Baudelaire's nihilism (Stauth and Turner, 1988). It also explains why the issues raised by Baudelaire's decadence found a central place in Walter Benjamin's *Das Passagen-Werk* (1982).

In the world of social sciences, differentiation was an important condition for the emergence of sociology and the idea of the 'social' as a separate and autonomous sphere. At the same time, modernism is a rejection of history. If modernization is differentiation, then postmodernism is cultural de-differentiation; it emerges with late consumer capitalism, and opposes avant-garde art and high culture (Jameson 1984; Lash and Urry, 1987). Postmodernism is thus often associated with a society in which consumer life-styles and mass consumption dominate taste and fashion (Kellner, 1983). With the spread of a modern mass technology of communications, it is not only that there is a great expansion of services and a leisure industry (and a concomitant new middle class), but there is a growing simulation of reality. This implosion of signs eventually undermines our sense of reality (Baudrillard, 1983). The result is that, in our media-dominated world 'the concept of meaning itself (which depends on stable boundaries, fixed structures, shared consensus) dissolves' (Kellner, 1989: 12). In this collection, Norman Denzin explores how the media reconstructs an image of reality (the yuppy world of finance capital), which not only reacts with reality, but attempts to re-establish an imaginary and nostalgic world of heroic capitalist enterprise.

Postmodernism in its populist form also threatens to shatter hierarchies of taste established by expert opinion. Although in his highly influential work on modern systems of consumer hierarchy, Pierre Bourdieu has tried to map the somewhat rigid national hierarchies of distinction (1984) in France, postmodernism in culture involves a playful (in fact, distasteful) mixing of kitsch culture with *haute couture*. Postmodern styles appropriate pop, but also mimic and reproduce it within high culture. Intellectuals in western societies increasingly intervene in the popular market to offer interpretations and meanings for the most transitory phenomena of mass culture – from MTV (Grossberg, 1989) to *Chariots of Fire* (Collins, 1989). However, as intellectuals are absorbed into popular culture, their traditional roles in the hierarchy of 'objective' expertise is also brought into question (Ross, 1989).

Yet, as Barry Smart points out, these meanings of modern and post-modern vary between different social science and humanities traditions. In America, postmodern criticisms in the 1960s of the institutionalization of high culture and the incorporation of modernism were reactions against the culture industry, and in this respect they were consistent with an older European avant-garde tradition. One should add the note that in Germany the defence of (an unfinished) modernity has assumed a much more open and overt political significance, as a defence against (what is seen to be) the anti-rationalism of the conservative and neo-conservative critique of modern society. David Ashley in this volume draws attention to Habermas's long-standing conflicts with the followers of Foucault and Baudrillard, and we might add Bataille and Derrida.

Thus, modernity is broadly about the massive social and cultural changes which took place from the middle of the sixteenth century, and it is consequently and necessarily bound up with the analysis of industrial capitalist society as a revolutionary break with tradition and a social stability founded on a relatively stagnant agrarian civilization. Modernity was about conquest – the imperial regulation of land, the discipline of the soul, and the creation of truth. In order to understand the contemporary critique of modernism, it is essential therefore to grasp the impact of Foucault on contemporary social theory, since it was Foucault who, through a number of brilliant studies of discourses (of psychology, penology, sexuality and so forth), challenged the rationalist pretensions of modern systems of power.

The question of postmodernism is a question about the possible limits of the process of modernization. Nevertheless, there appears to be persistent confusion about the content and scope of the terminology in this debate. In part, this confusion arises from the competitive struggle between intellectuals to control the debate, to exercise influence over the nature of the dispute, and to manage the 'cultural capital' in the marketing field which is associated with postmodernism. The proliferation of terms and their variable meanings are an effect of conflicts between different sectors of the intellectual market-place for influence (Featherstone, 1988). There is, however, a more important feature to this dispute over terminology.

Postmodernism has encouraged the view that the various fields and specialisms in the sciences are primarily strategies or conventions by which 'reality' is divided up, partly as a consequence of the intense struggle over truth by social groups in the quest for power. This view partly also explains the centrality of Nietzsche's will-to-power thesis within contemporary epistemology; the quest for truth is always the establishment of power. Nietzsche's emphasis on the arbitrary character of the grammatical structure of argument and rhetoric has remained an important part of the weaponry of postmodern forms of deconstructive criticism. Nietzsche's perspectivism laid the foundations for the contemporary emphasis on the textuality of life, on life as literature (Nehamas, 1985). In fact this scepticism towards the separation and autonomy of disciplines and fields is a defining characteristic of radical postmodernism, which broadly speaking is committed to 'a critique of Western representation(s) and modern "supreme fictions"; a desire to think in terms sensitive to difference (of others without opposition, of heterogeneity without hierarchy); a skepticism regarding autonomous "spheres" of culture or separate "fields" of experts' (Foster 1985: xv). If postmodernism is thus committed to open textuality, it is hardly possible to adopt a rigid or formal consensus about what postmodernity is. The very playfulness of postmodernism(s) precludes any premature foreclosure of its own meaning. Here again Nietszche's epistemology looms large: anything which has a history cannot be defined.

To express this issue somewhat differently, what many postmodern texts fail to make clear is whether we are in search of a sociology of postmodernism or a postmodern sociology (Featherstone, 1988), an issue which is discussed by Barry Smart in this volume. A sociology of postmodernism tends to locate postmodern culture in a context of disorganized capitalism, of consumer society and cultural mass production. The struggle over high and low culture is the cultural expression of new class or social divisions between the traditional defenders of high culture and a new mobile class which seeks to impose alternative standards and to ridicule the pretensions of 'serious' scholarship (Featherstone, 1987). Postmodern culture is the cultural product of the yuppy classes, who have enjoyed such enormous social success during the financial boom of the 1980s. Here again this 'reality' is expressed by films like *Wall Street*. This sociology of postmodernism, which attempts to understand the nature of our present crisis through an analysis, for example, of the structural location of the intellectuals (Bauman, 1988), is significantly different from a postmodern sociology, which might, amongst other things, seek to deconstruct such foundational assumptions, and which would regard 'the social' as problematic. However, the prospects of creating a 'genuine' postmodern social theory are equally difficult, for reasons that Habermas has potently outlined. He argues, for example, that Foucault is caught in the paradox of 'the performative contradiction', because Foucault is ultimately forced to use the tools of reason which he wants to overthrow. In short, can anti-foundationalism exist without foundations? In this introduction, I want to continue to pursue the idea of a sociology of postmodernism by examining the periodization of modernity (primarily within a Weberian framework). Roland Robertson's research on globalism and sociology, aspects of which are explored in his contribution to this volume, is especially important for locating sociology itself within various phases of the globalization. It is only by getting a perspective on modernization that we can begin to think about what post-modernization might sociologically entail; in my view, the most direct way into modernization is still via Weber's sociology of rationalization.

Periodizing modernization

Although Weber is often narrowly associated with a debate about the origins of capitalism in the famous Protestant Ethic thesis, it is more appropriate to interpret him as a theorist of modernization, of which the key component can be identified as rationalization. Modernity is thus the consequence of a process of modernization, by which the social world comes under the domination of asceticism, secularization, the universalistic claims of instrumental rationality, the differentiation of the various spheres of the life-world, the bureaucratization of economic, political and military practices, and the growing monetarization of values. Modernity therefore arises with the spread of western imperialism in the sixteenth century; the dominance of capitalism in northern Europe, especially in England, Holland and Flanders in the early seventeenth century; the acceptance of scientific procedures with the publication of the works of Francis Bacon, Newton and Harvey; and pre-eminently with the institutionalization of Calvinistic practices and beliefs in the dominant classes of northern Europe. We can follow this process further through the separation of the family from the wider kinship group, the separation of the household and the economy, and the creation of the institution of motherhood in the nineteenth century. Although the idea of the citizen can be traced back to Greek times via the independent cities of the Italian states (Turner, 1986), the citizen as the abstract carrier of universal rights is a distinctively modern idea. This historical sketch can be regarded as the kernel of Weber's account of modernization, especially from his *General Economic History* (1981) and *The City* (1958).

The essential feature of Weber's view of modernity is, however, its ambiguity. Modernization brings with it the erosion of meaning, the endless conflict of polytheistic values, and the threat of the iron cage of bureaucracy.

Rationalization makes the world orderly and reliable, but it cannot make the world meaningful. In some respects, therefore, Weber articulated in his historical sociology the very general ambiguities and doubts about modern capitalism which haunted the world-view of the nineteenth-century German mandarins (Ringer, 1969). The loss of *Gemeinschaft* and the threat of *Gesellschaft* were themes which were widespread, not only in German sociology, but more generally in the humanities and literature. While Weber had anticipated the black apocalyptic vision of the end of modernity (as a collapse into a meaningless iron cage of bureaucratic domination, as the rise of mediocrity, and as the control of the world by men without heart or spirit), he also in some respects avoided the nostalgia, that is widespread in the conservative *and* radical rejections of capitalism.

Rainer Maria Rilke's view of America and capitalist technology was typical in expressing a conservative, anti-modernism; in a famous letter he wrote that America had come to Europe via 'empty, indifferent things, artificial things that deceive us by simulating life' (Rilke, 1950: 898). This view of America has some resemblance to Baudrillard's *America* (1988), in that Baudrillard also writes about America in terms of simulation and artificiality, and yet the two visions are also very different. Baudrillard argues that the problem for the United States is 'the crisis of an achieved utopia, confronted with the problem of its duration and permanence' (1988: 77), whereas the European problem (the problem of the Old World generally) is the failure to achieve its ideals (in the French Revolution, in Soviet-style communism, or in the modern ideals of citizenship). Thus, Baudrillard condemns two types of nostalgia: the American nostalgia for the fine virtues and values of the Old World, and the European nostalgia for the promise of a New Land. Europeans are 'nostalgic utopians', professing everything is really possible, but never achieving anything.

Nostalgia thus emerges as a crucial product of modernization, because the strains and uncertainties of such rapid and large-scale change generates, especially in the intellectual classes, a nostalgia for the values of a more traditional society, in which the intellectual had an esteemed and worthy position as the guardian of high culture. As it has become devastatingly clear (with the invasion of Hungary in 1956, the events of 1968, the ethnic crisis in the Soviet Union, the catastrophe of the reaction against modernization on the part of the Chinese gerontocracy, and the collapse of the authority of communist parties in eastern Europe) that organized twentieth-century communism is a failure, nostalgic memories of more heroic days will become a more persistent theme of *fin-de-siècle* socialism (Jay, 1988). Nostalgia, memory and time occupy an important place in a number of contributions to this book. In particular, Roland Robertson draws our attention to the strange but prevalent interrelationships between nineteenth-century nationalism, the rise of sociology and the imaginary (and nostalgic) constitution of communities.

Of course, like modernism itself, there are many varieties of nostalgia. Kant in his pragmatic anthropology identified a positive nostalgia in which sympathetic nostalgia emerged as a crucial dimension of positive moral values, while for Maurice Halbwachs nostalgia was a therapeutic quest for our lost youth (Vromen, 1986). Robertson usefully identifies wilful nostalgia as an important ingredient in the modern invention of national traditions, and carefully charts the role of sociology in relation to the construction of modern national identities. In the twentieth century, as the horrors of Auschwitz were gradually discovered and perhaps more rapidly forgotten, there was a new nostalgia for innocence. He identifies a new consumerist nostalgia, which is combined in the American case with Reaganite conservatism. Norman Denzin's chapter is equally concerned with the new consumerist nostalgia, this time in the shape of such apparently realistic films as *Wall Street*. In a careful reading of the film, Denzin shows how this apparently raw, anti-capitalist film is in fact a nostalgic celebration of the family, heroism and decency. Films of this genre sustain the myth of traditional American capitalism, in which there are heroes who can still sustain a distinction between the moral and the immoral. The nostalgia of *Wall Street* lies in its forlorn quest for real values, real time or real sex. For Denzin, Baudrillard's argument that we live in a postmodern world of simulations rules out any possible quest for the real. We are already in hyper-reality (Eco, 1986).

The theme of nostalgia is further explored by Deena Weinstein and Michael Weinstein in this volume in their evaluation of Simmel's theory of postmodern society. They deny that Simmel shared what we may call the nostalgic paradigm of anti-modernism (Stauth and Turner, 1988), because Simmel both expressed, and to some extent accepted, the cosmopolitanism of Berlin, the spread of money values, and the emerging cultural phenomena of artistic expressionism and philosophical pragmatism. While Simmel was a critic of modern times, he was not, they argue, a pessimistic or nihilistic theorist. Simmel escaped the fate of a 'man without qualities'; he was a cultural diagnostician of the crisis of modern culture, far removed from the blind fatalism of Schopenhauer.

This periodization of modernity via a commentary on Weber's ambiguity as to the cultural significance of rationalization for a person of vocations has drawn attention to this theme of nostalgia, because what both modernists and postmodernists share in common is the assumption that there is a late twentieth-century crisis, and this crisis, while manifest especially in the complexity and artificiality of consumer culture, is also a crisis of politics. Is this crisis unique, or are there precursors of our modern sense of crisis? Is it valuable or possible to draw comparisons between (say) the crisis of the 1890s (with its early manifestations of modern antisemitism) and the contemporary crisis? I want to suggest, largely inspired by the work of Christine Buci-Glucksmann in *La raison baroque* (1984) and *La folie du voir* (1986), that for sociologists there are some fascinating parallels between the Baroque crisis of the first half of the seventeenth century, and the crisis of modernity at the close of the twentieth century.

Like our own time, the Baroque crisis, especially in Spain and France, was sparked off by unmanageable fiscal crises resulting from a transformation of the world economy, and it was associated with a chronic urban crisis of population growth and urban unrest. More importantly, Baroque politics were a response to the cultural crisis of the Protestant Reformation, and its associated individualism and commercialism. The creation of an absolutist state was the attempt by a threatened nobility to re-establish the old order and to re-create the authority of the old moral system by producing a mass culture of affects, which through the stimulation of the emotions, would ideologically reincorporate the various social groups and classes into an authoritarian system (Anderson, 1974; Maravall, 1986). The result was the theodicy of Leibniz (we live in the best of all possible worlds) as a justification of absolutism; the Sun King was the embodiment of Baroque virtue in which the king's body was the narrative script of the state (Marin, 1988); Shakespeare's *Hamlet* as an exploration of the Oedipal legend, passive intellectuality and the textuality of reality; Monteverdi's music as an alchemy of sound; and the sexualization of divinity in Bernini's adoration sculptures, especially in *The Ecstasy of St Theresa* (Buci-Glucksmann, 1986). These components of the Baroque style were explored in a classic text by Benjamin on the history of German tragic drama (Benjamin, 1955). The crucial issue is that Baroque art in its luxurious fantasies celebrated artificiality, mixing high and low culture, and playfully manipulated kitsch to produce, through its own version of the culture industry, a mass culture. Furthermore, the Baroque fascination with allegory, with *trompe-l'œil* creations, with mechanical devices and constructions, with artificial ruins, with melancholy, and with metaphor anticipated the postmodern fascination with texts about texts, with stories inside narratives, with simulations – in a word, with the socially constructed textuality of reality.

The main objection to such a comparison would be that modernization also involved democratization, and that, however faulty and underdeveloped, there are a set of institutions which in the modern world protect the citizen from the full onslaught of naked egoism, namely the market. Absolutism was an attempt to centralize power in the body of a king (or on rare occasions a queen) to the exclusion of intervening forces or institutions. Modern citizenship rules out absolutism, and hence the comparison is both weak and misleading. While this is a forceful objection, it is possible to argue that the modern political world is threatened by decisionism, by presidential government of the Reagan variety which is not sufficiently accountable, or by the authoritarianism of Thatcherite conservatism. The problem with democracy, as de Tocqueville clearly recognized in his analysis of America, is that the radical commitment to the principle of equality may destroy any tolerance of difference and opposition, in which case egalitarian democracy destroys liberal pluralism. Democracy may thus produce Terror (Lefort, 1988). This problem is an important feature, therefore, of Habermas's critique of postmodernism – a critique which is explored in this volume by David Ashley, Charles Turner and Barry Smart, and by Adam Seligman in his discussion of the relationship between the private and the public, the

particular and the universal. If modernity involves a principle of emancipation, because modern reason was an attack on ancient superstitions, then
Habermas wants to regard postmodernism as necessarily opposed to the
political framework of modernity, namely liberty, equality and freedom.

Postmodern politics: the death of the citizen?

In terms of practical consequences, the question concerning postmodernism's relation to radical politics is the most pressing issue of contemporary
social science. Several chapters in this issue address this problem, especially
insofar as postmodernism may transform the status of women (Ayşegül
Baykan and Lieteke van Vucht Tijssen), the nature of citizenship in the
semiotic society (P. Wexler) and urban politics (Scott Lash). The problem
may be briefly stated. If one believes that traditional society was based on
hierarchy, inequality and violence, then the modernist critique of tradition is
progressive. If, however, one regards the gas chambers as the final resting
point of modernization, then postmodern objections to modern instrumental rationalism are progressive. Again much rests on the definition of
postmodernism itself, and on the national context within which this debate is
taking place. In my view, it is crucial to our argument whether postmodernism is anti-modernism or after modernism.

As David Ashley points out, Baudrillard argues that the end of modernity
is simultaneously the end of the social and the termination of bourgeois
democracy, including the institutions of freedom of speech and human
rights. There is in fact much about Baudrillard, especially in his study of
America, which resembles a prophet crying in the wilderness, and it is
perhaps no accident that he claims that the American desert best represents
American civilization. As the Israelite prophets stood alone in the desert
cursing the wealth and corruption of Jerusalem, so Baudrillard stands in
fascinated horror before what he calls the astral spectacle of the American
consumer dream. He declares that 'My hunting grounds are deserts . . . I
know the deserts, their deserts, better than they do, since they turn their
backs on their own space as the Greeks turned their backs on the sea'
(Baudrillard, 1988: 63). If there is a submerged religious paradigm in
Baudrillard, then of course it is not only the case that his version of
postmodernism is not beyond modernism, but it is an anti-modernism.
Although Baudrillard fights against this possibility, one can read *America* as
Baudrillard's *moral* pilgrimage to the New Land. He condemns European
intellectuals for their bad nostalgia (their flawed moral paradigm), but his
own work can be read as a quest for the real, which disappears before his
eyes like a mirage in the desert. In other words, Baudrillard's version of
postmodernism is still a modernist interpretation of civilization in terms of
failures (Europe's lost revolutions) and achievements (America's realized
utopia).

However, Baudrillard is not the only possible version of postmodernism.

It is possible to be postmodern (without nostalgia for *Gemeinschaft*) without being anti-modern (without rejecting the achievements of bourgeois civil society; that is, the achievements of social relations based on *Gesellschaft*). It is too easy to dismiss the civil rights which did emerge with the development of bourgeois capitalism. As Habermas recognizes, the rationality of bourgeois civilization was a very real and radical challenge to the traditionalism of feudal society. Most critics of so-called bourgeois rationality typically find themselves in a contradiction, because they have to appeal to the very standards of argumentation which they want to challenge or dismiss. As Alasdair MacIntyre noted in his critical study of Herbert Marcuse, 'The institutionalization of rationality was one of the great achievements of bourgeois society' (MacIntyre, 1970: 91). To put this more controversially, critics of bourgeois capitalism too easily forget that it was the city market which gave the peasant free air, and it was the market (or more broadly exchange relations) which played host to individualism, universalism, liberty based on a social contract and freedom (Holton and Turner, 1989). It is this type of modernism which Marshall Berman, along with Marx, wants to celebrate. It is modernism which thus paradoxically lays the foundations of postmodernism by pure destruction, because 'All that is solid melts into air' (Berman, 1982).

If we can thus see postmodernity as beyond rather than against modernity, then we can also perceive the radical qualities of postmodern criticism. In a move which is clearly unfashionable, I want to conclude by claiming that postmodernism can be regarded as a form of post-liberalism or hyper-liberalism, and thus ultimately compatible with the radical contents of modernity. I refer to this solution as 'unfashionable', because most contemporary radicals want to avoid the connotations of the term 'liberal'. Thus, Foster warns us that 'postmodernism is not pluralism – the quixotic notion that all positions in culture and politics are now open and equal' (1985: xi). Yet, the classical liberal tradition of writers like J.S. Mill did not argue for a pluralism in which anything goes, but rather that differences should be both protected and promoted. It was precisely against the view that all cultural positions are equally acceptable (that is, against Bentham's notion that pushpin is as good as poetry) that Mill developed a moral defence of individual differences. The argument is *not* that Mill's liberalism was postmodern, but rather that the postmodern critique of hierarchy, grand narratives, unitary notions of authority, or the bureaucratic imposition of official values has a certain parallel with the principles of toleration of difference in the liberal tradition.

This radical aspect of postmodernism is often associated with the feminist critique of (male) notions of sameness and hierarchy. For example, in this volume Lieteke van Vucht Tijssen brings out a possible alliance between postmodernism and feminist radicalism, because postmodern epistemology provides a powerful case against unitary notions of 'man' and 'woman'. Thus, if we wanted a slogan that might express the ambitions of both a radical version of modernist liberalism and postmodern politics, it might be

'Here's to heterogeneity'. Consequently, if we can understand postmodernism as genuinely after- rather than anti-modern, it clears the ground for new political and social strategies which embrace difference, pluralism and the incommensurability of cultures and values. Postmodernism as after-the-modern might successfully avoid the paralytic nostalgia for *Gemeinschaft* which haunted anti-modern romanticism, while also making possible the development of a new style of politics which would be simultaneously post-Marxist and post-liberal.

Note

In developing my general view of the modern/postmodern debate, I am immeasurably indebted to Mike Featherstone, editor of *Theory, Culture and Society*, Willem van Reijen, the Rijksuniversiteit Utrecht, Roland Robertson, University of Pittsburgh, and to Georg Stauth, the co-author of *Nietzsche's Dance*. The chapters in this volume, except for the paper by Adam Seligman, were originally given as public lectures at the San Francisco conference of the American Sociological Association in 1989 in the special session on theories of modernity and postmodernity, which I organized. Various members of the ASA conference committee were particularly helpful in making the two sessions possible, and in particular I would like to thank Janet Astner, convention manager, for her support.

References

Anderson, P. (1974) *Lineages of the Absolutist State*. London: NLB.

Baudrillard, J. (1983) *Simulations*. New York: Semiotext(e).

Baudrillard, J. (1988) *America*. London: Verso.

Bauman, Z. (1988) 'Is there a postmodern sociology?' *Theory, Culture and Society*, 5 (2–3): 217–38.

Bauman, Z. (1989) *Modernity and the Holocaust*. Cambridge: Polity Press.

Bell, D. (1973) *The Coming of Post-Industrial Society*. New York: Basic Books.

Bell, D. (1976) *The Cultural Contradictions of Capitalism*. New York: Basic Books.

Bell, D. (1982) *The Social Sciences since the Second World War*. New Brunswick and London: Transaction Books.

Benjamin, A. (ed.) (1989) *The Lyotard Reader*. Cambridge: Polity Press.

Benjamin, W. (1955) *Ursprung des deutschen Trauerspiels*. Frankfurt am Main: Suhrkamp.

Benjamin, W. (1982) *Das Passagen-Werk*. Frankfurt am Main: Suhrkamp, 2 vols.

Berman, M. (1982) *All that is Solid Melts into Air: The Experience of Modernity*. London: Verso.

Bourdieu, P. (1984) *Distinction: A Social Critique of the Judgement of Taste*. London: Routledge & Kegan Paul.

Buci-Glucksmann, C. (1984) *La raison baroque, Baudelaire à Benjamin*. Paris: Galilée.

Buci-Glucksmann, C. (1986) *La folie du voir, de l'esthétique baroque*. Paris: Galilée.

Collins, J. (1989) *Uncommon Cultures: Popular Culture and Post-modernism*. New York and London: Routledge.

Eco, U. (1986) *Travels in Hyper-reality*. London: Pan.

Featherstone, M. (1987) 'Postmodernism and the new middle class', paper presented at the ISLP Conference on Postmodernism, Lawrence, Kansas.

Featherstone, M. (1988) 'In pursuit of the postmodern: An introduction', *Theory, Culture and Society*, 5 (2–3): 195–216.

Foster, H. (ed.) (1985) *Postmodern Culture*. London and Sydney: Pluto Press.

Grossberg, L. (1989) 'MTV: Swinging on the (postmodern) star', in I. Angus and S. Jhally (eds), *Cultural Politics in Contemporary America*. New York and London: Routledge. pp. 254–68.

Habermas, J. (1981) 'Modernity versus postmodernity', *New German Critique*, 22: 3–14.

Habermas, J. (1987) *The Philosophical Discourse of Modernity*. Cambridge: Polity Press.

Holton, R.J. and Turner, B.S. (1989) *Max Weber on Economy and Society*. London: Routledge.

Jameson, F. (1984) 'Postmodernism, or the cultural logic of late capitalism', *New Left Review*, 146 (July–August): 53–65.

Jay, M. (1988) *Fin-de-siècle Socialism*, New York and London: Routledge.

Kellner, D. (1983) 'Critical theory, commodities and the consumer society', *Theory, Culture and Society*, 1 (3): 66–84.

Kellner, D. (1989) 'Boundaries and borderlines: Reflections on Jean Baudrillard and critical theory', *Current Perspectives in Social Theory*, 9: 5–22.

Lash, S. (1987) 'Modernity or modernism? Weber and contemporary social theory', in S. Lash and S. Whimster (eds), *Max Weber, Rationality and Modernity*. London: Allen & Unwin. pp. 355–77.

Lash, S. and Urry, J. (1987) *The End of Organized Capitalism*. Cambridge: Polity Press.

Lefort, C. (1988) *Democracy and Political Theory*. Cambridge: Polity Press.

Lyotard, J.-F. (1984) *The Postmodern Condition: A Report on Knowledge*. Manchester: Manchester University Press.

Lyotard, J.-F. (1988) *The Differend: Phrases in Dispute*. Manchester: Manchester University Press.

MacIntyre, A. (1970) *Marcuse*. London: Fontana.

Maravall, J.A. (1986) *Culture of the Baroque: Analysis of a Historical Structure*. Manchester: University of Manchester Press.

Marin, L. (1988) *Portrait of the King*. London: Macmillan.

Nehamas, A. (1985) *Nietzsche: Life as Literature*. Cambridge, Mass.: Harvard University Press.

O'Neill, J. (1988) 'Religion and postmodernism: Durkheimian bond in Bell and Jameson', *Theory, Culture and Society*, 5(2–3): 493–508.

Owens, C. (1985) 'The discourse of others: Feminists and postmodernism', in H. Foster (ed.), *Postmodern Culture*. London and Sydney: Pluto Press. pp. 57–82.

Rilke, R.M. (1950) *Briefe*. Wiesbaden: Insel Verlag.

Ringer, R.K. (1969) *The Decline of the German Mandarins: The German Academic Community 1890–1933*. Cambridge, Mass.: Harvard University Press.

Ross, A. (1989) *Intellectuals and Popular Culture*. New York and London: Routledge.

Stauth, G. and Turner, B.S. (1988) *Nietzsche's Dance: Resentment, Reciprocity and Resistance in Social Life*. Oxford: Basil Blackwell.

Turner, B.S. (1986) *Citizenship and Capitalism: The Debate over Reformism*. London: Allen & Unwin.

Turner, B.S. (1989) 'From postindustrial society to postmodern politics: the political sociology of Daniel Bell', in J.R. Gibbins (ed.), *Contemporary Political Culture: Politics in a Postmodern Age*. London: Sage. pp. 199–217.

Vromen, S. (1986) 'Maurice Halbwachs and the concept of nostalgia', *Knowledge and Society: Studies in the Sociology of Culture Past and Present*, 6: 55–66.

Weber, M. (1958) *The City*. New York: Free Press.

Weber, M. (1981) *General Economic History*. New Brunswick and London: Transaction Books.

2

MODERNITY, POSTMODERNITY AND THE PRESENT

Barry Smart

The proliferation of millennial forms of thought, of predictions and prophecies, utopian formulations and crisis analyses proclaiming the end of an era may be a consequence, in part at least, of the imminence of the year AD 2000.[1] But it would be a mistake to consider contributions to debates on the nature of the present and answers to questions about 'what is happening now' to be simply a reflection of the approach of a particular temporal moment or event within an historically specific cultural formation, for it is evident that the idea of the present as a time of significant change has a longer history. If the view is taken that the time in which we live may not after all be a unique moment or an 'irruptive point in history', it nevertheless does remain a time in which on a number of fronts (for example socially, politically, culturally, economically), and in relation to a range of matters (for example epistemology, morality, ethics), significant forms of change can be identified. In brief, if our time, our present, is in an important sense a 'time like any other', it nevertheless may in turn be regarded as marked by transformations of various significant kinds. As one analyst has put it, 'the time we live in is very interesting; it needs to be analysed and broken down, ... [W]e would do well to ask ourselves, "What is the nature of our present?"' (Foucault, 1983: 206). It is to a consideration of one particular debate over the nature of the present that this chapter is directed.

Of the range of concepts and ideas introduced to explore the question of the present two sets of conceptual distinctions seem to have become particularly prominent and influential, namely those of industrial and postindustrial society and the modern and postmodern respectively.[2] The controversial conceptual distinction between 'industrial' and 'postindustrial' society has been employed to conceptualize a range of changes in socio-economic life deemed to be closely associated with, if not determined by, forms of technological innovation and deployment frequently analysed in abstraction from a prevailing capitalist mode of production. The even more nebulous conceptual distinction between the 'modern' and the 'postmodern' has been employed in respect of analyses of forms of social, cultural, and political change and appears to have displaced the former concern over a possible transition from 'industrial' to 'postindustrial' society at the centre of intellectual debate. It is also evident that some contributions to the debate over the present assume a close relationship, if not a correlation, between 'postindustrial' and 'postmodern' forms. Consider for example Lyotard's reference to the status of knowledge being altered as 'societies enter what is known as the postindustrial age and cultures enter what is known as the postmodern age' (1986: 3), a position which is paralleled by Frankel's comment that the debate over modernism and postmodernism 'has in many ways become an explicit debate over the nature of culture and social production in the emerging "postindustrial" society' (1987: 10). Whether the assumption of a relationship of interdependence, or for that matter of determination, between the emergence of postindustrial society and the constitution of postmodern cultural forms is justified is open to question. The precise form(s) of their possible articulation has yet to be demonstrated or established.

In a number of contributions to the debate Jameson is critical of the conception of postindustrial society, yet embraces the idea of postmodernism as an appropriate way of conceptualizing the cultural space of 'late' capitalism.[3] Jameson comments that rather than

> denounce the complacencies of postmodernism as some final symptom of decadence, or . . . salute the new forms as the harbingers of a new technological and technocratic Utopia, it seems more appropriate to assess the new cultural production within the working hypothesis of a general modification of culture itself within the social restructuration of late capitalism as a system. (1984a: 63)

This view receives a degree of endorsement in the work of Lash and Urry (1987: 299), who argue that the 'breakdown of older organized capitalist forms' is accompanied by the emergence of a postmodernist cultural sensibility. It is to an examination of the floating and fluctuating distinctions between the 'modern', 'modernism' and 'modernity', and the 'postmodern', 'postmodernism' and 'postmodernity', that my discussion will be directed.

Towards a history of modernity

A number of difficulties are encountered in the analysis of modernity and postmodernity, notably the presence of a constellation of related terms, a lack of specificity associated with the concepts employed, particularly in relation to their historical referents or periodization, as well as the existence of a number of conceptual distinctions between 'positive' and 'negative' manifestations of respectively modern and postmodern forms.[4]

In relation to modernity it has been suggested that there is a need to rethink the 'modern age', its emergence, development and current crisis in relation to its 'classical background in the metaphysics of "Graeco-Roman mind"' and early exploration in the texts of Augustine (Kroker and Cook, 1988: 36); to contemplate its fate as one of decline or continuing vitality and consider its impact on human experience (Featherstone, 1985; Burger, 1984–85; Berman, 1983); and to recognize that its project and positive promise still awaits fulfilment (Habermas, 1981). Although there has been a

tendency to equate the emergence of modernity with the Enlightenment and
the advent of a 'tradition of reason' at the turn of the eighteenth century,
other historical moments have been identified as marking the beginning of
what we have become accustomed to regard as the 'modern' age or era. As I
have implied above, Kroker and Cook take the view that the intellectual
horizon of the modern age extends back beyond the Enlightenment and the
respective works of Kant, Hegel, Marx and Nietzsche to the fourth century
and Augustine's radical reformulation of the philosophy of progress and
exploration of 'the *physics*, the *logic* and the *ethics* of modern experience'
(1988: 62). In a broad historical survey Toynbee argues that the beginning of
the 'Modern Age of Western History' occurs in the last quarter of the
fifteenth century amongst the people on the Atlantic seaboard of Europe
and derives from the emergence of a form of 'cultural pharisaism' and an
associated 'technological conquest of the ocean' (1954a: 144).

In a rather different analysis of the modern experience Berman (1983)
identifies three distinctive historical phases in the development of
modernity. The first extends from the beginning of the sixteenth to the end
of the eighteenth century, during which time 'people are ... beginning to
experience modern life'. A second phase is agreed to commence with the
French Revolution and the emergence of upheavals in social, political, and
personal life with which 'the great revolutionary wave of the 1790s' has been
associated. Finally Berman refers to the global diffusion of the process of
modernization and the development of a 'world culture of modernism' as a
third phase which precipitates more turmoil in social and political life, more
uncertainty and agitation, giving rise to new forms of experience.

It is evident that a number of historical moments have been identified as
synonymous with the emergence of modernity, although the most frequent
historical reference is to the post-Enlightenment era. It is also clear that the
terms 'modern', 'modernism', and 'modernity' are used at times as syno-
nyms. For example, Habermas (1981) in a discussion of the 'project of
modernity' refers interchangeably to 'aesthetic modernity', 'the modern
avant-garde spirit', as well as to the life world being 'infected by modernism'. A comparable tendency is evident in the work of Berman (1983), who
moves continually between references to modernity as a 'body of experience' and modernism as a developing world culture associated with a process
of modernization. Indeed one of the remarkable features of contributions to
debates on this issue is the extent to which key terms and ideas have evaded
clarification, and this applies not only in respect of the family of terms
associated with the 'modern' but in addition, if not to an even greater extent
in relation to the 'postmodern' and its conceptual constellation. In turn it
extends, as will become clear below, to the distinctions drawn between the
two sets of terms. Furthermore whilst there have been attempts to clarify the
conceptual fields concerned, the outcome has generally been either a
displacement of the problem, as in the case of Lash's (1987) address of
modernity and modernism which leaves relatively open the question of the
relationship of (aesthetic) modernism to 'postmodernity' or a 'postmodern'

sensibility, or as with Huyssen (1984) and Kellner (1988) a confirmation of the difficulties of conceptual clarification.

The term 'modern' derives from the late fifth century Latin term *modernus* which was used to distinguish an officially Christian present from a Roman, pagan past (cf. Calinescu, 1977; Habermas, 1981). Thereafter the term is employed to situate the present in relation to the past of antiquity, appearing and reappearing 'exactly during those periods in Europe when the consciousness of a new epoch formed itself through a renewed relationship to the ancients' (Habermas, 1981: 3–4). However, with the *Querelle des Anciens et des Modernes* and the emergence of the French Enlightenment a different conception developed, of modernity as a distinctive and superior period in the history of humanity. In relation to reason, religion, and aesthetic appreciation it was argued that the moderns were more advanced, more refined, and in possession of more profound truths than the ancients.[5] The quarrel over the respective merits of old and new effectively ended the blind veneration of classical antiquity and prepared the way for the eighteenth century Enlightenment philosophical project of developing the spheres of science, morality and law, and art in accordance with their respective inner logics in order to achieve a 'rational organization of everyday social life' (Habermas, 1981: 9).

In discussions of the emergence of modernity consideration is frequently given to the respective philosophical analyses of Kant and Hegel. But if Kant is acknowledged to have inaugurated the modern age, and Hegel is considered to have provided the first clear philosophical conception of modernity and to have identified its problem as 'self-reassurance' or the necessity of constituting its own grounds, it is the work of Baudelaire which is frequently considered to provide the turning point in the development of an understanding of modernity. Baudelaire has been credited with identifying 'the price for which the sensation of the modern age may be had' (Benjamin, 1973: 196); recognizing the distinctively 'transient, . . . fleeting, . . . contingent' character of modernity (Habermas, 1987: 8); illuminating 'modern life's complexities and conditions' (Berman 1983: 40); and for contrasting 'aesthetic modernity . . . to the practical modernity of bourgeois civilization' (Calinescu, 1977: 4). There are two observations to be made on the above. First, there is a clear implication of a substantial degree of overlap between considerations and critiques of modernity in philosophical and aesthetic discourse (cf. McCarthy, 1987). A similar observation might also be made in respect of debates about postmodernity. Second, a contrast between aesthetic or cultural modernity and socio-political modernity as 'two modernities' which are quite distinct and 'bitterly conflicting' (cf. Calinescu, 1977: 41) surfaces in Bell's analysis of the cultural contradictions which have emerged in contemporary (postindustrial) capitalism.

A comparable distinction is presented by Lash in response to the confusing profusion and conflation of references to the modern age, modernity, and modernism. The proposal outlined is that our age, the 'modern', should be understood not as modernity but in terms of modernism. Whereas modernity is presented as having been inaugurated in the sixteenth and seventeenth centuries, modernism is conceptualized as a reaction to our break with modernity, as 'something new', as a 'paradigm change in the arts which began at the end of the nineteenth century' (1987: 355), and which may be extended to encompass contemporary social practices. Where Lash makes reference to (aesthetic) modernism to conceptualize developments in social and cultural life which frequently have been regarded as an embodiment of the emergence of post-modernity, Giddens, addressing the interrelationship between sociology and modernity, documents the major parameters of modernity (namely, economic, administrative, military, and cultural) and attempts to defuse the problem of postmodernity by arguing that current controversies over the latter

> should perhaps ... be seen as the first real initiatives in the ambitious task of charting the cultural universe resulting from the ever-more complete disintegration of the traditional world. (1987: 28–9)

Before turning to an exploration of the postmodern constellation it is evident that consideration needs to be given to the question of modernism.

On modernism

The first positive references to modernism are to be found in 1888 in Dario's praise of the work of a Mexican writer, Ricardo Contreras, and subsequently in 1890 in references to *modernismo* as a movement in Latin America for cultural emancipation or autonomy from Spain. Hispanic modernism represents the common denominator of a variety of conflicting schools of French literature, 'a synthesis of all the major innovative tendencies that manifested themselves in late nineteenth century France' (Calinescu, 1977: 70). Barely two decades later criticisms were being expressed that the term meant something different to each person using it, that it referred to no specific school or movement, and at best constituted a periodizing term. For many critics of the time the term served no useful purpose and reflected merely a passing fashion. In response, Federico de Onis seeking to salvage the concept argued that there was an indissoluble link between modernism and modernity, that the former constituted the search for the latter, virtually a tradition in opposition to the traditional, and that Hispanic modernism constituted a specific manifestation of a universal literary and spiritual crisis to be found in 'art, science, religion, politics, and gradually in all other aspects of life' (Calinescu, 1977: 76). Many of the themes and issues identified above return in contemporary debates over an alleged 'postmodern condition'; for example art, science, religion, politics and other spheres of life are, once again, considered to be in crisis. Interestingly there is also a prominent transatlantic dimension associated with contemporary debates over modernity and postmodernity, a striking feature of which is the adoption of European analyses of modernity and modernism in the American context as contributions to an accumulating corpus on the postmodern condition.

A sociological sense of crisis in relation to contemporary culture, to modernism, is present in the work of Daniel Bell. Bell's position, paralleling to an extent Weber's own reflections on the distinctiveness of value spheres in modern life, is that modern society is composed of an uneasy amalgam of three distinctive realms, namely social structure, polity and culture. It is a disjunction or lack of fit between these three realms which accounts for the social tensions and conflicts characteristic of Western society over the past 150 years, and it is transformations in the realms of culture and social structure (which in Bell's conception includes the economy, technology, and occupational system) that are conceived to be the principal source of tension in the present. Bell's argument is that the modern impulses which have permeated Western civilization since the sixteenth century have been articulated in quite different ways in the respective realms of the economy and culture. A radical individualism in economics and a willingness to abandon traditional social relations has been accompanied by an opposition to, if not a fear of, forms of radical experimental individualism in the cultural sphere. On the other hand modernists in the cultural sphere whilst being willing to explore various dimensions of human experience have been critical of the utilitarian, materialistic, and disciplined character of 'bourgeois life'. If these economic and cultural impulses started out as 'aspects of the same sociological surge of modernity' they came in the course of their development to be antagonistic. Bell takes the view that the traditional source of legitimation of American capitalism has been eroded, that ascetic Protestant values sanctifying self-restraint, discipline, and work as a calling have been lost as a consequence of developments internal to capitalism itself ('the invention of the installation plan and instant credit' plus the emergence of mass production and consumption), and the subversion of bourgeois life by modernist culture.

Modernism is described by Bell as a cultural temper pervading all the arts; as opaque, unfamiliar, deliberately disturbing, experimental in form and disruptive of *mimesis*. It constitutes a response to late nineteenth century social changes in sense perception and self-consciousness which arose from space-time disorientations associated with fundamental transformations in communication and transport, and a crisis of self-consciousness following an erosion of religious beliefs and values respectively. The emphasis of modernism is upon movement and flux, on the absolute present, if not the future *as* present, and it is characterized by a 'refusal to accept limits, the insistence on continually reaching out . . . [to] a destiny that is always *beyond*: beyond morality, beyond tragedy, beyond culture' (Bell, 1976: 50). Implied within which is the status of modernism as an adversary culture, one which seeks to 'negate every prevalent style including, in the end, its own' (ibid.: 47).

Although a modernist artistic syntax which eclipses the distance between spectator and artist, or aesthetic experience and art work, is considered to be increasingly evident from the mid-nineteenth century, Bell regards the period between 1890 and 1930 as the high point of exploration and experiment in style and form. From this time on it is argued that there has scarcely been any innovation of any significance or value in the realm of culture, a claim which leads Bell to the conclusion that modernism is exhausted. What this seems to mean is that creative impulses have been dissipated through accommodation and institutionalization within the 'cultural mass', that the disturbing and shocking no longer disturbs or shocks, that anti-bourgeois rebellious impulses have now become mainstream, in brief that 'experimental forms have become the syntax and semiotics of advertising and haute couture' (1976: 20). To paraphrase Baudrillard, mass(age) seems to be the message.

It is important to emphasize that Bell does not really lament the exhaustion of modernism or the loss of its threatening edge. To the contrary it is the apparent passing away of a traditional bourgeois organization of life with its associated forms of rationality and sobriety that is the subject of regret. In discussing such issues a strong sense of disapproval of the moral temper and culture of modernism is conveyed by Bell, notably through references to modernism's anti-rational character (1976: 53); 'the apocalyptic moods and anti-rational modes of behaviour' associated with it (1976: 84); and its promotion of 'pre-rational spontaneity' in place of reason (1976: 143). But Bell's most critical comments are reserved for a cultural configuration which is said to carry 'the logic of modernism to its farthest reaches' (1976: 51), namely postmodernism. It is the development in the 1960s of a current of postmodernism (the 'postmodern temper'; the 'postmodern mood') mounting an 'onslaught on the values and motivational patterns of "ordinary" behaviour, in the name of liberation, eroticism, freedom of impulse and the like' (1976: 52) which is identified by Bell as precipitating a crisis of middle-class values. The idea that 'the postmodern' constitutes a cultural development which remains broadly within the 'logic of modernism' is a position not confined to the work of Bell alone.

Postmodernism and the problem of the 'new'

The question of a qualitative transformation in or transcendence of the modern is first articulated within aesthetic discourse, in debates over the emergence of seemingly novel literary and cultural forms. An early trace is present in de Onis's discussion of modernism as a broad period concept and postmodernism as 'a conservative reaction within modernism itself, when the latter settles down and becomes rhetorical like any literary revolution that has won out' (quoted in Calinescu, 1977: 77). As will become evident postmodernism is rarely rigorously differentiated from modernism, indeed within both aesthetic and sociological discourse there has been a marked tendency to conceptualize postmodernism as a 'part of the modern'.[6]

One of the problems of an age which conceives of itself as 'modern' in contrast to other eras or ages, which in consequence are constituted as 'pre-modern', 'traditional', 'primitive', and so on, is that of comprehending its relation to these other ostensibly distinctive socio-cultural and historical forms. And given that 'what "traditional" and "modern" should be taken to mean is a matter of chronic debate' (Giddens, 1987: 15), then it might seem excessively premature to devote consideration to a number of ideas and contributions which direct attention to the possibility that a 'dissolution of the traditional world under the impact of modernity' (1987: 28) has been followed by a permeation, if not a transformation, of the modern world by postmodernism. To achieve a clearer idea as to whether particular developments in social and cultural life constitute the emergence of a distinctively novel form of life beyond modernity it is necessary to take a closer look at the postmodern constellation.

If the concept of postmodernism first emerged in a literary context in reference to a conservative reaction within modernism, the term has subsequently been employed in relation to a broader range of texts and sensibilities, to characterize both affirmative and critical texts or narratives, to mark an historical period as well as an aesthetic style, and to conceptualize difference, a distinctive form beyond the modern, as well as similarity, a variant of the modern, in effect its limit form.

Reference to a particular historical period as 'postmodern' first appears in the work of Toynbee who contrasts the 'modern' chapter of Western history, dating from approximately the end of the fifteenth century to the turn of the nineteenth and twentieth centuries, with a subsequent 'post-Modern Age'. Here the 'modern' appears to be synonymous with 'bourgeois' or 'middle class' life, it being suggested that

> Western communities became 'modern' . . . just as soon as they had succeeded in producing a bourgeoisie that was both numerous enough and competent enough to become the predominant element in society. (1954a: 338)

In contrast the emergence of a 'post-Modern Age' is considered to be marked by the rise of an industrial urban working class.

The scenario outlined by Toynbee is that of a 'post-Modern Age' laying in wait for a prosperous, comfortable, and complacent modern middle class which had not only lost the necessary fund of 'creative psychic energy' required to drive the Western industrial system, but imagined that a 'safe, satisfactory Modern Life had . . . come to stay as a timeless present' (1954b: 421). The event which Toynbee considers disrupted the cosy complacency of the Western bourgeoisie is the outbreak of the 'first postmodern general war in AD 1914' (1954b: 422). This event and its sequel, the 'second act' which began in 1939, are described by Toynbee as having brought into focus a series of problems associated with the rapidity of technological change and the persistence of political and economic inequalities which, in so far as they threatened prevailing forms of life, raised the spectre of the mortality of Western civilization (cf. 1954b: 467).

Toynbee argues that Western technological advances precipitated a crisis in human affairs through the imposition of a rate of change beyond the 'adaptational capacity of a single life' (1954b: 468), a problem subsequently described by Toffler (1971) as 'future shock'. In addition the development of powerful new technologies raised the possibility of dramatically increasing productive capacity and made the customary levels of 'social injustice seem remediable and therefore intolerable' (1954b: 561). Whilst Toynbee makes reference to the material resource, demographic and industrial labour relations scenarios which shaped social and political accommodations to economic and technological changes, the major concern, as with Bell in his discussion of the revolutions of rising expectations and entitlements respectively (1976: 232–6), becomes that of the development of the 'public sphere'.[7]

A number of parallels may be drawn between the respective works of Toynbee and Bell. Both identify a comparable time or age of transition; the decline of a way of life, if not a civilization; and an erosion of the creative energy or 'zest for work' associated with the development of Western capitalism. Both seem to lament the demise of 'high' and/or 'traditional' cultural forms and view with concern the impact of new forms of cultural production and consumption associated with economic and technological innovation; and they each identify the public sphere or public household and its relationship to private interests and enterprise as an increasingly critical problem within Western capitalist social formations. But perhaps above all their positions are closest in respect of their mutual identification of the problem of a loss of belief as central to the crisis of Western civilization.[8] While in the respective works of Bell and Toynbee the concept of the postmodern carries negative connotations – for example the latter argues that such an age made it hard for 'any human soul to resist the temptation of becoming a fiend without succumbing to the opposite temptation of becoming a robot' (1954b: 757) – the use of the concept of postmodernism within social and literary theory and analysis is broader and covers a range of social and cultural developments of which some at least are conceived to be positive or progressive.

Transatlantic translations

The terms 'modernism' and 'postmodernism' are not only notoriously lacking in specificity, in addition they appear at times to carry very different connotations for continental European and American critics. 'Postmodernism' first came to prominence in the 1960s in criticisms advanced by American literary theorists of the institutionalization of 'high' culture and the incorporation of modernism within the mainstream (cf. Howe, 1971). As such, American 'postmodern' criticism of the effects of the culture industry stands in a relationship of similarity and continuity with an earlier European avant-garde. However, 'despite its radical and legitimate critique of the gospel of modernism, ... [it] must be seen as the endgame of the avant-garde and not as the radical breakthrough it often claimed to be' (Huyssen,

1981: 31). Standing in opposition to the neutralization of modernism's critical potential, to its transformation into a form of affirmative culture, postmodernism compensates for the absence of an indigenous avant-garde and challenges not modernism *per se* but a compromised version.

Characterized by a strong spatial-temporal imagination; an iconoclastic attack on the institution 'art'; technological optimism; and a cultural populism, postmodernism is considered to have been exhausted by the capacity of a 'technologically and economically fully developed media culture' to integrate, diffuse and market even the most serious challenges (Huyssen, 1981: 32; 1984: 20–3). Stripped of its avant-garde rhetoric postmodernism has been described as a logical culmination of the premises of romantic-modernist traditions; as a reactionary tendency which 'reinforces the effects of technocratic, bureaucratic society' (Graff, 1973: 385); and as a style which emphasizes diversity, displays a penchant for pastiche, and adopts an 'inclusivist' philosophy advocating eclectic use of elements from the past (Ghirardo, 1984/85: 189). The implication is clear, the seemingly endless assimilative propensity of contemporary society, with its capacity to convert attacks upon its values into 'pleasing entertainments' and ability to neutralize opponents and critics with the rewards of 'success' (cf. Howe, 1971: 16, 224), leads postmodernism to suffer the same fate as modernism.

Beginning in the 1970s there has been a proliferation of theorizing on the subject of postmodernism. In the case of literary theory and criticism it has been suggested that evidence of a shift towards theory may signify a 'falling rate of artistic and literary creativity' (Huyssen, 1981: 34), or perhaps it constitutes an attempt to retrieve some notion of avant-gardism through recourse to exotic continental brands of social theory. Ironically the French texts which appear to have stimulated theorizing on postmodernism in America (such as the works of Derrida, Barthes, Foucault) might more appropriately be regarded as addressing modernity or theorizing about modernism. Once again history appears to be repeating itself, for just as late nineteenth century modernism was constituted from literary tendencies present in France ('Parnasse, décadisme, symbolisme, école romane etc.' (Calinescu, 1977: 70)), so 1970s postmodernism appears to have derived its principal impetus from French writings concerned to explore the archaeology of modernity. Ironically the translation of ideas from one cultural milieu to another has been questioned by a figure frequently feted as the architect of postmodern social theory. In a panoramic portrayal of the (hyper)reality of American life Baudrillard argues that in terms of both culture and history America and Europe are significantly different, and that in consequence some things 'cannot be imported or exported'. Commenting specifically on the nostalgic leanings of American intellectuals towards Europe Baudrillard cautions that ideas, 'like fine wines and haute cuisine . . . do not really cross the ocean' (1988b: 79).

If an embrace of eclecticism, populism, and a principle of 'anything goes' may be regarded as symptomatic of a decline in creativity, as reflecting an acceptance if not a celebration of the current order of things, this by no means exhausts the polymorphous idea of postmodernism (cf. Foster, 1985: x). In contrast to a conception of postmodernism as 'conservative' an alternative might be posed, not of that postmodernism which effaces 'the older (essentially high-modernist) frontier between high culture and so-called mass or commercial culture' (Jameson, 1984b: 54), but rather of a 'progressive' or 'oppositional' postmodernism.

Postmodernism: resistance and reaction

A distinction may be made between oppositional and affirmative forms of postmodernism, between a 'postmodernism which seeks to deconstruct modernism and resist the status quo and a postmodernism which repudiates the former to celebrate the latter' (Foster, 1985: xi–xii). Examples of what have been termed a 'postmodernism of resistance' and a 'postmodernism of reaction' may be found in the respective works of Lyotard and Jameson.

In philosophy and social theory a concept of 'postmodernism' has been invoked to signify that the limits of the modern have been reached, that the pursuit of unshakeable foundations for analytic truth constitutes a fruitless project, one that will continue to remain incomplete in so far as the metaphysical presuppositions at the heart of Western philosophy are themselves problematic (Kellner, 1988; Featherstone, 1988). In addition it has been argued that the promise of modernity to achieve 'the emancipation of humanity from poverty, ignorance, prejudice, and the absence of enjoyment' (Lyotard, 1988: 302) is no longer considered to be feasible. Such grand hopes associated with global or totalizing forms of social theory and a politics of 'revolution' have been diminished by the realization that forms of knowledge, social conditions, human experiences and subjectivities are not as they were once thought to be. In brief, as Lyotard (1986) has suggested, the grand old narratives of modern social theory and philosophy have been rendered inoperative, they have lost their credibility. Whilst such an analysis may appear to render politics problematic, by for example undermining the position of the universalizing modern intellectual accustomed to wielding emancipatory metanarratives, the scope and resources for a politics of resistance remain. Lyotard suggests that

> The real political task today, at least in so far as it is also concerned with the cultural ... is to carry forward the resistance that writing offers to established thought, to what has already been done, to what everyone thinks, to what is well known, to what is widely recognised, to what is 'readable', to everything which can change its form and make itself acceptable to opinion in general ... The name most often given to this is postmodernism. (1988: 302)

Such a conception of postmodernism constitutes a counter-practice to official culture, if offers a critical deconstruction of tradition and is concerned with a 'critique of origins, not a return to them' (Foster, 1985: xii). It also serves to reaffirm the affinity between modernism and postmodernism (Jameson, 1985: 123).

Ranged against the idea of postmodernism as resistance is a critique of postmodernism as reaction. For Jameson (1984b) postmodernism is the cultural correlate of late, consumer or multi-national capitalism. In a range of papers Jameson has sought to retrieve and burnish the credentials of Marxist analysis as the sole remaining viable grand narrative by arguing that postmodern cultural forms replicate, reproduce and ultimately serve to reinforce the logic of consumer capitalism. The implication is that any vestige of autonomy ('semi-autonomy') possessed by the cultural sphere has been destroyed. But this does not mean that culture has thereby become marginal, to the contrary. Jameson argues that there has been a fundamental cultural mutation, a 'prodigious expansion' throughout the social realm, the effect of which has been that everything from economic value to the structure of the psyche has become cultural (1984b: 87), albeit through a process initiated by the logic of late capitalism.

Although critical of postmodernist cultural forms Jameson is not wholly dismissive of them, for example he rejects both the idea of their enthusiastic espousal as harbingers of a new technological or technocratic Utopia and their denouncement as decadent. What emerges is the view that new 'postmodern' forms of cultural production need to be located within a 'general modification of culture itself within the social restructuration of late capitalism as a system' (1984a: 63). Clearly for Jameson postmodernism is not to be conceptualized as a 'style', as one option among many, but rather as a cultural dominant of the logic of late capitalism. But such a conclusion does not mean that postmodernism is completely written off as simply reaction(ary). To the contrary, Jameson seems to be casting around for a functional equivalent to an older modernism which was 'critical, negative, contestatory, subversive, oppositional and the like' (1985: 125), but has yet to be convinced that whilst postmodernism reinforces the logic of consumer capitalism it can also resist it.

Postmodernism and sociology

One issue which has received relatively little consideration has been the implication of movement beyond the social, political, and epistemological limits of modernism for the discourse of sociology. If sociology emerged with modernity and found its epistemological space within the modern configuration of knowledge, what are its prospects *if* we are indeed confronting the 'end of the social' as Baudrillard (1983: 67–8) would have it, and/or a change in the forms of thought or conditions of knowledge associated with its emergence as Foucault (1973) and Lyotard (1986) respectively have implied? One suggestion which has been made is that 'we must relinquish the attractions of a postmodern sociology and work towards a sociological account of postmodernism' (Featherstone, 1988: 205), for a postmodern sociology risks being a contradiction in terms if we understand by sociology a systematizing, generalizing, social science. Featherstone is surely correct that a postmodern sociology would be required to abandon its generalizing social science ambitions. Yet the alternative, a sociology of postmodernism, is itself not free from controversy. To what extent can any (modern) sociology remain undisturbed or unchanged by the problematization of representation, the critique of 'grand narratives' and associated 'crisis of the foundations' (Lyotard, 1988: 280)?

The theme of sociology's postmodern crisis has been identified by Bauman (1988) as one which can not adequately be met by the strategy of 'business as usual', for the game and the customers have changed. Following Habermas's (1971) distinction between empirical-analytical, interpretive, and critical forms of analysis Bauman outlines the impact of postmodernism on three forms of sociology. For empirical sociology the objective needs must become to seek a 'new social application of its skills or . . . new skills' (1988: 229) to combat the declining requirement from the State for 'social-management knowledge'. The second category, 'interpreting sociology', takes two forms, one of which retains a vestige of social relevance in that it is concerned to enrich one's own tradition by rendering 'alien' forms and experiences comprehensible, a product for which Bauman implies potential customers may still exist. The second variant of 'interpreting sociology' is presented as making a virtue out of necessity, the decline in social demand for sociology providing an opportunity for, and legitimation of, a retreat into a self-serving disinterested patrol of one's own patch. The final form is that of a sociology of postmodernism which remains committed to a notion of social relevance and seeks to make the 'opaque transparent', a strategy which given the withdrawal of the State from the field effectively constitutes sociological discourse as a potentially critical and/or, 'subversive force' – this is the familiar figure of an 'emancipatory' sociology. However, in contrast to Habermas's 'emancipatory' pursuit of the endless project of modernity Bauman recognizes that a sociological analysis of postmodernity which seeks to 'preserve the hopes and ambitions of modernity' (1988: 231) must recognize that its strategy is based on values, assumptions and purposes, not laws, foundations and groundings. The emergence of a 'value-theoretical tradition' alongside an increasingly criticized 'onto-epistemological' tradition raises a number of questions (Fekete, 1988). The one which Bauman draws to our attention is: which forms of sociological inquiry are likely to be best placed to survive the 'postmodern flip' inflicted upon the modern paradigm?

Concluding remarks

Given the range of terms brought into play in debates and discussions over the possibility of the present as a time of significant change or transition, it is no surprise to find figures who are considered to be contributors to the confusion proclaiming that they do not understand what is meant by 'modernity' nor what kind of 'problem might be common to people described as postmodern' (Foucault, 1983).[9] Such responses should not be taken too literally and certainly in the case of Foucault one might suggest that speculation in one of his earlier works, that the entire modern *epistēmē* formed towards the end of the eighteenth century *might* be about to topple, contributed significantly to the development of the modernism–postmodernism debate. But Foucault did not assert that such a transformation was occurring, rather that a number of questions had been articulated to which it was not possible to provide answers, one possibility being that 'posing them may well open the way to a future thought' (1973: 386). From within a modernist paradigm it has not been possible to generate satisfactory answers to the questions posed and in consequence a plurality of diverse 'fringe' discourses have emerged, for example 'science fiction' (Baudrillard), 'paralogism' (Lyotard), and 'hyper-pragmatism' or 'pragmatism plus' (Fekete), not to mention Eco's (1987) references to the postmodern temptation to 'dream of a new medievalism'. This constitutes one way of interpreting the proliferation of contributions to the debate over the modern and the postmodern.

Another related way of understanding the present predicament is to recognize that what is encountered in the debate over the possibility of a distinction between modernity and postmodernity is a realization that the goals and values which have been central to Western 'European' civilization can no longer be considered universal, and that the associated 'project of modernity' is unfinished because its completion is inconceivable and its value in question. Such a realization is associated with an increasing awareness of significant changes in the relationships which have existed between 'modernized' Western and/or 'European' societies and non-Western or non-'European' societies. It is conceivable then that the preoccupation with the distinction 'modernity–postmodernity' reflects the growth of a concern over the possible emergence of a post-'European', if not a post-Western era. As Feher comments,

> True to the spirit of declining worlds, which learn to relativise their deities in the face of imported foreign gods, 'Europe' humbly inserts itself and its culture in yet another postmodernist innovation, in a 'wider context' of all cultures which are supposedly all equivalent. (1986: 44)

Furthermore, contrary to the view that America represents the form of civilization 'best adapted to the probability . . . of the life that lies in store for us' (Baudrillard, 1988b: 10), it might be argued that the waning of European hegemony, Europe's relative demise as the economic epicentre and cultural nucleus of Western modernity, subsequently has been followed by a 'crisis of the Pax Americana' (Eco, 1987: 76). If the 'Old World' of Europe no longer seems to be the bearer of universal values, the source and model for enlightenment and material progress, the 'New World' of America, in its turn, is encountering a number of substantial problems, notably a relative decline in economic fortune; military vulnerability and ineffectiveness in relation to forms of terrorist activity and a range of local or regional

conflicts; and political difficulties arising from changes in the established
pattern and balance of global forces associated with a thaw of the 'Cold
War'. Given the above the preoccupation with the 'postmodern' may be
symptomatic not so much of the demise or exhaustion of the 'modern', as a
belated recognition of its geo-political relocation, the shift of its creative,
innovatory momentum and influence to the Pacific rim and the developing
societies of the East.[10]

The idea of the present as 'postmodern' is now firmly on the agenda for
debate. Diverse and at times conflicting references to postmodernism and
postmodernity are to be found in a growing number of disciplinary fields and
across an increasingly broad range of discursive formations. But this should
not occasion 'panic'.[11] And it does not necessitate an unqualified endorsement of the polymorphous perversities associated with some manifestations
of the 'postmodern'. Rather, the critical implication is that complex transformations, questions, and problems deemed to be constitutive of the
present are not adequately articulated in prevailing forms of social theory,
indeed cannot be so. That is the kernel of the 'postmodern' challenge to
which a response is required.

Notes

1 See for example the very different contributions of Williams (1985); Baudrillard (1988a);
  Bell (1968, 1988); and the special issue of *International Journal of Comparative Sociology* on
  'The Global Crisis: Sociological analyses and responses' (25 (1–2), 1984).
2 Both sets are prominent in the works of American social theorist Daniel Bell (1973; 1976).
3 See Jameson 1984a, 1984b, 1988.
4 See Featherstone (1988); on the question of 'positive' and 'negative' manifestations of
  modernity–postmodernity see Calinescu (1977) and Graff (1973).
5 For a comparative discussion of 'moderns' and 'ancients' see Calinescu (1977); also Bock
  (1979).
6 See for example Lyotard (1986: 79); Lash (1987: 368); Graff (1973: 385); and Raulet (1986:
  162).
7 Toynbee argues that the growth of a public sphere, 'a ponderous public administration', led
  to a progressive exodus of the Western middle class from private enterprise and thereby
  threatened to spell the doom of capitalism, and by implication Western civilization (cf.
  1954b: 572–7).
    Bell's distinction between the two revolutions of 'rising expectations' and rising 'entitle-
  ments' allows him to avoid Toynbee's cynicism about the public sphere. However, whilst
  Bell develops a positive concept of the public household he argues that 'there are real crises
  ahead' and that such crises do not 'derive primarily from the "iron laws" of economics; they
  are the current dilemmas of private vices and public interests . . writ large' (1976: 236).
8 See for example Toynbee's references to the predicament confronting Western civilization
  in a post-Modern Age being resolved through a transfer of energy from economics to
  religion (cf. 1954b: 641). Whilst Bell is more sober in his formulation his remarks closely
  parallel those of Toynbee. Bell argues that the crisis of belief in Western civilization requires
  a return to religion if the problems arising from the existing 'shambles of appetite and self-
  interest and . . . destruction of the moral circle which engirds mankind' are to be resolved
  (1976: 171).
    For a discussion of the theme of religion and postmodernism in Bell's work see O'Neill
  (1988).

9 Consider for example the various qualifications and periodizations which follow from a conceptualization of the present as in-the-final-instance capitalist – 'organized', 'disorganized', 'State', 'monopoly', 'consumer', and 'late', not to mention 'post-industrial'.
10 For a discussion of the most prominent example of the relocation of modernism see Arnason (1987; 1987/88).
11 Even if panic is conceived to be 'the key psychological mood of postmodern culture' (Kroker et al., 1989: 13).

References

Arnason, J. (1987) 'The modern constellation and the Japanese enigma: part I', *Thesis Eleven*, 17.

Arnason, J. (1987/88) 'The modern constellation and the Japanese enigma: part II', *Thesis Eleven*, 18/19.

Baudrillard, J. (1983) *In the Shadow of the Silent Majorities . . . or the End of the Social and Other Essays*. New York: Semiotext(e).

Baudrillard, J. (1988a) 'The year 2000 has already happened', in A. and M. Kroker (eds), *Body Invaders: Sexuality and the Postmodern Condition*. London: Macmillan.

Baudrillard, J. (1988b) *America*. London: Verso.

Bauman, Z. (1988) 'Is there a postmodern sociology?' *Theory, Culture and Society*, 5(2/3).

Bell, D. (1968) 'The year 2000 – the trajectory of an idea' in D. Bell (ed.), *Toward the Year 2000: Work in Progress*. Boston: Houghton Mifflin.

Bell, D. (1973) *The Coming of Post-Industrial Society: A Venture in Social Forecasting*. New York: Basic Books.

Bell, D. (1976) *The Cultural Contradictions of Capitalism*. London: Heinemann.

Bell, D. (1988) 'The world in 2013', *New Society*, 82, 1303/4/5.

Benjamin, W. (1973) *Illuminations*. London: Fontana.

Berman, M. (1983) *All that is Solid Melts into Air*. London: Verso.

Bock, K. (1979) 'Theories of progress, development, evolution', in T. Bottomore and R. Nisbet (eds), *A History of Sociological Analysis*. London: Heinemann.

Burger, P. (1984–85) 'The decline of the modern age', *Telos*, 62.

Calinescu, M. (1977) *Faces of Modernity*. London: Indiana University Press.

Eco, U. (1987) *Travels in Hyperreality*. London: Picador.

Featherstone, M. (1985) 'The Fate of Modernity: an introduction', *Theory, Culture and Society*, 2(3).

Featherstone, M. (1988) 'In pursuit of the postmodern: an introduction', *Theory, Culture and Society*, 5(2/3).

Feher, F. (1986) 'The pyrrhic victory of Art in its war of liberation: remarks on the postmodern intermezzo', *Theory, Culture and Society*, 3(2).

Fekete, J. (1988) *Life after Postmodernism: Essays on Value and Culture*. London: Macmillan.

Foster, H. (1985) 'Postmodernism: A preface', in H. Foster (ed.), *Postmodern Culture*. London: Pluto.

Foucault, M. (1973) *The Order of Things: An Archaeology of the Human Sciences*. New York: Vintage Books.

Foucault, M. (1983) 'Structuralism and post-structuralism: an interview', *Telos*, 55.

Frankel, B. (1987) *The Post-Industrial Utopians*. Cambridge: Polity.

Giddens, A. (1987) *Social Theory and Modern Sociology*. Cambridge: Polity.

Ghirardo, D. (1984/85) 'Past or post modern in architectural fashion', *Telos*, 62.

Graff, G. (1973) 'The myth of the postmodernist breakthrough', *Triquarterly*, 26.

Habermas, J. (1971) *Knowledge and Human Interests*. London: Heinemann.

Habermas, J. (1981) 'Modernity versus postmodernity', *New German Critique*, 22.

Habermas, J. (1987) *The Philosophical Discourse of Modernity*. Cambridge: Polity.

Howe, I. (1971) *The Decline of the New*. London: Victor Gollancz.

Huyssen, A. (1981) 'The search for tradition: avante-garde and postmodernism in the 1970s', *New German Critique*, 22.

Huyssen, A. (1984) 'Mapping the postmodern', *New German Critique*, 33.

Jameson, F. (1984a) 'The politics of theory: ideological positions in the postmodernism debate', *New German Critique*, 32.

Jameson, F. (1984b) 'Postmodernism or the cultural logic of late capitalism', *New Left Review*, 146.

Jameson, F. (1985) 'Postmodernism and consumer society', in H. Foster (ed.), *Postmodern Culture*. London: Pluto.

Jameson, F. (1988) 'Cognitive mapping', in C. Nelson and L. Grossberg (eds), *Marxism and the Interpretation of Culture*. London: Macmillan.

Kellner, D. (1988) 'Postmodernism as social theory: some challenges and problems', *Theory, Culture and Society*, 5(2/3).

Kroker, A. and Cook, D. (1988) *The Postmodern Scene*. London: Macmillan.

Kroker, A. et al. (1989) *Panic Encyclopedia: The Definitive Guide to the Postmodern Scene*. London: Macmillan.

Lash, S. (1987) 'Modernity or modernism: Weber and contemporary social theory', in S. Whimster and S. Lash (eds), *Max Weber, Rationality and Modernity*. London: Allen and Unwin.

Lash, S. and Urry, J. (1987) *The End of Organised Capitalism*. Cambridge: Polity.

Lyotard, J.-F. (1986) *The Postmodern Condition: A Report on Knowledge*. Manchester: Manchester University Press.

Lyotard, J.-F. (1988) 'Interview', *Theory, Culture and Society*, 5(2/3).

McCarthy, T. (1987) 'Introduction', in J. Habermas, *The Philosophical Discourse of Modernity*, op. cit.

O'Neill, J. (1988) 'Religion and postmodernism: the Durkheimian bond in Bell and Jameson', *Theory, Culture and Society*, 5 (2/3).

Raulet, G. (1986) 'Marxism and the postmodern condition', *Telos*, 67.

Toffler, A. (1971) *Future Shock*. London: Pan Books.

Toynbee, A. (1954a) *A Study of History*, vol 8. London: Oxford University Press.

Toynbee, A. (1954b) *A Study of History*, vol 9. London: Oxford University Press.

Williams, R. (1985) *Towards 2000*. Harmondsworth: Penguin.

PART TWO

NOSTALGIA AND MODERNITY

3

READING 'WALL STREET': POSTMODERN CONTRADICTIONS IN THE AMERICAN SOCIAL STRUCTURE

Norman K. Denzin

> Money itself isn't lost or made, it's simply transferred from one perception to another. This painting here, I bought it 10 years ago for 60 thousand dollars. I could sell it today for 600. *The illusion has become real and the more real it becomes, the more desperate they want it.* (Gordon Gekko, in 'Wall Street,' 1987, italics added)

> Reality no longer has the time to take on the appearance of reality: it captures every dream even before it takes on the appearance of a dream. (Baudrillard, 1983: 152)

Released on December 3, 1987, just 44 days after the worst day (October 19) in the history of the New York Stock Exchange (Glaberson, 1987: 1),[1] Oliver Stone's movie 'Wall Street',[2] set in 1985, portrays the heyday of Wall Street's frantically bullish market in the 1985–1986 period.[3] The villain in the story, Gordon Gekko,[4] is loosely modeled on real life investor, arbitrager Ivan F. Boesky, who was convicted of insider trading violations in late 1986. As the film begins its protagonist, Bud Fox, the hero who falls, is employed as a broker in a second-tier Wall Street firm, yet yearns to make it to the big time. From a working class family,[5] he sells his soul so to speak, to become an employee of Gekko's. In the process he learns how to commit securities fraud, and is easily persuaded to pass along illegally acquired information obtained from his father about the operations of 'Bluestar' airlines. These moves very quickly make him very rich, but lead to his arrest for conspiracy to commit securities fraud and for violating the insider trader's sanctions act; tricks he learned from Gekko. In the film's final scene he is taken to the courthouse by his father and mother, to whom he has repented and from whom he has sought, and received, forgiveness.

'Wall Street' is a modern day morality tale; according to many critics, a story of seduction, corruption and redemption (Ebert, 1987: 21). A tale fitted to the actual doings of real life people in America's premier capitalist marketplace. Interpreted as a 'radical critique of the capitalist trading mentality' by one film reviewer (Ebert, 1987: 21), the movie in fact is a conservative apologia for the very social structure it purports to critique. The following argument organizes my reading of this text.

On the surface, the movie appears to be a hardhitting, realistic treatment of a corrupt market structure, built on ethical contradictions in late post-modern multinational capitalism. However, contrary to appearances, the film resolves its ethical dilemmas in a traditional capitalist fashion. It aligns the forces of rugged individualism and family (Carl Fox, Bud's father), on the side of the young man who capitulated to the unethical, illegal desires of fradulent commodity trading. It turns Bud's story into a moral fable and suggests that if your family stands behind you, and if you seek forgiveness, then all's well that ends well.

By failing to seriously interrogate the inner market structures that produce unethical commodity trading, and which fuel the desire for money and fame, the text leaves unexamined the ethical contradictions that lie at the heart of late market capitalism. In so doing the text narrativizes the fictional morality that underlies the late postmodern age. It resorts to the Oedipal logic of competing father figures, one evil, the other good, and resolves its tenuous ethical position through a nostalgia which returns the wayward son to the family hearth.

A subversive reading of the film's text suggests that the stories Hollywood tells the members of the popular culture about the problems its capitalist social structures are having are just that, fictions.[6] These tales have become valuable commodities in a nostalgic age which has lost its footing, morally and aesthetically, in a swirling system of avarice and greed which knows only one ethic, the profit motive. By keeping alive the myth of the repentant son who returns to the values of family and individualism, this film, and others like it,[7] creates for the members of the popular culture a sublimating fantasy structure which represses the 'real' destructive forces of a world economy gone wild and out of control.

In order to establish these points it will be necessary to examine in some detail how the film tells its story, which falls into three parts: the seduction of Bud, his corruption and fall, and his redemption. I will examine the various readings the film received by popular culture film critics, and then return to my subversive interpretation.

Seduction

Stone immediately plunges his viewer into the world of 'Wall Street.' Frank Sinatra's 'Fly me to the moon,'[8] is heard over opening credits, as a New York City skyline, filmed in grainy, muted orange and amber colors, emerges in the foreground, to slowly dissolve into close-up, hand-held camera shots of persons jostling on Manhattan streets, crowded into elevators, shouting bids on the floor of the stock exchange, talking to clients with necks cupped against the telephone, eyes staring at the green screens of computer monitors, young brokers hawking clients for five minutes of their time while they explain the international debt market and the hope of a quick sale of a stock on the rise. Out of this jungle of voices and people, captured in an electronic world, emerges young Bud Fox, who has just been shorted on a deal. Turning to his young friend Marvin, he moans: 'American Express's got a hit man out looking for me. My dream is to one day to be on the other end of that thing.' Along walks Lou, an old broker, 'Jesus you can't make a buck in this market . . . Too much cheap money sloshin' around the world . . . Putney Drug, you guy's might want to take a look at. They got a good new drug. Stick to the fundamentals. That's how IBM and Hilton were built. Good things sometimes take time.' Marvin replies, 'The big game hunters bag the elephants, not guys like us. Gordon Gekko. Thirty seconds after the Challenger blew up he's on the phone sellin' NASA stocks short.' Bud sings Gekko's praise: 'But 47 million he made on the milk order, 23 on the Imperial deal before he was 40. The guy makes 20 times what Dave Winfield makes in a year, and, he talks to everybody.' Marvin: 'And he had an ethical by-pass at birth.'

This conversation sets the context for what is to come. Bud is on the make. Gekko is his hero. All that remains is for the two to meet. But first Bud's father, Carl, must be introduced. After work, the same day, at a local bar where the members of his father's airline union meet to drink, Bud and his father have the following conversations. Carl: 'Told ya not to get into the racket in the first place. Ya coulda been a doctor or a lawyer. If you'd started at Bluestar you coulda been a supervisor by now, instead of bein' a sales-man.' Bud: 'I'm not a salesman. I'm an account executive.' Carl: 'You get on the phone and ask strangers for money. Right? You're a salesman. I don't get it kid. You borrow money to go to NYU. Last year you made 50 grand and you still can't pay off your loans.' Bud: '50 grand doesn't get you to first base in the Big Apple.' Father: 'Come back home and live rent free. Jesus Christ, 50 grand. The whole world's off its rocker. You know I made a total of $47,000 last year.' Bud: 'There's no nobility in poverty any more. One day you're gonna be proud of me.' Father: 'It's yourself you gotta be proud of Huckleberry. How much ya need?' Bud borrows $300. Carl then tells him of a forthcoming FAA announcement which will have a positive effect on Bluestar's financial status.[9]

The conflict between father and son established, Gekko must make his entrance. Bud makes his way, after calling for 59 days in a row, into Gekko's ultramodern office, which is lined with original art works by Jim Dine, Julian Schnabel and Joan Miró. He gives him a box of Cuban cigars as a birthday present, and a tip on a 'hot stock.' Gekko rebuffs him, 'Tell me somethin' I don't know. It's my birthday. Surprise me.' Bud: 'Bluestar Airlines.'[10] The next day Gekko calls Bud, 'I want you to buy 20,000 shares of Bluestar.' Bud shouts, to Marvin, 'I just bagged the elephant.' The camera shifts to a shot of the Statue of Liberty.[11]

Playing handball with Gordon, days later, he is told that 'The most valuable commodity I know of is information.'[12] Bud, who has just lost 150 thousand dollars on a deal, pleads with Gordon to 'Give me another chance.' Gordon: 'You want another chance. Then you stop sendin' me information and you start getting me some.' The next day Gordon asks Bud to get him information on his rival, Sir Larry Wildman, a British broker. Bud replies, 'It's not exactly what I do. I could lose my license. If the FCC found out I could go to jail. That's inside information isn't it?' Gordon answers, 'You mean like when a father tells his son about a court ruling on an airline? Somebody hears I'm going to buy TELEDAR Paper and decides to buy some for himself. Is that what you mean? I'm afraid unless your father's on the board of directors of another company, you and I are gonna have a very tough time doin' business together.' Bud answers, 'What about hard work?' Gordon: 'What about it? You work hard. Bet you stayed up all night analyzing that dog shit stock you gave me, Uh. Where'd it get ya? My father. He worked like an elephant pushin' electrical supplies. He dropped dead at 49 with a heart attack and tax bills.'[13] Gordon drops Bud off. 'Nice meetin' you, buddy.' Bud comes back to the limo, and knocks on the window. 'Alright, Mr Gekko. [Voice squeaks] You got me.'[14]

Corruption and the fall

The story moves quickly from this point. Bud is given Gordon's mistress, Darien. He buys a 950 thousand condo.[15] He is given a secret account in the Cayman Islands to pass Gordon's deals through. Gordon begins a take-over of TELDAR Enterprises. At a Board of Directors meeting he gives this speech:[16]

> The new law of evolution in corporate America seems to be the survival of the unfittest. Well in my book you either do it right or you get eliminated . . . The point is, ladies and gentlemen, is that greed, for lack of a better word, is good. Greed is right.[17] Thank you very much. [Round of applause. Sinatra's voice begins singing 'Let me fly you to the moon.'][18]

Bud convinces Gordon to attempt to buy Bluestar airlines. In a pivotal scene Carl and Gordon meet at Bud's new condo. Gordon makes his pitch for the take-over of Bluestar.[19] Carl rejects it.[20] He states: 'Well, I guess if a man lives long enough he gets to see everything. What else you got in your bag of tricks Mr Gekko? There came into Egypt a pharaoh who did not know . . . The rich have been doin' it to the poor since the beginning of time.'

The clash between Bud's two father figures is brought to a dramatic head in the following exchange between father and son. Bud: 'Congratulations Dad. You just did a great job embarrassing me. Look, save the workers-of-the-world-unite speech for the next time. You are gonna get axed, just like Branniff, and if it isn't Gekko it's gonna be some other killer.' Carl: 'He's usin' you kid. He's got your prick in his back pocket, but you're too blind to see it.' Bud: 'No, what I see is a jealous old machinist who can't stand the fact that his son has become more successful than he has.'[21]

Redemption

In a crescendo of scenes the film moves to its conclusion. Gordon betrays Bud, Carl and Bluestar, immediately setting in motion plans to liquidate the entire firm.[22] Learning of this, Bud goes to Gordon's rival, Sir Larry, and secures his commitment to buy the firm, which he does, leading Gordon to lose millions of dollars in a single day's trading on the floor of the stock exchange.[23] The day after the Bluestar deal, Bud is arrested by the SEC.[24] He and Gordon have a final violent meeting in Central Park.[25]

> *Gordon*: How ya, Buddy? ... Ya sandbagged me on Bluestar. I guess you think you taught the teacher a lesson that the tail can wag the dog ... You could have been one of the great ones Buddy. I look at you and I see myself. Why?
> *Bud*: I don't know. I guess I realized [wipes blood from face and hands] I'm just Bud Fox. As much as I wanted to be Gordon Gekko, I'll always be Bud Fox [throws handkerchief on ground, walks away].

Having rejected Gordon, it remains for Bud to be reunited with his father. The film's last scene provides this reunion. Bud, his father and his mother are on the way to the federal courthouse.

> *Carl*: You told the truth and gave the money back.
> *Mother*: You helped save the airline and the airline people are gonna remember you for it.
> *Carl*: That's right. If I were you I'd think about the job with Bluestar that Wildman offered you.
> *Bud*: Dad, I'm goin' to jail and you know it.
> *Carl*: Ya, maybe that's the price son. Its gonna be hard on ya, that's for sure, but maybe in some kind of screwed up way that's the best thing that coulda happened to ya. Create instead of living off the buying and selling of others.

Bud walks up the steps of the courthouse. A long camera shot pulls up to the courthouse, then the Manhattan skyline, then pans the Wall Street corridor. 'THE END' appears on the screen, with the following lines 'Dedicated to Louis Stone, Stockbroker, 1910–1985.'[26] A Talking Heads song, 'This must be the place,' plays over the closing credits,[27] in stark contrast to Frank Sinatra's 'Fly me to the moon,' which opened the film.

The critics read the film

Even before it was released, 'Wall Street' was surrounded by a laudatory discourse that was apparently determined by two factors: Oliver Stone's reputation as one of Hollywood's new star directors and scriptwriters, and the subject matter of his new film.[28] Consider the following leads either to reviews of the film, or stories about it: '"Wall Street" takes aim at value system' (Ebert, 1987); 'A Season of Flash and Greed' (*Time*, 1987b); 'Greed' (Canby, 1987); 'A Bull Market in Sin' (*Newsweek*, 1987); 'Wall Street's gutter ethics' (Newman, 1987); 'In The Trenches of Wall Street' (*Time*, 1987a); 'Making "Wall Street" Look Like Wall Street' (Cowan, 1987); 'Oliver Stone Easing Out of Violence' (Bennetts, 1987); 'Wall Street Reviews "Wall Street" ' (Fabrikant, 1987); 'A View From the Trenches' (Rattner, 1987).

The subject matter could not have been more timely. Wall Street, the new battle ground for Yuppie America, and 'Reaganomics', were collapsing, and with the collapse a part of the new American dream was being shattered. History and fiction overlapped in the film, and if history was not passing judgement on what was happening on the American scene, Stone was. How did the critics read his production?

Go back to the leads for the reviews: 'A view from the trenches,' 'A bull market in sin,' 'Wall Street's gutter ethics,' and read the praise: 'A sensationally entertaining melodrama about greed and corruption in New York' (*New York*, 1987: 87); 'May not be a work of art, but it's the most enjoyable movie of the year . . . The psychology of seduction is appallingly convincing' (*New York*, 1987: 88);[29] 'An upscale morality tale' (Canby, 1987). But underneath these gritty, glittering headlines the critics found fault, especially in the film's narrative and final moral position.[30] Canby (1987: C3) suggested that it would 'entertain achievers who don't want to lose touch with their moral centers, but still have it all.' *Newsweek* (1987: 78): 'Underneath the shiny, contemporary surface is a musty old Hollywood movie about good and evil, full of stock characters and cliches.' *Variety* (1987): 'Watching "Wall Street" is about as wordy and dreary as reading the financial papers accounts of the rise and fall of an Ivan Boesky-type . . . with one exception. Instead of editorializing about the evils of greed . . . it lectures, which is great as a case study in business school but wearisome as a film.' Quarreling with the film's praise for the superior morality of the working class, as given in Bud's last speech to Gekko, Sprinkler (1988: 365–6) argues that 'Herein lies the most acute flaw in Stone's conception . . . the plot finally revolves around a small allegory of class: honesty, fairness, and loyalty are working class values; ruthlessness, cunningness, and selfishness are the preserve of financiers.'

As might be expected, so-called Wall Street experts also reacted negatively to the film. Rattner (1987) argued that 'investment banking is tough, but not nearly as brutal as the film makes it. . . Airlines aren't bought and sold in an afternoon . . . the movie focuses on a distinctly small slice of the Street.'[31] This opinion was also echoed by the 130 investment bankers and brokers who watched the film in a private showing: 'The people here do an honest day's work,' was one comment (Fabrikant, 1987: 5). Another broker stated, 'It is upsetting because it makes the excesses of Wall Street look like an everyday occurrence' (Fabrikant, 1987: 5), and still another suggested that the subject of the film was 'too foreign to be a hit elsewhere in the U.S. You have people on farms in Iowa going to movies. How can they relate to this?' (Fabrikant, 1987: 5). Finally, 'At the end the movie takes a stern but realistic line on the ethical questions it raises' (*New York*, 1987: 88), but, 'The movie crashes in a heap of platitudes that remind us that honesty is, after all, the best policy' (Canby, 1987: C3).

Back to the story

Unnoticed in the seduction–corruption–redemption morality tale motif that structures many of the above reviews is the fact that the seduction occurred before the film began, that corruption was already present in Bud's workplace, and his redemption, signaled by the return to his father's values, is undermotivated.[32] Listen again to Bud's first speech in the film: 'My dream is to one day to be on the other end of that thing.' In his next speech he recites Gordon Gekko's accomplishments: 'The guy makes 20 times what Dave Winfield makes in a year.' He was seduced before the story began. He was already corrupt. He knew it and his father knew it, as did Marvin and Lou, and Gordon knew it the moment he set eyes on him. He had bought into the value system that Stone wishes to critique in his Boesky–Gekko character. Gordon neither seduced, nor corrupted him, for he was a player waiting to become guilty, as soon as the circumstances permitted.

The narrative falters, then, from the very beginning. This being the case, Stone's morality tale never gets off the ground as it seeks to explain Bud's corruption by Gekko's effects. Despite his attempts to locate minor corruption in the workplace, what he never succeeds in establishing is how the broader social-historical moment itself created the conditions for Bud's fall. By never going outside the workplace, except to the pivotal conversations with Carl, Stone is left with a simplistic morality tale which espouses the virtues of hard work over easy money. In the very moment when it rushes forward to redeem Bud, in his final speech to Gordon, the film's simplicity and redundancy become most apparent.

As a result, the film is neither a 'radical critique of the capitalist trading mentality,' nor a telling fictional treatment of a passing moment in American history. But it is more than a conservative apologia for 'Wall Street.' It is a form of myth-making which absorbs into its very center the central features of a postmodern world which threatens to destroy itself from within.[33] The postmodern moment not only commodifies information, as Gekko teaches Bud, but it commodifies time, individuals, life styles, status and prestige, and human feelings. This commodification process turns on the representations that are given to 'real' things. But since the real has become a commodity that is transformed into a thing with a market value, all that is purchased are the illusions of things and the money they cost. As Gekko notes, he creates nothing. He only buys and owns. What he buys are illusions. Money is the ultimate illusion for it signifies nothing but more money, and money no longer resides in a real world of signified things. It refers only to itself (see Simmel, 1978). There is only illusion.

Carl doesn't know this. His old-time values reference a time that never will be, the time when people create, instead of living off the buying and selling of others. The film's closing nostalgic move, which inserts a false historical moment into the narrative, is pure ideology. Neither Stone nor his critics understood the structure he criticized; he wants, like they do, a time when things are real, have real value, and when real things reflect the real value of hardworking individuals. That time is gone.[34]

Gekko understood part of the new equation, the illusion part. What he hasn't grasped is the unreality of the things he owns, and the unreality of the process which produces the satisfactions he experiences when he buys, sells and destroys. That is, Gekko's is an ideological illusion, a commodity attached to a conservative Darwinian political belief system which holds that the strongest survive and the weakest die. In fact nothing in this system has any reality whatsoever; not even Gekko. In the endless chain of signifiers that money attaches itself to, persons become commodities who have no referent outside the chain of signification. They differ from one another only in terms of the signifiers they can attach to themselves, but the signifiers only sustain one illusion over another; nothing is permanent.

Carl, Gordon, Bud and Oliver Stone believe in permanence. Stone's permanence, and the one he transferred to Bud and Carl, is old fashioned American capitalism. And here is where the myth-making becomes so critical. As long as capitalism can sustain the illusion that there are two types of illusions, one moral, the other immoral, one permanent, the other not, it appears able to sustain the belief that everything is fine (see Marcuse, 1964; Baudrillard, 1975; Lash, 1988; Featherstone, 1988; Turner, 1987; Stauth and Turner, 1988; Denzin, 1988). As long as there are Oliver Stones who can tell stories like 'Wall Street,' nobody has anything to worry about. Don't worry about the simplistic morality tale he tells, don't worry about whether it will play in Iowa, or if he only describes a tiny slice of reality. All that matters is that there are people who know it won't play in Iowa, and these same people know that only a small number of traders really act like Gekko.

Such beliefs sustain the system and that is why this is an important film. Stone's myth turns attention away from the very structure that is no longer reachable, from the unimaginable, for if the world were really filled with Gordon Gekkos we would all be in trouble. But we are not in trouble because there are the Carl Fox's and the SEC out there and they will police this corrupt system and bring our wayward Yuppies back into line.

What if there was no system to be brought back into? What if the illusion has become real, and there is only illusion? What if there is no fallback system? This is the ultimate terror that Stone pulls back from, but then he never saw it. What prevented him from seeing what he thought he saw? Go back to the two songs, Sinatra's 'Fly me to the moon,' and The Talking Heads' 'This must be the place.' Compare the lines, the historical moments occupied by the singers, and the positioning of the two songs at the beginning and end of the film. Sinatra, the ultimate signifier of conservative, male, mainstream, middle class American culture croons 'Fly me to the moon'. Stone intends the lyric to be more than a song about a man's love for a woman. They are applied directly to Bud. He wants to play among the stars, be a Gekko, a sixteenth century Italian entrepreneur. He wants to live life on the other side. He worships money and power. He wants these things to be true and real. Stone wants the viewer to believe that Bud has found these things that he adores not to be true. In fact his text does not establish this, for what Bud learns is that Gekko is not true. There is no support in the film for the conclusion that Bud has rejected all that this thing called money can buy. He will probably accept the corporate position with Bluestar that has been offered. He has simply reinserted himself back into the very structure that Stone wants the viewer to think he has rejected.

The vehicle for the re-entry is The Talking Heads' song, with the theme 'Home is where I want to be.' Home is where Bud is at the end of the film. Feeling numb, saying little about what has happened, he has plenty of time now it's for love, not money. Having drifted in and out (away from home), he's back where he started, with mother and father. The prodigal son, like a tamed animal, has returned home.[35]

Consider the source of these lines. The Talking Heads are widely known as a subversive 'leading avant garde, post punk, rock and roll group, whose nihilistic images have recently turned to a more romantic celebration of love, community, family and the individual's place in the group.'[36] Yet the music of this group signifies a sound which is quite different from Sinatra's. Hip Stone has used radical rock to offer the final commentary in his critique of American capitalism. This is a surface, glossed reading. Underneath, the message from Sinatra to The Talking Heads can be read as being equivalent. Both voices celebrate the same values, love and family. The paradox of Sinatra's lines lie only in the fact that Bud, at the end, returns to their original meaning. His journey through the film is simply an exploration of their alternative meaning, the one Stone gives them when he allows them to play over his opening shots of 'Wall Street.' Hence while the 'Heads'' lines appear to offer a radical conclusion to a radical film, underneath they simply stitch together the opening and closing parts of the film into a tightly bound structure which is conservative from beginning to end.

Two problems remain. The first, how Stone created his subject called Bud Fox. The second, the multiple meanings contained in the phrase 'Wall Street.' After Althusser (1971: 171) it can be argued that the capitalist ideology Bud has accepted has constituted him, a concrete individual, as a subject who has been 'hailed by' or called to an ideological site where his subjectivity may be enacted. Stone suggests that he was corrupted by this site: a perfect ideological dupe, he fell into Gordon's trap, learned Gordon's voice and realized himself through the language and material wealth Gordon gave him.

In order for this argument to work the film must have a category of ideologically pure subjects who have not been contaminated by the 'greedy' side of capitalism. But where are they? Carl, the working class hero, makes over $47,000 a year and believes that real men make real things with their hands, and don't live off the buying and selling of others. His airline buys and sells tickets, routes and services. Lou, the other spokesperson for purity, gives hot tips on a good stock. Carl and Lou trade in information and commodities, just like Gordon. They are ideological dupes of another version of capitalism, that version Stone wants to maintain and valorize. Indeed their version of capitalism sustains the other version that Stone despises, Gekko's sharks who destroy in the name of greed. One version could not exist without the other. In the end the film is about a simplistic clash between two ideological versions of the same thing. Stone wants to destroy one version in the name of the other; in fact he ends up supporting both. It could have been no other way. Stone, as a concrete individual, has been constituted by 'his' popular culture as a subject who valorizes that culture while criticizing it. In so doing he used all of the ideological equipment the popular culture could make available to him, even up to and including the voices of Sinatra and The Talking Heads.

Now the metaphor 'Wall Street.' The word signifies more than a place that points to the world's leading financial center. It points to the ethical doings that go on in that place, and there are two kinds of doings that happen there; those that are ethical and those that are unethical. These are the meanings Stone manipulates in his movie. But there is a third meaning, the one hinted at above, and the one that Stone refuses to touch. This is the meaning that says that 'Wall Street' is a purely imaginary ideological site, which has no concrete referent in the real world. This is the meaning that points to the political economy of signs, not money in the postmodern world (Baudrillard, 1975, 1981). In this political economy only signs, representations and simulations of the real circulate. In fact this is the reality of 'Wall Street.' Go back to the floor of the Stock Exchange, and re-examine the green computer screens of the young brokers at Bud's firm. Numbers flashing across screens, numbers which can be erased with the touch of the finger, or a loud voice. Numbers which point to imaginary properties or imaginary things. Companies with made-up names, whose productivity is measured by imaginary numbers concerning losses and gains. Money going in and out of hidden accounts. Money attached to nothing by imaginary numbers attached to made-up accounts, built on the transactions and imagined doings of imaginary companies. Careers built on who can best manipulate this imaginary political economy of signs.

This is what 'Wall Street' is. A site where a political economy of signs ceaselessly circulates across an imaginary computerized space where nothing is any longer real. This 'cool universe of digitality has absorbed [and] won out over the reality principle' (Baudrillard, 1983: 152). As Gekko says, 'The illusion has become real and the more real it becomes, the more desperate they want it.'

This is the frightening world 'Wall Street' refers to and this is the world Stone pretended to open up in his movie. This cool universe, unfeeling, imaginary, and 'real' in its peculiar, quaint, ideological way will destroy all of us, and when it does it will do so in the name of family, love, hardwork, and honesty.[37]

Notes

I would like to thank Katherine Ryan-Denzin, Lawrence Grossberg, Wayne Woodward, Peter K. Manning and James W. Carey for their assistance, comments and suggestions on earlier drafts of this statement.

1 The crash led to a serious reappraisal of the US's marketing system, assertions that the new computer technology was partly responsible for the crash, concerns about global securities markets, and debates over the structure that regulates such trading (see Glaberson, 1987: 20). The *New York Times* ran a five-part series on the 'Lessons of October 1987' (see Glaberson, 1987; Sterngold, 1987; Sanger, 1987; and Lohr, 1987). In 1989 the same structure that Stone described in his film seems to be in place. All that has changed is the number of brokers who have been arrested for the kinds of violations detailed in the film.

2 Oliver Stone director, produced by Edward R. Pressman, screenplay by Stanley Weiser and Stone, released by 20th Century-Fox, starring Charlie Sheen (Bud Fox), Michael Douglas (Gordon Gekko), Martin Sheen (Carl Fox), Daryl Hannah (Darien Taylor), Terence Stamp (Sir Larry Wildman), Hal Holbrook (Lou Mannheim), Sean Young (Kate Gekko), John C. McGinley (Marvin), James Spader (Roger Barnes), Sylvia Miles (Realtor), running time 124 minutes, Oscar for Douglas, one of the top money-making films of the 1988 season, and a current top video rental.

3 The film takes it name from a place, Wall Street, a metaphor which stands for something else, the world's leading financial center, and in recent years the place where America's ethical standards, 'or lack of them has been determined' (Newman, 1987). At the same time the real place, Wall Street, refers to a 'seven-block alley of skyscrapers on the seaward tip of Manhattan Island' (Newman, 1987). The movie 'Wall Street' stands in this double relationship to a 'real' place and the doings that go on in that place. It captures the importance of money, class, morality and mobility in the postmodern age, while it punctures the dreams that money can make happen. By collapsing reality and fantasy into a single commercial venture, which also incorporates Stone's own life story, the film opens a window into and dramatizes a version of contemporary postmodern life that is more read about than seen. It capitalizes on the viewer's voyeuristic desire to gaze into the worlds of the rich and the famous. Bud (see below), and his father, become, under this formulation, the viewers' alter egos, for they do the gazing, and their reactions become ours.

4 A *gecko* is a lizard that feeds on insects and sheds its tail when trapped. Ivan Boesky was convicted of conspiring to file false documents with the federal government. The case in question involved insider trader violations, connected to Boesky's trading of junk bonds with Drexel Burnham Lambert Inc. In 1985 Boesky won the top moneymaking award on Wall Street ($100 million earnings). His former aide, Michael Milken, was convicted of similar violations in 1988. As part of a sentencing agreement Boesky was granted immunity from federal criminal prosecutors, as was Milken (see *Wall Street Journal* 1987).

5 His father is an airline mechanic and the leader of the local union at Bluestar airlines.

6 By subversive I mean a reading that opposes the dominant readings brought to the text by audience members and film critics (see Denzin, 1988).

7 Other films, also in 1987, which stress the values of family, individualism and work, include 'Moonstruck,' 'Fatal Attraction,' 'Broadcast News,' 'The Untouchables,' 'Lethal Weapon,' 'Stakeout,' 'The Secret of My Success,' 'Tinmen'; in 1988, 'The Accidental Tourist,' 'Everybody's All American,' 'The Boost,' 'Dominic and Eugene,' 'Running On Empty'; and already in 1989, 'Field of Dreams,' 'Rainman,' 'Beaches,' 'When Harry Met Sally,' 'Indiana Jones and the Last Crusade,' and (problematically) 'Do The Right Thing.'

8 'Fly me to the moon. Let me play among the stars. Let me see what spring is like on Jupiter and Mars.'

9 A crash a year earlier was caused by manufacturer's error. The ruling will allow the company to go for new airline routes. Bud asks, 'You sure about this announcement?' Carl: 'You got that mischievous look in your eye.'

10 He then gives him the information he had earlier gained from his father about the forthcoming FAA decision.

11 In the next scene Bud and Gordon are in a restaurant. Gordon gives him a check for one million dollars: 'That should cover the Bluestar buy. Put a coupla 100 thou on those bow wow stocks you mentioned. Pick the dog with the least fleas. Use a stop-loss so down-size a 100 thou, and buy a decent suit. Put the rest of the money in a tax-free fund. I wanta see how you do before I invest in ya. And save the cheap salesman talk. You do good you get perks. Lots and lots of perks.'

12 Gordon offers his theory of how the market works in the following lines. 'The public's out there throwin' darts at boards sport. I bet on sure things . . . It's trench warfare out there pal.'

13 Several scenes later, in a move which aligns Bud's father with Gordon's father, Carl has a heart attack.

14 Gordon's view of love is given in the following lines. He and Darien are walking along Wall Street. 'You and I are the same, Darien. We are smart enough not to buy into the oldest myth runnin', love. A fiction created by people to keep 'em from jumpin' out of windows.'

15 Looking out of Manhattan, from his balcony, after having just left Darien in his mammoth bed, he asks, 'Who am I?'

16 He begins his speech with the following lines, which reflect the film's attempts to be historical, radical and chic at the same time: 'Ladies and gentlemen. We are not out here to indulge in fantasy, but in political and economic reality.'

17 In a speech to a group of business students in 1985 Boesky stated, 'Greed is right, by the way, I think greed is healthy. You can be greedy and still feel good about yourself' (Glaberson, 1987: 20). Stone's use of these lines is a classic instance of intertextuality, where the real spills over into the fictional, and the world of fiction is then used to judge the reality of the 'real' world.

18 Moved by this speech, and now working day and night, Bud announces to Darien, who has just complained that she is going psychotic, from a lack of REM sleep, that 'You think I'm gonna broker for the rest of my life? Come on Darien. I'm gonna be a giant. An entrepreneur in the Italian sixteenth century sense of the word. A mover, a shaker.' Darien, as if in an attempt to top Bud, later describes her goals in these words: 'I'd like to do for antiques what Laura Ashley did for interior fabric. Produce a line of high quality antiques at a low price.' Despite its glossy, surface representations of successful women, the film really takes a traditional, anti-feminist stance on women, work and their relations with men. Darien, after all, is Gekko's mistress, and achieved everything she has through his material wealth and her sexuality. James W. Carey underscored this point for me.

19 'You've got a loss of 20 million dollars, dividends cut to zero, and you're bein' squeezed dead by the majors.'

20 In his rejection he also repudiates the new voice Bud has acquired; the voice of Gekko.

21 The bitterness between the two increases. Carl: 'What you see is a man who never measured the size of man's success by the size of his wallet [yelling].' Bud: 'That's because you never had the guts to go out into the world and stake your own claim.' Carl [stares at him]: 'Boy if that's the way you feel, I must have done a really lousy job as a father.' Bud: 'Dad. I'm asking you. I'm begging you.' Carl: 'I don't go to sleep with no whore and I don't wake up with no whore. That's how I live with myself. I don't know how you do it. I hope I'm wrong about this guy.'

22 Bud confronts Gekko, and gets the following speech: 'The richest one percent of this country owns half our country's wealth.'

23 As this occurs Carl has his heart attack. Bud makes up with him in the hospital room. In this speech Bud relinquishes Gekko's voice and takes back Carl's.

24 In a degradation ceremony he is led in handcuffs out of the office, through a long gauntlet-like corridor of onlooking co-workers.

25 In this penultimate scene, he wears a 'wire.' Afterwards he is told by federal agents that 'You did the right thing, Bud.'

26 Stone's father, a retail stockbroker and conservative Goldwater Republican, who left his son with the following dictates, 'Love justice, Do Mercy, Walk humbly with thy God' (*Vogue* 1987: 172).

27 'Pick me up and turn me around, guess I must be havin' fun. . . Hi ho, we drift in and out. I'm just an animal looking for a home.'

28 He had won Academy Awards in 1987 for writing and directing 'Platoon,' and in 1985 he had received critical acclaim for 'Salvador' (*Vogue* 1987: 166). Even before the film was released it was common knowledge that Stone was going for realism. He employed stockbrokers as advisors (Cowan, 1987: 16), privately screened the film for Wall Street luminaries (Fabrikant, 1987), consulted with brokers over the lines he wrote, had Charlie Sheen spend two days with David Brown, a former Goldman Sachs trader who pleaded guilty to insider trading in 1986 (*Time*, 1987a: 76–7), trotted out 'real' Manhattan characters like James Rosenquist and Richard Feigen (Canby, 1987), and consulted with novelists Joseph Heller and Kurt Vonnegut on his characters and the words they spoke (Cowan, 1987).

29 This same reviewer, in discussing Stone's morality play, invoked the earlier Hollywood production 'Sweet smell of success' (1957), which also exposed the evils of power and the seduction of the pure.

30 Even though the narrative was perceived as flawed, reviewers praised the performances of Douglas and the two Sheens (see Denzin, 1990, ch. 2 for a discussion of how film reviewers write their criticisms).

31 Rattner, managing director at Morgan Stanley & Co, also compared the film to Tom Wolfe's *Bonfire of the Vanities*, which 'in a single phrase – Masters of the Universe – defined the investment mentality as aptly as all 125 minutes of "Wall Street"' (Rattner, 1987: 80); and Sprinkler (1988: 367) suggested that the viewer interested in the psychology of Wall Street read Matthew Josephson's 'unparalleled classic about nineteenth century capitalism, *The Robber Barons* [1934]. One will quickly see that nothing much has changed on the street from that day to this.'

32 I thank Katherine Ryan-Denzin for pointing this out to me. There is little that indicates why Bud would suddenly capitulate to his father's value-system.

33 Human experience gets lost in the endless swirl of signifiers, which signify nothing but themselves. Bud had to leave that world in order to be saved. Gekko remained inside it and was (presumably) destroyed by it.

34 As Baudrillard (1987/88: 22) observes, 'history [has become] instantaneous media memory without a past.' This means, in part, that the media's signified representations of the past (i.e. coldwar clips from the Berlin Wall) lack referentiality in contemporary lives. Nostalgia, which re-enacts a purified past, establishes that sense of presence which has no presence (see Denzin 1988 for a discussion of the forms of nostalgia that circulate in the postmodern moment).

35 The animal theme is prominent throughout the film's text, including the Darwinian, evolutionary theory of greed, the elephant metaphor, and Gekko's recurrent use of the word 'dog' to characterize certain kinds of stock. Gekko's profane excretory phrases are closely connected to the animalistic metaphors. They contribute to the general impression that Gekko, a profane, dirty being, is outside society.

36 Lawrence Grossberg, in conversation (paraphrased), August 2, 1989.

37 Compare here the recent 'H.U.D.' (Housing and Urban Development) scandal, where a new group of 'immoral' capitalists succeeded in manipulating the housing market in a way that excluded real people from real homes (see Gerth, 1989).

References

Althusser, Louis (1971) *Lenin and Philosophy*. New York: Monthly Review Press.

Baudrillard, Jean (1975) *The Mirror of Production*. St. Louis: Telos Press.

Baudrillard, Jean (1981) *For Critique of The Political Economy of Signs*. St. Louis: Telos Press.

Baudrillard, Jean (1983) *Simulations*. New York: Semiotext(e).

Baudrillard, Jean (1987/88) *America*. London: Verso.

Bennetts, Leslie (1987) 'Oliver Stone easing out of violence.' *New York Times*, 13 April: C 13.

Canby, Vincent (1987) Review of Stone's 'Wall Street.' *New York Times*, 11 December: C 3.

Clark, Mike (1987) 'Stone's Stock Soars,' review of 'Wall Street.' *USA Today*, 11 December: 16.

Cowan, Allison Leigh (1987) 'Making "Wall Street" Look Like Wall Street.' *New York Times*, 30 December: C 16.

Denzin, Norman K. (1988) ' "Blue Velvet": Postmodern Contradictions.' *Theory, Culture and Society*, 5: 461–73.

Denzin, Norman K. (1990) *Film and the American Alcoholic*. New York: Aldine de Gruyter.

Ebert, Roger (1987) ' "Wall Street" takes aim at value system': review of 'Wall Street.' *Chicago Sun Times*, 11 December: 20–1.

Fabrikant, Geraldine (1987) 'Wall Street reviews "Wall Street." ' *New York Times*, 10 December: D 1, 5.

Featherstone, Mike (1988) 'In pursuit of the postmodern: an introduction.' *Theory, Culture and Society*, 5:195–215.

Gerth, Jeff (1989) 'Risks to H.U.D. rose after its shift of responsibility to private sector.' *New York Times*, 31 July: 5.

Glaberson, William (1987) 'The plunge: a stunning blow to a gilded, impudent age.' *New York Times*, 13 December: 1, 20.

Josephson, Matthew (1934) *The Robber Barons*. New York: Macmillan.

Lash, Scott (1988) 'Discourse or figure? postmodernism as a "regime of signification." ' *Theory, Culture and Society*, 5: 311–36.

Lohr, Steve (1987) 'Investors retreating from foreign markets.' *New York Times*, 16 December: 1, 32.

Lyotard, Jean-François (1984) *The Postmodern Condition: A Report on Knowledge*. Minneapolis: University of Minnesota Press.

Marcuse, Herbert (1964) *One-Dimensional Man*. Boston: Beacon Press.

Nash, Nathaniel C. (1987) 'A new urgency for reforms in policing securities trades.' *New York Times*, 17 December: 1, 34.

Newman, Peter C. (1987) 'Wall Street's gutter ethics.' Review of 'Wall Street.' *Maclean's*, 28 December: 61.

Newsweek (1987) 'A bull market in sin.' Review of 'Wall Street,' 14 December: 78–9.

New York Magazine (1987) 'Review of "Wall Street." ' 14 December: 87–8.

Rattner, Steven (1987) 'A view from the trenches: an investment broker winces at "Wall Street." ' *Newsweek*, 14 December: 80.

Sanger, David E. (1987) 'The computer's contribution to the rise and fall of stocks.' *New York Times*, 15 December: 1, 52.

Simmel Georg (1978) *The Philosophy of Money*. London: Routledge & Kegan Paul.

Sprinkler, Michael (1988) Review of 'Wall Street,' in Frank N. Magill (ed.), *Magill's Cinema Annual: 1988*. Pasadena, CA: Salem Press, pp. 364–7.

Stauth, Georg and Turner, Bryan S. (1988) 'Nostalgia, postmodernism and the critique of mass culture,' *Theory, Culture and Society*, 5: 509–26.

Sterngold, James (1987) 'Seeking a stronger safety net for the system.' *New York Times*, 14 December: 1, 34.

Time (1987a) 'In the trenches of Wall Street.' 20 July: 76–7.

Time (1987b) 'A season of flash and greed.' Review of 'Wall Street.' 14 December: 82–3.

Turner, Bryan S. (1987) 'A note on nostalgia.' *Theory, Culture and Society*, 4: 147–56.

Variety (1987) Review of 'Wall Street.' 9 December.

Vogue (1987) 'Talking to Oliver Stone.' December: 166, 172.

Wall Street Journal (1987) General news index: 1124–25.

Wolfe, Tom (1988) *Bonfire of the Vanities*. New York: Knopf.

4

AFTER NOSTALGIA? WILFUL NOSTALGIA AND THE PHASES OF GLOBALIZATION

Roland Robertson

We have no history. Our history begins today. (A Japanese to a German physician, [1876]; Smith, 1983: 9)

Like nostalgia, diversity is not what it used to be. (Clifford Geertz, 1986: 114)

For the nostalgic, the world is alien. (Bryan S. Turner, 1987: 149)

When the real is no longer what it used to be, nostalgia assumes its full meaning. (Jean Baudrillard, 1983: 12)

In this discussion I want to continue the exploration of what Stauth and Turner have called 'the nostalgic paradigm.' Stauth and Turner (1988a: 29) argue that sociology 'is dominated by a common episteme which provides the leading motif for the separate and jarring discourses of various sociological approaches.' There is, they say, wide variation in 'the terminologies' of the latter but those 'are actually dominated by a uniform problem, which is the problem of nostalgic memory' (Stauth and Turner, 1988a: 29). This is a heavy claim – so strong that even its proponents do not, I take it, mean to say that *all* of contemporary sociology and social theory or *all* contemporary practitioners in those intellectual areas are equally implicated in the reproduction of the nostalgic attitude. Nonetheless I believe that with allowance for some rhetorical exaggeration Stauth and Turner are persuasive. That being so, and insofar as one tends to think that there must be something wrong with an academic discipline which is so strongly tied to the nostalgic attitude, it follows that we should not merely render it more explicit – that is, describe it – we should also 'provide a critique of nostalgia in order to set sociology on a different course' (Stauth and Turner, 1988a: 29). The present paper takes up that challenge, by offering an interpretation of the circumstances which have promoted nostalgia both on social-theoretical and on real-life empirical fronts.

The global setting of wilful nostalgia

The thematization of the problem of nostalgia which Stauth and Turner have initiated is, in their own terms, situated within the context of an extended discussion of the relatively unexplored influence of Nietzsche in the history of social theory, an exercise which at the same time involves an advocacy of a Nietzschean outlook as far as the future of sociology is concerned.[1] My own task here, however, is to consider the issue of nostalgia both more directly and from a rather different angle. Specifically, I will try to expand upon the argument of Stauth and Turner by addressing the issue of the foundations of what Tom Nairn (1988: 347) has called the 'modern, wilful kind' of nostalgia. In so doing I will be particularly concerned with the global dynamics and significance of that phenomenon.

In his penetrating analysis of the British monarchy (more diffusely, of Britain – indeed, 'Ukania' – as a whole) Nairn (1988: 347) argues that the kind of nostalgia which was to be found in, say, the late eighteenth century 'hadn't been more than a century or so behind the times.' Using Viscount Bolingbroke as an exemplar of late eighteenth century English nostalgia, Nairn says that 'the actual wreckage of the world he had lost was all about him, some of its rooms inhabited, apparently still recuperable.' In contrast, with the late *nineteenth* century interest in *the invention of tradition* (Hobsbawm and Ringer, 1983) there arose a kind of nostalgia which had scant, if any, concern with what Christopher Lasch (1988: 178) has appropriately called a 'conversational relationship with the past.' Rather, this was a period – lasting from about 1880 to the early or mid-1920s – when there was considerable concern about issues surrounding national identity and national integration across the world; except for black Africa, which was an arena for the projection of the identities of the imperialist powers. But it should also be pointed out that in Africa, as well as in parts of Asia and Oceania, these issues appeared not just as concrete extensions of Western identities – as in the idea of 'the white man's burden' – but also, with the arrival of early functionalist anthropology, as forms of identity and integration *conferral*. In other words, while Western imperialism of the late nineteenth and early twentieth centuries involved the political and symbolic incorporation of African and other territories into the national identities of the imperialist nations, it also, on the other hand, involved the attribution to primal societies of cohesive functionality – which exercise actually combined a modernist notion of function with a nostalgic injection of Western *Gemeinschaft* (Ardener, 1985).

Sociology as we now know it crystallized precisely during the period of which I have spoken. Specifically, the period during which modern *wilful* nostalgia developed in earnest was also the period when so-called classical or canonical sociology was formulated (in Western and, to some extent, Central Europe) – along 'grand narrative' lines. In view of that circumstance, I present three main arguments.

First and most generally, I maintain that there was indeed a close link between those two developments – that they mutually amplified each other in the main centers from which emanated the major traditions of social theory (notably Britain, France, Germany and, to some extent, the USA). Wilful nostalgia among national elites fed into the work of leading sociologists and vice versa. In that connection it is of fundamental importance to note that from around 1880 there was considerable and increasing concern among the elites of a large number of societies with the establishment of grandiose national symbols, monuments, ceremonials, and so on (Hobsbawm and Ringer, 1983). From Washington DC across Europe to Tokyo the late nineteenth century witnessed the kind of wilful, politically driven nostalgia of which Nairn has spoken elaborately in reference to Britain – and fleetingly to Japan (Nairn, 1988: 271). As Stephen Kern (1983: 277) has written in his study of the emergent global culture of that period, 'the self-images of nations in the full spectrum of time – past, present, and future – changed after 1880 . . .' However, it is also the case that there were significant differences across nations concerning the sense of the past: 'Examination of the sense of the past of the major belligerents in World War I reveals a striking contrast between the temporalities of the nations of each alliance system and underlying causes of resentment and misunderstanding' (Kern, 1983: 277). Thus while nostalgic concern was widespread – most explicitly among the major European powers such as Britain, France, Germany, Russia, Italy and Austria-Hungary – there was significant variation with respect both to the intensity and the type of concern with the past.

While Kern, Nairn and the contributors to the pathbreaking volume edited by Hobsbawm and Ringer are correct in emphasizing the last quarter of the nineteenth century as the crucial phase in the rise of modern wilful nostalgia, it has to be said that strains leading to explicit concern with national identity and tradition became manifest somewhat earlier than that in some Asian societies, of which China and Japan were (and remain) the most important. In both China and Japan, Western intrusions during the 1850s created an intense 'response to the West' (Schwartz, 1964: 9) – which in Japan led, in turn, to a remarkably effective invention of national myths in the early Meiji period (Gluck, 1985), but which in China led to increasing uncertainty and instability. That does not, of course, mean that a concept such as tradition was readily available to East Asians; for it was only in the late nineteenth century that the nineteenth-century Western category of 'tradition' was actually translated into Chinese (Schwartz, 1964: 50). On the other hand it is worth noting that the term 'nostalgia' (*hsiang-ch'ou*) has been a conspicuous topic in Chinese literature since at least the time of Confucius in the sixth century BC (about which more later) – although in registering this I am certainly not equating traditionalism with nostalgia.

Second, I argue that in the period in question some of the leading motifs of Western social theory – notably the predicaments expressed in the thematization of the *Gemeinschaft–Gesellschaft* and related distinctions, on the one hand, and the search for integration-promoting national identities, on the other – diffused to other parts of the world (such as embryonic and actual Turkey, China and Japan) in such a way as to provide the beginning of a global discourse (much more explicit than Foucault's episteme) concerning what a modern society should 'look like' and how it should operate. The early impact of Western sociology in that regard is probably the most overlooked of all aspects of the history and historiography of social theory. For it may well be that during its classical period sociology made its greatest general impact upon international and public affairs; although, as I have suggested, it was itself greatly affected – indeed, restricted – by the national and international circumstances of the time. In that regard what is of particular interest in the present context is the differential impact of the thinking of the sociologists of the classical period – particularly Herbert Spencer – on the national newcomers to 'international society,' of whom Japan was in various respects the most important (Gong, 1984). Japan had, of course, a long and 'successful' history of manipulating its own history and of expressing its substantive identity – its 'essence' – in *forms* drawn from other cultures, most importantly China (Pollock, 1986). But the new Meiji elites were particularly explicit about and adept at reconstructuring 'the' national tradition, which policy eventuated in the production of a highly serviceable nostalgia about such matters as the imperial system, Shinto as a native religion, the samurai ethic and the Confucian ethos as a way of consolidating Japan's 'national essence' and strengthening it, as an entirely 'unique' society, against the outside world (Smith, 1983; Buruma, 1989: 44; Gluck, 1985).[2]

Japan's newcomer status and the ability of its leaders to combine or transcend the *Gemeinschaft–Gesellschaft* predicament gave it certain advantages over the European latecomers, of whom the most important was obviously Germany – and from which it actually learned quite a lot with respect to national-identity formation. At the same time, Japan also managed to reverse much of its historical relationship with China, in that Japan's apparent success in 'responding to the West' became a problematic model *for China*; one important aspect of which was that a very large portion of the Western ideas which reached China after 1900 came via Chinese students' experiences in Japanese universities and Chinese translations of Japanese translations from European languages (Wang, 1966; Schwartz, 1964). In the later period of World War II Germany and Japan were, of course, to become the leading Axis powers – both committed in their own ways, as 'deprived' nations, to 'the transcendence of the modern' or, more precisely, the calculated, synthetic transcendence of the uniquely *modern* myth of the tension between *Gemeinschaft* and *Gesellschaft*. And it is of relevance to the present discussion that questions concerning both Japanese and German identities – including the issue of nostalgia – have in recent years become more, rather than less, globally salient (Buruma, 1989). That salience has been profoundly enhanced by the strong moves towards German reunification which began towards the end of 1989 and the prospect of Japan and a reunified Germany eventually becoming the two most powerful nations on earth. Both Japan and Germany stand out as nations which stress ethnic or racial homogeneity rather than heterogeneity; both have been adept at the political exploitation of nostalgia.

Newly unified in the 1870s but lacking a readily serviceable national myth and a relatively unbroken past of the kind enjoyed by England (or Britain),

France and Russia, 'it was impossible for [Germany's] citizens to believe . . . that their country has always been and always would be' (Kern, 1983: 278).[3] Thus the highly influential sets of sociological ideas produced in Germany at that time were remarkably pessimistic about the future and modernity in general (Liebersohn, 1988). The *Kulturpessimismus* of Max Weber – *the* most influential of German sociologists – 'projected an indefinite glacial epoch for the whole of mankind' (Merquior, 1980: 187); while the attempt by critical theorists – 'after Auschwitz' – to resume the old 'Enlightenment project' has, on the other hand, been dominated in Germany by such ideas as 'modern myth' and 'total community.' As John Rajchman (1988: 184) has recently argued in specific reference to Jürgen Habermas, 'something of a retrospective "invention" ' is involved in the theorization of such motifs. In fact, Rajchman goes so far as to maintain that 'the great German *Angst* or lack of 'self-reassurance" ' is best seen as 'the *product* of the "discourse on modernity" ' – suggesting that the will to nostalgia is, indeed, a distinctive issue of modernity (although it is as much a product of the early-modern phase of *globality* and the contemporary ramifications of the latter). Even more directly, Buruma (1989: 43) persuasively accuses Habermas of contradictorily promoting both 'enlightened nationalism' and 'uncritical emotionalism.' That old German contradiction centers upon the idea of Germany as a politico-legal entity, on the one hand and, on the other, as 'a *Heimat*, devoid of politics, a land . . . anxiously searching for identity.'

One of the major features of modernity which has had a particularly powerful impact with respect to nostalgia is undoubtedly the *homogenizing* requirements of the modern nation state in the face of ethnic and cultural diversity. In the wake of the French and American Revolutions in the late eighteenth century there spread across the Western world the idea of people living as citizens of nationally constituted societies. More specifically, it was during the period 1750 to 1920 that nationalism triumphed as an ideal, involving the attempt to overcome local ethnocultural diversity and to produce standardized citizens whose loyalties to the nation would be unchallenged by extra-societal allegiances. As William McNeil (1985: 34) has remarked, 'something . . . happened in western Europe about 1750 to alter prevailing patterns of civilized society' – a central ingredient of his own account of the interruption of the historical norm of people living in polyethnic collectivities being the power exerted on European elites by what he calls 'the classical ideal.'[4] 'As classical Latin and Greek became the staple of schooling, the pagan authors of Rome and Greece [offered] educated Europeans an ideal of life built around participation in a self-governing city-state' (McNeil, 1985: 36).

There can be little doubt that the classical ideal continued to have its impact upon European elites right into the period of classical sociology (1880–1920) and thus upon the development of twentieth century social theory as a whole. Its impact upon classical German theory is apparent in Max Weber's concern with the cultural homogenization of the German nation – in terms of which his orientation to the Polish and Jewish 'questions' can be readily understood, if not applauded (Abraham, 1987); while I have already remarked upon its hold over critical theory – most explicitly in the work of Habermas. It can be shown that a large portion of Emile Durkheim's work was informed by Fustel de Coulanges' *The Ancient City* (1980), while the classical element in Durkheim's sociology has considerably affected the nostalgia-tinged work of Robert Bellah, most notably in his role as senior author of *Habits of the Heart* (Bellah et al., 1985) – a work which is openly attuned to the 'Grecophilia' (Holmes, 1988: 36) of Alasdair MacIntyre's *After Virtue* (1981) and *Whose Justice? Which Rationality?* (1987).[5] I cannot, however, provide here comprehensive documentation of the hold of the classical ideal over social theory as mediated to recent sociology via the symbiotic relationship between the rise of classical sociology and the global consolidation of the homogeneous national society in the period 1880–1925. However, it is important to note that nostalgia was built into the very *origins* of what McNeil has described as the classical ideal. Emphasizing that the latter has continuously involved the overlooking of the foreigners and slaves who lived in ancient Athens (and Rome) in their periods of imperial glory, McNeil points out that nostalgia for 'a homogeneous rural society' was a very significant aspect of the thinking of the major Athenian authors. They 'flourished while the transition from a homogeneous rural society was underway; indeed their work was stimulated in large part by the strains and pains inherent in that transition' (McNeil, 1985: 23).

I contend, third, that the processes of globalization – the processes which by now have led to the world becoming a 'single place,' a 'singular system,' a 'world society,' a 'global ecumene,' or whatever – were set in high motion, reached their crucial phase of take-off, during the period lasting from about 1880 through the first quarter of the twentieth century. Moreover, I maintain that globalization has been a primary root of the rise of wilful nostalgia. Indeed, wilful nostalgia *as a form of cultural politics* has, in a special sense, been an aspect of globalization. While it is appropriate for certain analytical purposes to think of politically motivated nostalgia on the part of actual or potential national elites as arising from a mixture of the perceived need for national integration, on the one hand, and the threat of relativization of national identity by the compression of 'international society,' on the other, it is also the case that what I call *the universalization of particularism* (Robertson, 1987, 1989a) is *an ingredient of* the compression which has come to be conceptualized as globalization (Robertson and Chirico, 1985; Robertson and Lechner, 1985). In other words, the emphasis upon nationalsocietal identity which has been such a salient feature of intra-national and international relations in modern times may be fruitfully conceptualized at the global level as a component of *institutionalized societalism* (Lechner, 1989) – the institutionalization of globally diffused (and often coercively imposed) expectations concerning the structure and functioning of societies, including *the expectation of uniqueness* of identity.

Thus globalization cannot be adequately defined as simply the compression (or implosion) of the world as a whole into a singular entity. Rather, it has to be seen more specifically, as having a particular form. Before expanding upon that idea I want to emphasize again that sociology as an academic discipline entered *its* most crucial phase of early institutionalization during what I am calling the take-off period of modern globalization and that it did so in reference to the general theme of modernity and the more specific individual-society problem, rather than in explicit acknowledgment of globalization. The extent to which the classical sociologists were, in fact, concerned with the wider, global circumstance is quite an important issue; but I want, in any case, to press the point that classical sociology was, in a special sense, a manifestation of the early-modern globalization process.

In arguing that globalization is a particular form in terms of which a kind of world order became institutionalized, I do not, of course, mean that the world became – or has become – integrated in a naive functionalist sense. Rather, I am referring to the heavily (indeed, violently) contested 'implementation' of a pattern in terms of which humanity is or should be 'organized'. Moreover, I want to convey the idea that in principle there were alternatives to the one that actually obtained in the take-off phase of the making of the world into a singular system (Moore, 1966). What, in any case, was the *actual* form? Briefly stated, my claim is that by the end of the nineteenth century or thereabouts there were established four major reference points – standing in problematic relationships with each other – as far as 'international society' was concerned. These were: the nationally constituted society; the individual; the system of international relations (world politics); and humankind. The period 1880–1925 was one in which the world was increasingly patterned along these lines. It was a remarkable period, in the first place, because of the extensive development of rapid means of communication across much of the globe – the wireless, the airplane, and so on – and of various forms of international agreement and organization concerning the world-as-a-whole, such as the institutionalization of World Time and the rapid completion of the globewide expansion of the use of the Gregorian calendar (Zerubavel, 1981; Kern, 1983). Second, and of more direct relevance, there began to be firmly established in the declining years of the nineteenth century a global 'standard of civilization' (Gong, 1984) concerning the basic constitutional and state-structural features of national societies; the rights and modes of participation of individuals in societies; a conception of international relations as globewide in their reach (hence the fact of the first *world* war occurring toward the end of the period in question); and the increasing thematization of humankind, or humanity (concretely in such contexts as the Geneva and Hague conventions, the World Court and, towards the end of the period in question, the League of Nations).

Thus not only was there a universalization of particularism, in the sense of acknowledgment – indeed, expectation – of the formulation of particularistic societal identities (against the background of expectations concerning basic *similarities* in the constitutional structures of modern societies and of the virtues of 'internationalism'), there was also *a particularization of*

universalism in that the world as a whole was given sociopolitical concreteness in various formal and informal respects. For example, the institutionalization of World Time involved, of course, the time-*zoning* of the world –
thus systematically combining the universal with the particular. Similarly,
the global generalization of a common calendar 'fell short of' the overriding
of all particularistic, mainly religious, conceptions of calendrical rhythm
(Hertz, 1932); while standardization of constitution-making 'allowed for'
expressions of civil-religious national identities (Markoff and Regan, 1987;
Robertson, 1989a). However, sociology began to gain a firm footing in this
period with remarkably little acknowledgment of such crucial developments. Only here and there in the period of classical sociology do we find
such acknowledgment and then only loosely. Durkheim, for example, was
clearly interested in the significance of a new form of what he called
'international life.' He was also concerned with the increasingly salient
category of humanity; as was Georg Simmel, partly in deference to
Nietzsche (Robertson and Chirico, 1985). On the other hand, there is much
yet to be done in sifting the work of the pioneers of modern sociology with
respect to their sense of the global changes of their time. (The history of
sociology may yet, as I have implied, have to be rewritten along such lines – a
new intellectual tradition to be invented.) To take a single example, the
influential (but much neglected) British sociologist, L.T. Hobhouse wrote in
1906: 'Humanity is rapidly becoming, physically speaking, a single society –
single in the sense that what affects one part tends to affect the whole'
(Hobhouse, 1906: 331). Nevertheless I think it safe to say that, with the very
important (but problematic) exception of Marx, there was little explicit
sociological concern about globalization (and, of course, Marx mainly wrote
before the period 1880–1925), while Marxist 'internationalism' was seriously
– some would say fatally – wounded by the nationalism of the period in
question. For the most part, sociologists were interested – often in very
nostalgic ways – in the coming of diffuse modernity to Western societies and
the problems of integration and meaning occasioned by the new kind of
relatively standardized national society.[6]

Nostalgia and the changing form of globalization

Turner (1987) has traced quite a lot of the history of the concept of nostalgia,
emphasizing its close association with the idea of melancholy in classical and
later thought, and its medical, literary and religious significance in the West.
Following Fred Davis's discussion of nostalgia in symbolic-interactionist
perspective (1974), Turner (1987: 149) points out that nostalgia in its literal
meaning as homesickness 'was defined in medical analysis by Johannes
Hofer in the seventeenth century as the symptoms (melancholy, weeping,
anorexia and despair) of home-sick Swiss mercenaries, fighting in regions
remote from their homelands' – to which it might be added that nostalgia
does not appear to have been used with any frequency in the English

language (as indicating homesickness) until the eighteenth century (Onions, 1966: 615). Turner regards the quasi-medical notion of nostalgia as homesickness as 'somewhat debased' – since, in line with a richer tradition of discourse about melancholy, we ought to talk philosophically and sociologically about nostalgia as 'a fundamental condition of human estrangement' (Turner, 1987: 150). Although he is rather convincing in that regard, it should, however, be emphasized that the notion of *homelessness* as a basic form of estrangement or alienation *has* been particularly evident in the very traditions of Marx and Heidegger where Turner seeks to locate nostalgia. (Needless to say, I am not explicitly referring here to homelessness in the recent sense of being without a dwelling-place in which to live.) Indeed, the most explicit and lengthy discussion of homelessness (a less specific phenomenon than homesickness) as a *psychological* product of modernization and as itself a *producer* of 'nostalgia . . . for a condition of "being at home" in society, with oneself and, ultimately, in the universe' was written largely within the Germanic intellectual tradition of concern with the themes of alienation and estrangement. I refer, of course, to *The Homeless Mind*, by Peter Berger et al. (1973: 83). It also bears repeating that in at least one non-Western civilization the idea and condition of nostalgia have been pervasive. The Chinese term *hsiang-ch'ou* involves the combination of the words for homeland and sorrow – indicating a desire to return to a familiar place in one's earlier life. It also possesses a more pathological connotation: that one experiences sorrow whenever one is tempted to think of one's original homeplace.[7]

Turner (1987) and Stauth and Turner (1988b: 47) suggest that there are four main presuppositions of what they call the nostalgic paradigm: the idea of history as decline; the sense of a loss of wholeness; the feeling of the loss of expressivity and spontaneity; and the sense of loss of individual autonomy. I want to press this scheme a little further by relating the sociological and philosophical thematization of these notions in the period 1880–1925 to what Nairn (1988: 168) has described as 'a great tide of synthetic nostalgia' which reached its peak at the end of the nineteenth century. In turn I want to discuss briefly the kind of wilful nostalgia which we find in the present period – my argument being that we are currently in a new phase of accelerated, nostalgia-producing globalization. More specifically, I suggest that we are witnessing, and participating in, a *second* major phase of modern globalization – which is closely related to the rise of postmodernist ways of thinking. This second phase of globalization – which began in the 1960s – involves the reconstruction and problematization of the four major reference points of globalization (societies, individuals, international relations and humankind) and the strengthening of the particular-universal 'dialectic.' These developments are generating a somewhat different and diffuse kind of wilful, synthetic nostalgia – amounting to something like the global institutionalization of the nostalgic attitude. All the more reason, then, to eliminate nostalgia from social theory and thematize it as an 'object' of sociological analysis. Let us *study* it – not allow it to determine our theory and research.

(One particular problem with this plea is that it may appear to run strongly against the grain of recent attempts to indigenize sociology in a number of African, Asian and other societies. Insofar as attempts to indigenize are *driven* by nostalgia, then I object to them, but there is no intrinsic reason for indigenization to be so propelled.)

In my view the multidimensional image of nostalgia provided by Stauth and Turner is very illuminating. However, it does not go far enough with respect to the issue of periodization; while I have already maintained that the issue of wilfulness in the political manipulation of nostalgia is an extremely significant additional factor that has impinged upon the development of social theory, most notably in Germany. Moreover, Turner's (1987) declaration that the world is alien to the nostalgic needs to be unpacked so as to double the meaning of 'the world' – the world as the mundane ingredient of modernity *and* the world as a concrete, singular system resulting from globalization (Robertson, 1985, 1990b). Before coming directly to these matters let me give a hint as to the kind of nostalgia which is particularly evident in the late twentieth century – in a period in which the phrase 'nostalgia isn't what it used to be' has become a commonplace (Davis, 1974). I do this via Fredric Jameson.

> The appetite for images of the past, in the form of what might be called simulacra, the increasing production of such images of all kinds, in particular in that peculiar postmodern genre, the *nostalgic film*, with its glossy evocation of the past as sheer consumerable fashion and image – all this seems to me something of a return of the repressed, an unconscious sense of the loss of the past, which this appetite for images seeks desperately to overcome. (Jameson, 1988: 104)

As Jameson emphasizes, *culture* is a 'privileged area in which to witness' the current appetite for images of the past, although he also argues that global capitalism is deeply involved.[8] The point that needs to be made in that cultural regard is that even though one can undoubtedly find more than a dose of nostalgia in the 'interdiscipline' of cultural studies, it is from the latter that some of the more interesting – and, in the best sense, subversive – challenges to the nostalgic paradigm in sociology are being issued. In the simplest terms, much of sociology *is* nostalgic, whereas much of cultural study involves the *thematization* of nostalgia. In any case, it is clear that late twentieth century nostalgia is intimately bound-up with consumerism. Compared to wilful, synthetic nostalgia as an ingredient of late nineteenth and early twentieth century cultural politics, contemporary nostalgia is both more economic – in the sense of being a major product of transnational capitalism (which is *itself* bound by the global institutionalization of the play between the universal and the particular) – and more 'democratically' cultural (or simulational). That does not, of course mean that wilful, politically driven nostalgia has been overwhelmed. How could one say that at a time of flag-waving nostalgia about a mythical American past; Ukania-myth making; the politically astute manipulation of the idea of Japanese uniqueness; the use of nostalgia in legitimating ethnonationalism inside the Soviet Union; the cultivation of Chinese purity; and so on? (Not to speak of more definitely global types of nostalgia, to which I will refer in a moment.) So my point is that the latter kind of nostalgia promotion is now embedded in – although it has been partly responsible for – a more pervasive and diffuse, consumerist type of nostalgia. Prior to the late nineteenth century – before the onset of modern globalization – one tended to find a more directly existential type of nostalgia, arising more 'naturally' from estrangement or alienation. That does not mean that existential nostalgia was then *replaced by* wilful nostalgia (itself to be replaced by consumerist-simulational nostalgia). Rather, existential nostalgia was – for the most part nationalistically – *incorporated into* wilful nostalgia; which is now being incorporated – for the most part capitalistically – into consumerist, image-conveyed nostalgia, the last being wrapped into the global institutionalization of the universalization of the particular and the particularization of the universal.

I have been arguing that what Nairn has called wilful nostalgia can best be understood and accounted for in reference to the take-off phase of recent globalization during the period 1880–1925 and that we are now in a later phase which is producing a more diffuse, almost globally institutionalized kind of nostalgia. I cannot, however, produce anything resembling a comprehensive formulation of the current phase in the present discussion. All that I can do is to register some of the major considerations which, in my view, would have to be included in such an exercise; acknowledging – indeed, emphasizing – that, given the remarkable fluidity of 'world affairs' at this moment of writing (1989), any analytical contribution to this issue itself becomes part of the process of contemporary global-reality construction. Perhaps this point can best be illustrated in terms of the debate which has been sparked by Francis Fukuyama's (1989) argument concerning *the end of world history*. Writing – at least in part – as deputy director of the US State Department's policy planning staff, and also as a devotee of Alexandre Kojève's (1947) interpretation of Hegel, Fukuyama has spoken of the 'powerful nostalgia' which he has felt 'for the time when history existed' (Fukuyama, 1989: 18). The apparent end of the Cold War, centered upon the clash between the USSR and the USA and the supposed triumph of 'the Western idea' (Fukuyama, 1989: 3), has left him sensing that it is *nostalgia* which 'will continue to fuel competition and conflict even in the post-historical world for some time to come' (Fukuyama, 1989: 18). According to Fukuyama (1989: 18), the 'very prospect of centuries of boredom ... will serve to get history started once again.'

Fukuyama's statement and the extensive debate which it has engendered (Atlas, 1989) amount to powerful support for the argument that nostalgic has indeed become increasingly evident in the global-human condition. In other words, nostalgia has increasingly assumed a global-cultural significance, quite regardless of its ontogenetic importance as a natural part of any individual's autobiography or lifestyle (Davis, 1974: 31–71). Although he pays no attention to the experience of globality (Robertson 1990b), Fred Davis's definition of 'collective nostalgia' is relevant here: 'Collective nostalgia ... refers to that condition in which ... symbolic objects are of a highly public, widely shared, and familiar character, those symbolic resources from the past that ... can trigger wave upon wave of nostalgic feeling in millions of persons at the same time' (Davis, 1974: 122–3). Insofar as Davis has provided a sociological account of the conditions which, in the twentieth century, have produced and are producing collective (or, from a somewhat different perspective, phylogenetic) nostalgia, he largely confines himself to what he calls the erosion of the sense of *home* as 'a specific geographic locale with its own distinctive atmosphere' (Davis, 1974: 124) and thus of '*home*sickness *per se*' by the 'constant movement in sociographic space' as an ingredient of modernity and the rise of the 'nostalgia industry' (Davis, 1974: 119). I want to use Davis's discussion of nostalgia as a 'friendly foil,' bearing in mind that the Fukuyama debate indicates that large numbers of people can become nostalgic about such a large-scale – indeed, global – phenomenon as the Cold War. In fact Davis directly invites his readers to respond in such a way when he implies that we may now be in a stage of 'interpreted nostalgia,' involving the attempt to objectify it with '*analytically oriented* questions' about its foundations, significance, and so on (Davis, 1974: 24).

While Davis is undoubtedly correct in drawing attention to the erosion of the concreteness of 'home' and thus the problems involved in continuing to think of nostalgia as homesickness *per se*, as is well-exampled in the Fuku-yama debate, there is also a respect in which the idea of home *has* recently become evident. (Again, it should be said that I am not talking of the recent concern with the homeless as people without real, physical dwellings; although that concern is not totally unrelated to the matters under discussion here.) I refer particularly to the salience of 'home' in the growing Green movement and its deployment by such movements as Greenpeace. The earth as home or as *the relationship between* humankind and the natural environment (animate and inanimate) has become one of the most dissemi-nated symbolic motifs of our time. The world as *the place* in which we all live is being increasingly promoted on all kinds of fronts – in attempts to legitimate the centrality of particular nations via thematization of environ-mental problems to the world-as-a-whole; in programs for legitimating green, until recently extra-parliamentary, oppositions; in 'pre-contractual' justifications for the global scope of extra-national corporations; in munici-pal, prefectural and (in the American sense) state efforts to compete for a slice of the global-economic pie; in the efforts to restore geography to its 'rightful place' in the curriculum; and so on. By the same token – but in a certain sense on the other side of the coin – we witness the development of something like a global pro-family and pro-neighborhood movement, talk about Europe as *a home*; religious movements concerned with the unifica-tion of the entire world; and so on. In other words, the notion of home is very much alive and well. Nostalgia is simply not what it used to be – it is *more than* what it used to be. It has been doubly globalized. It has become both collective on a global scale and directed at globality itself.

Baudrillard (1983: 12–13) has recently observed that 'when the real is no longer what it used to be nostalgia assumes its full meaning. There is a proliferation of myths of origin and signs of reality; of second-hand truth, objectivity and authenticity.' That observation is embedded in Baudrillard's own theory of 'the precession of simulcra' (Baudrillard, 1983; 1988). However, I do not wish to explore or apply that perspective in the present context. Instead, I argue that one vital ingredient of the contemporary shift as far as 'reality' is concerned consists in the accelerated speed and changing form of globalization. Late twentieth century globalization – the most recent phase of modern globalization – exacerbates the nostalgic tendency in a number of ways. The very fluidity of global change invites, as we have seen, nostalgia for the meaningfulness of the global order which was problematically patterned in the period 1880–1925 and which was then the occasion for hot and cold war until quite recently. More specifically, nostalgia is produced in particular references to the four major components of the globalization process which I have previously identified – national societies, individuals, the system of international relations, and humankind as a species.

I suggest, in brief, that four sets of interrelated change are currently occurring with respect to the main aspects of globalization. *National societies* are increasingly exposed internally to problems of heterogeneity and diversity and, at the same time, are experiencing both external and internal pressures to reconstruct their collective identities along pluralistic lines; *individuals* are increasingly subject to competing ethnic, cultural and religious reference points; *the system of international relations* is becoming more and more fluid and 'multipolar'; and the idea of *humankind* as a species is being subjected to contested thematization and scrutiny. It may be the case that this overall *form* of globalization will not hold – that we will enter a qualitatively different stage in the 'evolution' of humanity. Meanwhile, nostalgic resistance to globalization – whatever its form – will continue (Robertson, 1990b). The global vocation of the social theorist is, on the other hand, to be *positively* – as opposed to negatively and nostalgically – analytical and *critical*.

Notes

1 It should be noted that Bryan Turner has also, with Robert Holton, deployed the writings of Talcott Parsons in a separate critique of sociological nostalgia (Holton and Turner, 1986: 209–34). I have written in a similar vein of Parsons's sociology as being distinctively anti-nostalgic (Robertson, 1989b). In developing their argument that Parsons was 'against nostalgia, for the modern world, and unambiguously post-classical,' Holton and Turner maintain that his sociology also constitutes a decisive step beyond both the communitarian position in moral philosophy – as represented by Alasdair MacIntyre's *After Virtue* (1981) – and the modernistic, perspectival stance of Nietzsche, to which MacIntyre is thoroughly opposed (Holton and Turner, 1986: 215). It is not my task here to discuss the extent to which Turner's virtually simultaneous advocacy of Nietzschean and Parsonian positions is sustainable; although I think that it might be. The title of the present paper is, of course, a negative reference to MacIntyre's *After Virtue* – in the sense of indicating an attempt to both ground the nostalgic critique of modernity and argue for the elimination of nostalgia from social theory *per se*.

2 The encounter with Asia – most notably, Japan – also facilitated a nostalgic yearning on the part of Westerners for a more 'homely' Western past (not dissimilar to an Enlightenment hankering after oriental 'harmony'). See Yokoyama (1987) for an excellent study of some British attitudes towards Japan in the Victorian period.

3 This may well be an exaggeration. Simon Schama's rich discussion of Dutch identity in the seventeenth century is specifically concerned with 'the community of the nation, an entity not supposed to have existed before the French Revolution' (Schama, 1987: 6) – the implication being that 'the community of the nation' was an important sociocultural phenomenon, at least in the West, prior to the period beginning around the time of the French Revolution. However, even though I take Schama's suggestion seriously I regard the kind of 'nationalism' which developed prior to the late eighteenth century as having only very incipient significance as far as globalization is concerned. *Modern* globalization did not begin to enter its relatively concrete phase until the appearance of explicit ideas concerning *the relationship between nationalism and internationalism* at the end of the eighteenth century (Kohn, 1971).

4 In line with Schama (1987), McNeil (1985: 7) acknowledges that 'the idea that a government rightfully should rule only over citizens of a single ethos took root haltingly in western Europe, beginning in the late middle ages.' He also points out that that ideal has weakened considerably in western Europe since the early 1920s, but that it has gained elsewhere, especially in the ex-colonial areas of Africa and Asia. (In spite of the USA's much-heralded ethnic and racial heterogeneity, I include it as a national society which has greatly stressed the importance of a homogeneous citizenry – negatively marked by the widely-held conception of *un*Americanism.)

5 Bellah's work has also been deeply affected by the covenantal myth (Bellah, 1974). Indeed, it is important to acknowledge that the ancient Jewish – and more directly the sixteenth century, Puritan – myth concerning communal covenants with God has had a powerful effect on American sociology. It should be noted, on the other hand, that Talcott Parsons attacked Bellah for 'absolutism' in emphasizing so strongly the moral-communal aspect of Durkheim's sociology (Coleman, 1980; Parsons, 1977). Parsons never romanticized either ancient Israel or Greece in spite of his great emphasis upon their evolutionary significance as 'seed-bed societies' – although he did cling somewhat nostalgically to some elements of the covenant theme in his own version of the idea of civil religion. See also the argument of Vidich and Hughey (1988: 245) that 'there is an irreconcilable tension between the religious foundations of community and the very purposes of post-Enlightenment scholarship' and that 'scholarship is in this sense the enemy of community.' Baudrillard (1988: 79) draws attention to another nostalgic aspect of contemporary American intellectual thought – namely, 'the unhappy transference' involved in 'the nostalgic eye' which is cast towards European history and metaphysics. European intellectuals, on the other hand, tend to 'remain nostalgic utopians, agonizing over [their] ideals, but balking, ultimately, at their realization' (Baudrillard, 1988: 78).

6 Even Herbert Spencer, who was undoubtedly the most globally influential of the sociologists of the period in question, was not the cool embracer of 'rational modernity' that he is often made out to have been. For example, he advised the early Meiji elites in Japan to cling strongly to their religious traditions (Spencer, 1966: 417), while in talking about his own Britain Spencer assumed 'the actual nourishment that came from the more organic harmony of a medievalism that had not altogether disappeared' (Hartz, 1964: xv). Nonetheless, the overt thrust of Spencer's ideas about progress and evolution provided both a theoretically viable conception of the relations between national societies (namely one of competitive, adaptive struggle) and a sense of a human destiny to which individual societies should contribute (Blacker, 1964: 34–5, 59, 62). The global significance of the mainly British idea of progress has been made especially clear to me by Norman Stockman.

7 I am indebted to Chang Wang-Ho for his assistance in exploring the history and meaning of the idea of nostalgia in China. A full analysis of the global significance of nostalgia would require comparative, historical and etymological research on the centers of social theory.

8 For an innovative discussion of 'the return of the sacred' in reference to the current debate about globalization, see Kavolis (1988). See also Kavolis's (1987) critique of some of my own

work on globalization, and my reply (Robertson, 1987). For a more detailed account, see Robertson (1990c). See also Robertson (1990a).

References

Abraham, Gary A. (1987) 'Max Weber and the Jewish Question.' Ph.D Dissertation, University of Pittsburgh.

Anderson, Benedict (1983) *Imagined Communities*. London: Verso.

Ardener, Edwin (1985) 'Social anthropology and the decline of modernism,' in Joanna Overing (ed.), *Reason and Morality*. London: Tavistock Publications. pp. 47–70.

Atlas, James (1989) 'What is Fukuyama saying?' *New York Times Magazine*, October 22: 38–54 and 42–3.

Baudrillard, Jean (1983) *Simulations*. New York: Semitext(e).

Baudrillard, Jean (1988) *America*. London: Verso.

Bellah, Robert N. (1974) *The Broken Covenant*. New York: Seabury.

Bellah, Robert N., Masden, Richard, Sullivan, William M., Swidler, Ann and Tipton, Steven M. (1985) *Habits of the Heart: Individualism and Commitment in American Life*. Berkeley: University of California Press.

Berger, Peter L., Berger, Brigitte and Kellner, Hansfried (1973) *The Homeless Mind*. New York: Random House.

Blacker, Carmen (1964) *The Japanese Enlightenment: A Study of the Writings of Fukuzawa Yukichi*. Cambridge: Cambridge University Press.

Buruma, Ian (1989) 'From Hirohito to Heimat.' *New York Review of Books*, 36 (16): 31–45.

Coleman, John A. (1980) 'The renewed covenant: Robert N. Bellah's vision of religion and society,' in Gregory Baum (ed.), *Sociology and Human Destiny*. New York: Seabury Press. pp. 86–109.

Davis, Fred (1974) *Yearning for Yesterday: A Sociology of Nostalgia*. New York: Free Press.

Fukuyama, Francis (1989) 'The end of history?' *The National Interest*, 16 (Summer): 3–18.

Fustel de Coulanges, Numa Denis (1980) *The Ancient City*. Baltimore: Johns Hopkins University Press.

Geertz, Clifford (1986) 'The uses of diversity,' *Michigan Quarterly*, 25(1): 105–23.

Gluck, Carol (1985) *Japan's Modern Myths: Ideology in the Late Meiji Period*. Princeton: Princeton University Press.

Gong, Gerrit W. (1984) *The Standard of 'Civilization' in International Society*. Oxford: Clarendon Press.

Hartz, Louis (1964) 'Introduction,' in Benjamin Schwartz, *In Search of Wealth and Power*. Cambridge: Belknap Press of Harvard University Press. pp. xi–xx.

Hertz, J.H. (1932) *The Battle for the Sabbath at Geneva*. London: Humphrey Milford Oxford University Press.

Hobhouse, L.T. (1906) *Morals in Evolution: A Study in Comparative Ethics*, Volume I. New York: Henry Holt and Co.

Hobsbawm, Eric and Ringer, Terence (eds) (1983) *The Invention of Tradition*. Cambridge: Cambridge University Press.

Holmes, Stephen (1988) 'The polis state,' *New Republic*, June 6: 32–9.

Holton, Robert J. and Turner, Bryan S. (1986) *Talcott Parsons on Economy and Society*. London: Routledge & Kegan Paul.

Jameson, Fredric R. (1988) 'On *Habits of the Heart*,' in C.H. Reynolds and R.V. Norman (eds), *Community in America: The Challenge of Habits of the Heart*. Berkeley: University of California Press. pp. 97–112.

Kavolis, Vytautas (1987) 'History of consciousness and civilization analysis,' *Comparative Civilizations Review*, 17 (Fall): 1–19.

Kavolis, Vytautas (1988) 'Contemporary moral cultures and "The Return of the Sacred",' *Sociological Analysis*, 49: 203–16.

Kern, Stephen (1983) *The Culture of Time and Space, 1880–1918*. Cambridge: Harvard University Press.

Kohn, Hans (1971) 'Nationalism and internationalism,' in W. Warren Wagar (ed.), *History and the Idea of Mankind*. Albuquerque: University of New Mexico Press. pp. 119–34.

Kojève, Alexandre (1947) *Introduction à la lecture de Hegel*. Paris: Editions Gallimard.

Lasch, Christopher (1988) 'The communitarian critique of liberalism,' in C.E. Reynolds and R.V. Norman (eds), *Community in America: The Challenge of Habits of the Heart*. Berkeley: University of California Press. pp. 173–84.

Lechner, Frank J. (1989) 'Cultural aspects of the modern world-system,' in William H. Swatos, Jr. (ed.), *Religious Politics in Global and Comparative Perspective*. New York: Greenwood Press. pp. 12–74.

Liebersohn, Harry (1988) *Fate and Utopia in German Sociology, 1870–1923*. Cambridge: MIT Press.

MacIntyre, Alasdair (1981) *After Virtue: A Study in Moral Theory*. Notre Dame: University of Notre Dame Press.

MacIntyre, Alasdair (1987) *Whose Justice? Which Rationality?* Notre Dame: University of Notre Dame Press.

McNeil, William H. (1985) *Polyethnicity and National Unity in World History*. Toronto: University of Toronto Press.

Markoff, John and Regan, Daniel (1987) 'Religion, the State and political legitimacy in the world's constitutions,' in Thomas Robbins and Roland Robertson (eds), *Church–State Relations*. New Brunswick: Transaction Books. pp. 161–82.

Merquior, J.G. (1980) *Rousseau and Weber: Two Studies in the Theory of Legitimacy*. London: Routledge & Kegan Paul.

Moore, Wilbert E. (1966) 'Global sociology: the world as a singular system,' *American Journal of Sociology*, 71: 475–82.

Nairn, Tom (1988) *The Enchanted Glass: Britain and its Monarchy*. London: Hutchinson Radius.

Onions, C.T. (ed.) (1966) *The Oxford Dictionary of English Etymology*. Oxford: Oxford University Press.

Parsons, Talcott (1977) 'Law as an intellectual stepchild,' *Sociological Inquiry*, 47: 11–58.

Pollock, David (1986) *The Fracture of Meaning: Japan's Synthesis of China from the Eighth through the Eighteenth Centuries*. Princeton: Princeton University Press.

Rajchman, John (1988) 'Habermas's complaint,' *New German Critique*, 4–5 (Fall): 163–91.

Robertson, Roland (1985) 'The sacred and the world system,' in Phillip Hammond (ed.), *The Sacred in a Post-Secular Age*. Berkeley: University of California Press. pp. 347–58.

Robertson, Roland (1987) 'Globalization theory and civilization analysis,' *Comparative Civilizations Review*, 17 (Fall): 20–30.

Robertson, Roland (1989a) 'Globalization, politics and religion,' in James A. Beckford and Thomas Luckmann (eds), *The Changing Face of Religion*. London: Sage. pp. 10–23.

Robertson, Roland (1989b) 'A new perspective on religion and secularization in the global context', in J.K. Hadden and A. Shupe (eds), *Secularization and Fundamentalism Reconsidered*. New York: Paragon House.

Robertson Roland (1990a) 'The globalization paradigm: thinking globally,' in David G. Bromley (ed.), *Religion and the Social Order: New Directions in Theory and Research*. Greenwich, CT: JAI Press. pp. 1–10.

Robertson, Roland (1990b) 'Globality, global culture and images of world order,' in Hans Haferkamp and Neil Smelser (ed.), *Social Change and Modernity*. Berkeley: University of California Press.

Robertson, Roland (1990c) 'Mapping the global condition: globalization as the central concept,' *Theory, Culture and Society*, 7(2–3).

Robertson, Roland and Chirico, JoAnn (1985) 'Humanity, globalization and worldwide religious resurgence: a theoretical exploration,' *Sociological Analysis*, 46: 219–42.

Robertson, Roland and Lechner, Frank (1985) 'Modernization, globalization and the problem of culture in world-systems theory,' *Theory, Culture and Society*, 2(3): 107–18.

Schama, Simon (1987) *The Embarrassment of Riches: An Interpretation of Dutch Culture in the Golden Age*. London: William Collins.

Schwartz, Benjamin (1964) *In Search of Wealth and Power: Yen Fu and the West*. Cambridge: Belknap Press of Harvard University Press.

Smith, Robert J. (1983) *Japanese Society: Tradition, Self and the Social Order*. Cambridge: Cambridge University Press.

Spencer, Herbert (1966) *A System of Synthetic Philosophy*. Osnabruck: Otto Zeller.

Stauth, Georg and Turner, Bryan S. (1988a) *Nietzsche's Dance: Resentment, Reciprocity and Resistance in Social Life*. Oxford: Basil Blackwell.

Stauth, Georg and Turner, Bryan S. (1988b) 'Nostalgia, postmodernism and the critique of mass culture,' *Theory, Culture and Society*, 5 (2–3): 509–26.

Turner, Bryan S. (1987) 'A note on nostalgia,' *Theory, Culture and Society*, 4(1): 147–56.

Vidich, Arthur J. and Hughey Michael W. (1988) 'Fraternization and rationality in global perspective,' *International Journal of Politics, Culture and Society*, 2 (2): 242–56.

Wang, Y.C. (1966) *Chinese Intellectuals and the West: 1872–1949*. Chapel Hill: University of North Carolina Press.

Yokoyama, Toshio (1987) *Japan in the Victorian Mind: A Study of Stereotyped Images of a Nation, 1850–80*. London: Macmillan.

Zerubavel, Eviatar (1981) *Hidden Rhythms: Schedules and Calendars in Social Life*. Chicago: Chicago University Press.

5

POSTMODERNISM AS HUMANISM? URBAN SPACE AND SOCIAL THEORY

Scott Lash

In what follows I should like to argue that much of what is usually regarded as postmodernist culture is really part and parcel of modernism. That is, I should like to maintain that what is characteristically understood in terms of a cultural paradigm (postmodernism) which has become pervasive in the past decade or two is in fact much more characteristic of the set of modernist movements of the turn of the last century.

Perhaps a majority of today's analysts (1) define postmodernism in terms of anti-humanism: (2) say it is anti-historical; (3) see it in terms of an (often inaccessible) avant-garde; and (4) claim that it is self-referential. My claim is that it is *modernism* – not a recent, but a late nineteenth century, phenomenon – which is anti-humanist, anti-historical, initiated by avant-gardes, and self-referential. Postmodernism, on the other hand, (1) is an attempt to restore humanism; (2) is a try at reconstituting the historical dimension; (3) rejects avant-gardes in favour of 'convention'; and (4) is, not self-referential, but *other*-referential.

Let me address these defining characteristics – humanism, historicity, avant-gardes and referentiality – in sequence. Let me also jump ahead of my argument and preview my conclusions, which are that postmodernism *fails* in its humanist, historical, conventional and other-referential undertakings. The unanticipated consequences of postmodernist cultural practices are instead (1) a phoney humanism; (2) a de-semanticized historicity; (3) not convention, but 'an avant-garde leading from the rear'; and (4) a quest for a, so to speak, 'disappearing' referent.

Humanism

What is meant by 'humanism' is a fairly straightforward matter. Writers on art and architecture – as diverse as Panofsky, Aldo Rossi, Michael Graves, Peter Eisenman, Lewis Mumford and many others – are in broad agreement on this centuries old, conventional notion of humanism. Humanism has to do with Alberti, Erasmus and Grotius. It has to do with the ontological primacy of 'man' over the Christian God. It has to do with the Renaissance and the eighteenth century search for Classical and humanist values in Greek Antiquity.

It has very little at all to do with what French structuralism of the 1960s labelled as 'humanist'. The structuralism of Althusser, Barthes, Foucault and even Bourdieu defined itself in contradistinction to the agency-centred social theory – of Sartre, Merleau-Ponty, Hippolyte – of the generation of their teachers. They called these older theorists 'humanists'. But action-theoretical social thought is not at all necessarily humanist. Action-theoretical philosophy and sociology (and this would apply to Jon Elster and the ethnomethodologists) assumes a highly abstract notion of agency which is incompatible with humanism. Humanism looks back to Classical Greece in which the view of human agency was not abstract but foundational. Moral agency here was not abstract, but rooted in the foundations of a social *Sittlichkeit*. Moral, aesthetic and cognitive action were not conceived in abstraction, the one from the others, but as integrally intertwined. Rational agency was not conceived in the same kind of abstraction from the body. The nature/culture diremption was not so radically stated. And so on.

Neither structuralism nor the twentieth century theories of agency, of which the structuralists were so critical, are humanist. Both structuralism and these action theories are instead quintessentially *modernist*. Habermas's and Benjamin's discussions of modernism juxtapose Ancients and Moderns. And humanism in its classicism, its foundationalism, its rootedness in Socratic Greece, is not modern, but fundamentally ancient. Modernization, I have argued, following Weber and Habermas, is a process of cultural differentiation and autonomization. Now humanism, whether in fifth century Greek, Renaissance or eighteenth century neo-classical guises, represents a certain level of cultural modernization (pre-Socratic Greece and medieval Europe is less differentiated hence less modern and more 'ancient' than the Ancients); that is, a certain level of differentiation and autonomization of cultural spheres – for example, the sacred is differentiated from the profane, and secular culture from religious culture. But it also entails the foundationalisms mentioned above.

Modern*ism*, a turn of the last century phenomenon, represents the culmination of this process of cultural differentiation. At this point the spheres are fully autonomized. Modernism is thus fully non- or anti-foundational and cultural spheres are fully abstracted from one another. This is exemplified in the full autonomy of modernist art; that is, in the aesthetics of 'art for art's sake' and 'truth to the (aesthetic) materials'. It is exemplified in the birth of sociology and its assumptions of the autonomy of the social. Hence Durkheim's 'social facts' are *sui generis*. And epistemologies and ethics are not foundational and categorical in the Kantian sense, but are socially conditioned or sociologistic. Thus the abstract and autonomous agency of the action theorists is only the other side of the modernist (relatively) autonomous structures of the structuralists. Abstraction and autonomy are the rule in both cases. In this sense, modernist social theory only reproduces the contradistinction of modernist painting. Here action theory is homologous to the abstract agency assumptions of Expressionism, and structuralism to the facet-plane constructions of cubism.

Humanist architecture and humanist urban space are, on the lines of this argument, (a) anthropomorphic, (b) anthropocentric, and (c) anthropometric. Modernist architecture rejects, while postmodernist architecture embraces, anthropomorphism, anthropocentrism and anthropometrism.

Anthropomorphism

In various historical epochs art and architecture has been more or less humanistic in the sense of anthropomorphism. Thus Panofsky has written that Egyptian art was based on a geometric principle and much of medieval art structured on algebraic lines. Aesthetic notions in Classical Greece, the Renaissance and eighteenth century classicism were anthropomorphic, in that images in art, and forms in architecture, resembled man. Corbusier's modernist definition of architecture, like Egyptian and medieval art, stands counterposed to humanist anthropomorphism. Corbusier's is a different (from Egyptian and medieval) type of formalism, in which architecture is 'the magnificent, knowledgeable and correct play of volumes under light'. The parallel with, for example, cubist painting is unmistakable.

Postmodern architects – and it is no coincidence that its predominant form is neoclassicism (for example, Terry Farrell, Quinlan Terry) – advocate a return to anthropomorphism. Thus Aldo Rossi cites Alberti's humanist credo in which the base, shaft and capital of the orders (columns) reproduce the foot, body and head of human beings; in which the proportions and symmetry of the buildings is modelled on the symmetry of the human body. In this classicism, postmodernism harkens back to the humanist aesthetics of beauty in place of modernist experimentation aesthetics. This is true also in the human figure painting of postmodern artists such as Warhol, Bacon, Baselitz and Freud.

Anthropocentrism

This is a question of to whom (or what) a cultural object is addressed. Medieval and Egyptian (encased in tombs so surely not addressed to man) cultural objects were addressed to deities. Modernist architecture is similarly not addressed to human beings. It is valued instead for formalist criteria – the 'play of volumes'. Similarly modernist painting and cinema wants experimentally to decentre the viewer rather than produce images which, along the lines of Albertian Quattrocento perspective, are tailored to viewing by the human eye. However, architects and analysts of architecture who are sympathetic to postmodernism argue that modernist architecture does not address, does not speak to, anyone at all. That is, modernist architecture is syntactical. Postmodernists such as Graves advocate an architecture based not on properties of syntax, but (like in Classical architecture) on semantics. The idea for Graves, Rossi, Charles Moore and Leon Krier is that such a syntactical architecture must function, culturally, for human beings and especially in the fostering of the formation of stable individual and collective identity. This sounds suspiciously like the description of the premodernist social environment advocated by neo-conservative social analysts such as Daniel Bell and Christopher Lasch. Thus Charles Moore, from the 'first generation' of postmodern architects, writes:

> The psychic spaces and the shape of buildings should assist the human memory in restructuring connections through time and space . . . so that those of us who lead lives complicatedly divorced from a single place in which we can find roots, can have . . . through the channels of our memories, through the agency of building, something like these roots restored. (Moore, 1980: 208)

Anthropometrism

This is a question of the *scale* of the built environment. On this count, the postmodernists want 'user-friendly' space, scaled down to human size. Thus Rossi again approvingly cites Alberti's humanist view, in which 'the city [and the individual] is a microcosm of an harmonic universe'. Postmodern humanist anthropometrism is, on the one hand, opposed to the monumentality of Baroque architecture or Third Reich neo-classicism. It condemns equally, on the other, the autonomy of modernist urban space from any conception at all of what is human in scale; thus the emptiness of modernist public places such as the South Bank complex in London or squares such as Chicago's Civic Center or, in the extreme, East Berlin's Alexanderplatz, which 'kill', so to speak, public space. The critique of modernism has, in contrast, advocated the anthropometric scaling down of such space through street cafes, events, basketball courts (like in downtown New York) and street musicians. The critique of modernism has advocated the creation of what William H. Whyte (1980) calls, in *The Sociology of Small Public Spaces*, 'schmoozing space', that is, nooks and crannies contiguous to the mainstream of pedestrian traffic where people can stop and 'schmooze'.

Historicity

It is not postmodernism but modernism which has advocated the radical break with history. Let us be certain in this context to distinguish movement and change from history. The modern – as advocated by Berman and (the acceptable face of) Marxism – is a metaphysics of change and movement, but is a rejection of history. Anti-modernist cultural neo-conservatives such as Bell, Lasch, MacIntyre and Allan Bloom – advocate the recovery of the historical dimension, in the interest, not of movement or change, but of stability. Hence Bell and Lasch lament the disappearance of the historical sense in which identity is stabilized by the sensibility of being 'the son of my father who is the son of his father' and so on.

Modernism, for its part, rejects history in order to embrace movement and change. Modernism in Vienna, Paris, Berlin and a number of other European cities, as the nineteenth century drew to a close, was ushered in by a series of effective 'secession' movements. These movements consisted of a rejection of 'academic' standards by artists and architects. This was at the same time a rejection of state sponsored art, in that given national states controlled the academy which taught art or architecture as well as which paintings were to be exhibited at the annual 'salons'. Official, 'academic' painting and architecture in each of these cases was historicist. Paintings were commonly of historical scenes. Architecture taught by the Paris École des Beaux-Arts and its non-French equivalents repeated styles from previous historical epochs. Thus French Impressionism (and realism), Viennese Art Nouveau (*Jugendstil*) and German Expressionism, all took from the institutional context of the reaction against historical art. In each case the rejection was in favour of a modernist or proto-modernist aesthetic of working through the possibilities of the aesthetic materials.

Postmodernism, on the other hand, proposes a return to historical values. The event which consecrated the arrival of modernism in the US was the Museum of Modern Art's International Style exhibition in 1932. The event, according to the editors of *Oppositions*, which heralded the coming of postmodernism also took place at the MOMA some 45 years later. This was the Beaux-Arts exhibition of 1977. Significantly, the École des Beaux-Arts was the central institutional context of the historicist architecture that modernists rejected. Corbusier in the 1920s and 1930s saw the Beaux-Arts academic style as the main enemy in much the way that the secession movements several decades earlier were revolts against the academy. And the Beaux-Arts style was above all historicist. Training at the École produced architects such as Cass Gilbert and William Van Alen, authors of 'delirious' New York's awesome neo-Gothic skyscrapers such as the Woolworth and Chrysler buildings. Such training is noticeable in the neo-romanesque features of Louis Sullivan's Auditorium Theatre in Chicago. Beaux-Arts influence informs Speer's monumental Third Reich neo-classicism.

But Beaux-Arts architecture was histori*cist* rather than histori*cal*. That is, its architects reproduced one of a set of varied styles from different historical epochs in the present. The rise of historicist architecture ran parallel to the rise of historicist social theory, in the work of, for example, Dilthey. The very plurality of historical styles suggested a rejection of universalism and an acceptance of a certain relativism corresponding to the 'forms of life'-type relativism of the social theorists. The return to history that the postmodernist architects advocate, however, rejects historicism and relativism. The search instead is for universals in history. And these universals are humanist. Hence the neglect of gothic and romanesque forms for neo-classicism by the postmodern architects.

This universalism of the postmodernists is a bit confusing perhaps in the light of criticisms against them made by Habermasians. Such criticisms have taken them to task for being anti-universalist. But there are (at least) two types of universalism. Universals can be sought, by modernists such as Corbusier and Habermas, in the 'ought', in the utopian moment of a possible future. Such universals constitute the moment of critique in Corbusier's harmonically juxtaposed volumes or Habermas's ideal speech situation. But universals can also be sought in the past, like in the model of humanism described above. Because modernist universals are abstract does not mean that all universals have to be abstract. The (historical) humanism outlined above is universalist in the sense that a certain set of values is held to be valid for all historical periods and in all geographic places. Full spatio-temporal validity is also the assumption of modernist universals.

But postmodernist (humanist) universalism is grounded in the rejection of modernist abstraction. The search for historical universals of the architects is matched by painters among the German *neue Wilden* such as Anselm Kiefer. It is purveyed by the social theorists such as MacIntyre and Leo Strauss. Strauss and his follower Allan Bloom are critical of modern natural rights theory because of the very abstraction of the rights involved. Their advocacy of a return to Platonic political philosophy is an endorsement of the more humanist and '*sittlich*' (that is, grounded in social practices) notion of rights implicit in Classical thought. Alisdair MacIntyre is critical of the assumptions of abstraction (and absence of *Gemeinschaft* and *Sittlichkeit*) in Enlightenment thought. For MacIntyre, Nietzsche and the modernists do not, *à la* Habermas, constitute the reversal of the Enlightenment project. They are emblematic instead of the radicalization of Enlightenment abstraction. They bring about the total break of ethics and epistemology with any kind of foundations. MacIntyre, as well, has advocated a return to the social groundedness of Classical Greece, this time of Aristotle's ethics and the *Sittlichkeit* of the *polis*.

Thus the critique of modernism – in architecture and in social theory – embraces a return to the historical sense that the modernists have abandoned. This critique is perhaps most appropriately, though surely cryptically, formulated by the populist/vernacular postmodern architect Robert Stern. Stern writes that modernism is based on 'the dialectic of the "is" and the "ought"', and postmodernism on 'the resolution of the "is" and the "was"'.

Avant-gardes

One tends almost naturally to see postmodernism in terms of a set of new avant-gardes, in architecture, painting, etc., setting themselves up in counterposition to an entrenched modernist establishment. Surely postmodernism is in an important sense a somewhat populist critique of modernism. But so were surrealism and dada in the 1920s and these were quintessentially movements of avant-gardes. Equally, Derrida, Foucault and other post-structural theorists are commonly called postmodernists, and they have been widely understood to be a Parisian, theoretical avant-garde;

a conception reinforced by their own aesthetic pretensions and their loyalties especially to surrealism.

Avant-gardes, however, not only originated with modernism, but their whole ethos is quite integral to its logic. The aforementioned universalist abstraction of the modernist 'ought' is, at the same time, the regulating principle of avant-gardes. Both aesthetic and political avant-gardes presume a universalism, which unlike humanism, is abstracted from the social. Avant-gardes, which are abstracted and thus separate from socio-political everyday life, impart forward movement to the latter. Thus for Marxism, class struggle, and later the proletarian political party, is the (avant-garde) 'motor' of history. Much the same characterizes aesthetic avant-gardes which, separate from the everyday convention of the state and social *Sittlichkeit*, are to impart movement to the latter. In both cases the principle of modernization, or autonomization and differentiation, is the rule.

If modernization is a process of differentiation, then postmodernism is one of cultural *de*-differentiation. And such de-differentiation precludes the possibility of avant-gardes. The postmodernist denigration of avant-gardes stands in counterposition to the modernist autonomy of the creative 'author'. Modernism presupposes an Adornian production aesthetics, in which power lies in the hands of the (avant-garde) producers of cultural goods. Postmodernism is not only homologous to consumer capitalism, but lodges power in the consumers of cultural goods. Postmodern aesthetics are thus reception aesthetics and this entails the absence of avant-gardes. Hence the 'populism' of Robert Venturi and Denise Scott-Brown in their assignment of an important role to the public in deciding the shape of the built environment. 'Convention' would seem to be the antonym of avant-garde. Venturi and Scott-Brown castigate the idea of avant-garde architect as legislating hero and instead note, inconspicuously, 'we like convention'.

Avant-gardes, further, mean change, much in the sense of Marshall Berman's ever-transmuting modernist utopia. But postmodern architect Robert Stern wonders what indeed is so great about such 'constant change and experimentation'? And the (equally postmodern) maverick Leon Krier calls for the termination of avant-gardes and 'their barbarous profusion of innovations that culminate in the kitsch which perverts every level of life and culture'.

Modernist avant-gardes, as noted above, have always been constituted in opposition to 'the academy'. Thus Corbusier, though admitted to the École des Beaux-Arts, was trained in the art school of his home town in Switzerland. And Van der Rohe underwent a crafts-oriented training. Postmodernism, on the other hand, has literally grown up in the academy; that is, in the architecture departments of the most establishment of American universities. Thus the chief voices of postmodernism have been the *Harvard Architecture Review* and Princeton's *Oppositions*. One can only lament here, along with Russell Jacoby, the academy's destruction – though he points the finger rather more at postmodern theorists such as Jameson – of the modernist critique of 'the last intellectuals'.

Modernist avant-gardes presuppose the primacy of movement. This is foregrounded in discussions of the modernist city by analysts like T.J. Clark, Carl Schorske, Berman and Bell. Key to the modernist built environment on these accounts is the street, and the promise of never stopping circulation, both of vehicles and pedestrians. Postmodern space would, by contrast, it seems, hold out the promise of *stasis*. Roland Robertson has held that Japanese culture was postmodern *avant la lettre*, and this ontology of stasis would seem to be borne out by the organization of space in Japan. Thus the Japanese street, unlike modernist Western streets, is organized, notes Augustin Berque in *Vivre l'espace au Japon* (1982), not for moving through, but for living in. What takes place often in squares, airports or malls in the West – shops, markets, public sociability – commonly takes place in residential streets in Japanese cities.

With modernization, as Western space became more and more a medium, not for living, but for moving through, streets took on names and houses numbers. To this day in Japan, streets have no names and houses no numbers. Japanese residences and places of business do have addresses, typically with three digits and a name. The name refers, however, not to a street, but to a quarter. The first of the three digits refers, in its turn, to a district in this quarter. The second to a square block in the district. The final digit designates the building on this square block. It does so, not in spatial and linear sequence, but in chronological order according to when the house was built. Thus *Business Week* has noted the popularity of fax machines in Japanese offices. Japanese companies must send Western (and Japanese) visiting clients photocopies of maps showing how to find their corporate headquarters.

Referentiality

If post-structuralist theory is postmodernist – and most commentators think so – then the Derridean 'il n'y a pas un hors du texte' would be the postmodernist canon. This would also be canonical self-referentiality. The absence of an *hors-du-texte* would mean a semiotics consisting solely of signifiers, in which utterances have their effect totally apart from any relationship they may have to signified and referent. In fact signified and referent are banished as *hors du texte*, and meaning is generated through the differential values of elements and spaces in networks of signifiers.

But Derridean self-referentiality has, mostly, its roots in Saussure. And Saussure, for his part, is a canonical modernist. Modernist differentiation and autonomization reached its peak in the early decades of this century, as cultural spheres and discourses achieved their fullest autonomy. Hence there is at this time Kelsen's pure theory of law. There are the beginnings of a political science which does not, as did early modern political philosophy, elide the political and the social. There is the onset of autonomy of the social in Durkheimian social facts and sociologistic ethics and epistemologies. And there is the autonomy of language, both from referent and signified (where it had been lodged in the nineteenth century historical linguistics (that is, philology) of the Grimms and others) in Saussure's course in general linguistics. There is finally the theorization of all of these autonomous and modernized cultural spheres in Max Weber's ethics of responsibility. Weber speaks of each sphere becoming self-legislating (*Eigengesetzlichkeit*). And self-legislation is the other side of self-referentiality.

The doctrine of the non-existence of the *hors-du-texte* is pre-eminently exemplified in modernist architecture. For van der Rohe, for example, the form of a building was to follow not function – which would be an *hors-du-texte* – but the structure of the building itself. That is, Mies's understanding of, say, glass was not in terms of light maximization for a building's users, but was instead involved with aesthetic, formal and structural properties. He thus wrote of glass as a building material permitting not 'the play of light and shadows as in ordinary buildings . . . but the play of reflections'. 'It [glass]', he continued, 'also permits a particular massing of the building as viewed from the street.' The role of glass, then, as building material, was to reveal structure. And this surely is the language of self-referentiality. Similarly, Corbusier's rendering of the house as a *machine à habiter*, focused less on the functions of the machine for its users than on the relationship of the elements of the machine to one another. This looks suspiciously like Saussurean *langue* – Corbusier even calls the elements 'terms'. The five elements of the *machine à habiter* in a 1925 Corbusier exhibition were (1) the *pilotis*, (2) the free plan, (3) the free façade, (4) horizontal strip window and (5) roof garden.

Postmodernism, in contrast, revels in the *other*-referentiality of the *hors-du-texte*. Thus the signified is resurrected in the rejection of modernist syntactical architecture for an architecture of semantics. Postmodernism also heralds the return of the (repressed) referent in the representational painting of pop art and the *neue Wilden*, or of Americans like Eric Fischl and the new popularity of Edward Hopper.

Modernism signifies, in brief, via a principle of semiosis, and postmodernism via mimesis. Semiotic signification is self-referential and takes place through the differences among signifying elements in a *langue*. Mimetic signification is other-referential and takes place through the resemblance of signifier to referent. Postmodern signification takes place largely through images, through spectacle. And the more closely signifiers resemble images (compare abstract versus figural painting) the greater the extent to which signification proceeds via mimesis. Thus the Lacanian and Barthesian analysts associated with *Screen* could not be further from the truth in their main claim that cinema signifies like a language. It would be difficult to find a cultural practice indeed – with its images, its movement, its sound, the size and high definition of its images – that signifies *less* like a language than cinema. Cinema and video signify almost not at all semiotically, but almost fully mimetically. And postmodern signification through images could not be further from self-referentiality. It could not give a greater role to the *hors-du-texte*.

Conclusions

When Michel Foucault heralded the 'end of man' in *The Order of Things* (1970) – and celebrated the subject's removal from social-scientific centre-stage by structuralist anthropology, psychoanalysis and semiotics – he was celebrating the triumph, not of postmodernity, but of modernity. The principle of 'man', or 'humanism', with its corresponding mirror-of-nature (which is also Quattrocento) epistemology and ontology, is part and parcel, not of Foucault's modern, but of his *classical* episteme. The bulk of *The Order of Things* deals with the classical and modern epistemes. Foucault's critique of Marx takes place significantly in the sections on the classical episteme. Elsewhere, in Foucault in *Discipline and Punish* (1977), Marxism is criticized for its *pre*-modern, statist conception of power. Foucault's famous chapter in *The Order of Things* of the replacement of the sciences of man by autonomous sciences of 'structure' comes of course under the modern episteme. Lyotard's analyses comprises a similar logic. Here Marxism is a 'metanarrative' to be replaced by autonomous and 'local' language games. Thus in Foucault's terms and those of the argument of this paper, Marxist metanarratives would be pre-modern and the local language games modern. Lyotard's aesthetics of 'paralogy' fully parallel a modernist aesthetics of experimentation. The only problem is that what is classical (humanist) or pre-modern Lyotard mistakenly labels modern, and what is modern he mistakenly labels postmodern.

In any event Lyotard's *Postmodern Condition* (1984) was a hastily written report for a Canadian social policy agency, and bears none of the depth of insight and analysis of his major works such as *Discours, figure* (1971). Foucault's *Order of Things* is a twentieth century 'Great Book'. And here the radical separation of subject from object at the outset of his very Kantian modernity already foreshadows the death of humanism. As Foucault's modern episteme unfolds, the subject of Kant's categorical epistemology and ethics achieves autonomy from categorical (that is, unconditional) status, and becomes socially conditioned in Weber's neo-Kantian *wertrational* and *zweckrational* social action. The other side of this autonomous actor is the social structures of Durkheimian sociology, which achieve their own autonomy from all of the humanist foundationalisms described above.

Foucault, then, as structuralist is pre-eminently modernist, as is the self-referentiality and basis in autonomous Saussurean linguistic structures of Derrida's post-structuralist '*écriture*'. These modernists, like the modernist architects, celebrate, implicitly or explicitly, the downfall of humanism. The postmodernists, I argued at length above, want to resurrect it. Have they succeeded?

The answer to this would seem largely to be in the negative. Let us review our categories. As regards *humanism*, the attempt of postmodern architects at reconstituting the anthropometric and anthropocentric scale and fabric of our cities has turned into the highly individualistic and atomized isolation of the buildings of the 1980s financial districts. This has been only a radicalization of modernism's loss of foundations. Modernist architecture came under the spell of industrial society's polarization of manufacturing capital and labour. Industrial capital in the initial tertialization – the proliferation of high rise buildings for white collar employees of manufacturing firms – of our city centres. And industrial labour in the modernist public housing blocks of first Germany and then Britain, the US and elsewhere. In contradistinction, postmodernist architecture has been subject to the imperatives of a *post*-industrial economy, of the internationalization of fictive commodities, of financial, business and culture services, of the property developers.

As regards historicity, one must be suspicious of the authenticity of engagement of postmodern architects such as Moore and Graves with historical universals. Their more populist counterparts, such as Helmut Jahn, Robert Stirling, Venturi and Philip Johnson are quite openly 'playful' with historical elements. They operate with historical signifiers only for 'effect' or 'impact' on the public. Their focus surely is not on meaning. Theirs is a de-semanticized historicity.

As regards avant-gardes, Venturi has admitted that his buildings are intended for two publics, one elite and the other mass. The elite reception group is similar to the audience for the modernist avant-gardes. The same is true of a number of recent postmodernist films such as *Diva*, *Blade Runner*, *Blue Velvet* and *Robocop*. They too are, unlike Godard's or Bergmann's modernist films, aimed simultaneously at two audiences. The assumption, of course, is much of the significance of these postmodern cultural objects, like that of modernist avant-gardes, will not be accessible to the mass audience. Finally, the engagement with populist commercialism of the postmodernists was not unknown among modernist avant-gardes, and is exemplified in say the Hoffmann and Moser's design in the Vienna Secession and the mass-production turn of the later Bauhaus. Thus the claim of the postmodernists to reject avant-gardes is not substantiated in their own cultural practices. Perhaps most apposite is British architecture critic Martin Pawley's comment that the postmodernists are an 'avant-garde leading from the rear'.

And what, finally, about the attempt to break with modernist self-referentiality? The attempt of postmodern architecture to re-connect with historical meanings (or signifieds) has, as has often been noted, wound up in the trivialization of the latter. Similarly the putative reunification of signifier with referent, that is of representation with reality, in (postmodernist) pop art turns out to be a very problematic referentiality indeed. That is, the referent in for example Warhol's silk screens, the Elvises and Marilyns and Maos, turn out to be images, or signifieds themselves. This sort of reference differs considerably from modernist self-referentiality. In the latter, attention is called to the signifying practice; in the former, to entities external to the signifying practice. For example, in Godard's modernist cinema, attention is continually drawn to the fact that what the spectator is seeing is not reality, but a cinematic signifying practice. In a postmodernist film like Beneix's *Diva*, the spectator is not told that he/she is watching a cinematic convention or a signifying practice, but is instead drawn into the murky reality of the film itself. Elements of *Diva*'s *mise-en-scène* turn out to be lifted from Nicholas Ray's *Rebel without a Cause*. But this draws attention not to *Diva* as a signifying practice (or set of conventions), but to the fact of how much (this) reality, itself, is like an image. Thus the quest for stabilization of reference is travestied by the very 'flimsiness' inherent in the very nature of the postmodernist signifieds and referents.

We can finally now begin to present an answer to Habermas's *j'accuse* of neo-conservatism versus the postmodernists. Yes, we have seen, important strains of postmodernism are cast, in parallel with social theorists such as Bell, Lasch, MacIntyre, Strauss and Bloom, in the intention of some sort of anti-modernist and effectively conservative cultural restabilization. We have equally seen that this attempt in cultural restabilization has largely misfired. The unintended consequences of these attempts has been not the humanist utopia of a *sittlich*, balanced and harmonic *polis*, but something closer to the dystopic landscapes and mediascapes of Jean Baudrillard's nightmare commentaries. The unintended consequence of the postmodernists has been not the resurrection of Italian Renaissance or neo-classical urban space, but the chaotic imbalance and chronic instability of Ed Koch's New York. It has been the world of the profane juxtaposition of a home for the homeless framed in a Ridley Scott's *Blade Runner* urban wasteland with the glitzy spectacle of Donald Trump's towers and the arriviste downtown silicon networks of Tom Wolfe's *Bonfire of the Vanities*.

Is there, then, in postmodernist culture no *radical* potential to match the disruptive possibilities and ethos of change in modernist experimentation? Must its vision, if not neo-conservative, be fully one of cultural pessimism? Again here, I would like to propose a response in the negative. The modernist challenge to the cultural status quo lay in its experimentation with the signifier, with its destabilization of representation. Postmodernism's putative restabilization of the signifier winds up, in its consequences, in *de*stabilizing the referent, be it in Lichtenstein's comic book figuration or Philip Johnson's recent buildings. Thus the logic of modernism inheres in its problematization of the representation, while the logic of postmodernism inheres in its problematization of the reality. In other words, the postmodernists, whether intentionally or not, can direct our attention to a changing social reality of consumption increasingly comprised by the proliferation of images. And to a social reality of production which is, to an ever greater degree, semiotic in content. This problematization of the real, through art, through cultural forms, could indeed have considerable disruptive and radical potential.

References

Berque, Augustin (1982) *Vivre l'espace au Japon*. Paris: Presses Universitaires de France.
Foucault, Michel (1970) *The Order of Things*. London: Tavistock.
Foucault, Michel (1977) *Discipline and Punish: The Birth of the Prison*. London: Tavistock.

Lyotard, Jean-François (1971) *Discours, figure*. Paris: Klincksieck.
Lyotard, Jean-François (1984) *The Postmodern Condition*. Manchester: Manchester University Press.
Moore, Charles (1980) 'Beyond the Modern Movement: forum discussion', *Harvard Architectural Review*, 1: 190–217.
Whyte, William H. (1980) *The Sociology of Small Public Spaces*. New York: Conservation Forum.

6

SIMMEL AND THE THEORY OF POSTMODERN SOCIETY

Deena Weinstein and Michael A. Weinstein

The revival of interest in Georg Simmel's thought that has occurred in the English-speaking world since the early 1970s has brought to the forefront of attention his contributions to cultural theory. Among the commentators on Simmel's work Donald Levine (1971) has integrated Simmel's sociological studies and his philosophy of life around the dialectical tension between 'life' and 'form'; Peter Lawrence (1976) has provided fresh translations of some of Simmel's major essays on culture and has interpreted them in the context of the European civilization of his time; and David Frisby (1981) has given a careful and rich account of Simmel's intellectual spirit in the light of contemporary hermeneutical categories. The growing literature on Simmel's legacy is characterized by a welcome tendency to consider his thought as a whole rather than to abstract from it particular substantive or methodological contributions to sociological inquiry, and to establish firmly that a concern with the problematicity of modern culture is a unifying theme in his varied studies in philosophy, aesthetics, and sociology. Contemporary Simmel scholarship offers a sound basis for a further project of making some of the critical nuances of his reflections on culture more precise. A more intensive examination of key aspects of Simmel's cultural theory will not only provide a more adequate picture of his thought, but will show its relevance to present interpretations of culture.

Current scholarship on Simmel is characterized by the legitimate aim of placing his work in the context of the times in which it was written. The approach of cultural history performs the salutary function of preventing misplaced abstractions, but it often fails to grasp the significance of a thinker for future generations. Any thinker is embedded in his age, sharing with his contemporaries participation in distinctive discursive formations which are intelligible both in terms of regnant social conditions and the given level of cultural development in all of the phases of what Simmel called, in the manner of Hegel, 'spiritual life.' However, a thinker may also push beyond the confines of his era and anticipate the problems which will preoccupy future reflection. Cultural history, as it is practiced today, with the guiding intention of circumstantializing a thinker, tends to neglect fruitful antici-pations. Although it is difficult both to make a thinker intelligible through his socio-cultural circumstances and to show how he transcended them, those two endeavors are essential to a complete interpretation: history must strive to be adequate to the temporal determinations of its object, but historiography rejoins that the past is necessarily interpreted through present concerns.

Lawrence (1976: 5) evinces the present direction of Simmel scholarship when he writes that 'Simmel is of interest as a representative, though not always a typical representative, of both European culture before the war of 1914–18 and of Wilhelminian Germany, though there is some opposition between these two environmental forces.' That understanding of Simmel will tend to assimilate his thought to the special problems of German national unification and the 'cultural pessimism' which arose in Germany as the Bismarckian formula of a thinly-disguised authoritarianism fell apart in the years preceding World War I. Frisby (1981), indeed, makes Simmel into the arch cultural pessimist by interpreting his spirit through the free-floating retreatism of Robert Musil's Ulrich, 'the man without qualities.' One need not deny that Simmel reacted painfully against 'the First World War which shattered the civilization he revered,' or even that he sometimes 'displayed a characteristically German apathy towards contemporary politics' (Lawrence, 1976: 6). Much of Simmel's temperament is fully attuned to his period and he acknowledges that fact in his late writings. However, among his famous contemporaries such as Max Weber, Ferdinand Tönnies and Werner Sombart he was distinguished by a decided lack of nostalgia and by a penetrating interest in emerging cultural phenomena, for example expressionism in art and pragmatism in philosophy, which casts doubt on the picture of him as a man who could not summon the nerve to engage himself in the great struggles of his time. If Simmel was a representative of his epoch, both as German and as European, he was also a pathfinder beyond it, most particularly in his late works on cultural theory, written during World War I. As Georg Stauth and Bryan Turner (1988: 16) note, he 'may be regarded as the first sociologist of post-modernity.'

The anticipations of future discourses in Simmel's work are articulated with greatest precision in two of his most sensitive essays on cultural theory, 'The crisis of culture' (1917) and 'The conflict of modern culture' (1918). In these writings Simmel emerges not as a cultural pessimist but as an internal critic of modernism, anticipating in 'The crisis' the existentialism of Martin Heidegger, and in 'The conflict' contemporary 'postmodernist' perspectives. The following discussion will suggest that, far from suffering a failure of the will to engagement, Simmel in his later years struggled deeply with the tensions of modern life, agonizing over them and introjecting them into the core of his intellectual personality, and seeking restlessly, though unsuccessfully, to overcome them. Simmel's unwillingness or inability to take a stand in any of the movements of his period or to found a school or a movement of his own do not bespeak, as Frisby (1981) has it, the spirit of the *flaneur* or the impressionist, who distances himself from the currents of life because he finds them too multifarious and fluctuating to embrace in a consistent praxis;

or, as Lawrence (1976) claims, a 'characteristically German apathy.' Instead, the absence of partisan commitment in his intellectual life stems from his placement of the problematicity of modernity in cultural conflict rather than in economic, political, or social dynamics. Simmel traced the crisis of modernity to an internal contradiction in culture and he strove to discern signs of its possible reconciliation: he was not so much 'the man without qualities,' the victim of a cultural pathology, as a Nietzschian diagnostician and therapist seeking cultural health, an agonistic healer, similar to his Spanish contemporary Unamuno.

The following discussion will interpret 'The crisis of culture' and 'The conflict of modern culture' as parallel texts which address the same phenomena of modernist culture – expressionism, post-metaphysical philosophy, and post-Christian religiosity – in distinctively different ways. 'The crisis,' which is Simmel's most careful reflection on World War I, interprets modernism in terms of the categories of his pre-war thinking, recalling *The Philosophy of Money* and 'The metropolis and mental life,' but infusing those categories with a moral commitment leading out to the existentialism of the post-war generation. Here Simmel's thought is a bridge between the past and the immediate future, anticipating the drive away from relativism and skepticism, and toward commitment that would mark the inter-war period. 'The conflict,' which is the most unique and original work in Simmel's canon, pushes beyond the parameters of his other writings, leaving off from the past and breaking entirely new ground in its profound acknowledgment of the positivity of modernism and of its essential failure: in this text the postmodernist discourse erupts. In 'The crisis' Simmel is still a representative, though certainly not a typical one, of his generation, though he is struggling painfully beyond it. In 'The conflict' he is contemporaneous with our own cultural situation, which gives us the privilege of understanding him more fully than previous generations have been able to do.

The exhaustion of form

'The crisis of culture,' which is one of four essays collected in Simmel's *The War and Spiritual Decisions*, has been generally ignored by commentators, who find the notes of German nationalism that are sounded in his writings on World War I to be uncharacteristic of his supposed cosmopolitan bias and, perhaps, embarrassing. Lawrence (1976), however, points out that Simmel's 'war enthusiasm' in 'The crisis' is 'reasoned rather than rabid.' The essay, indeed, far from being a defense of the war spirit is exemplary of Simmel's late cultural theory, framed in the context of how the War affects the basic dialectical tensions in modern life. Simmel shows in 'The crisis' how war reveals the presuppositions of peacetime life in a 'highly developed objective culture.' His project is similar to that of 'The metropolis and mental life' (Simmel, 1971), in which he traced the impact of the social form of the modern urban setting on individual subjectivity, only now the form mediating cultural conflict is war. The basic terms of that conflict are the same in both essays – the opposition between objective and subjective culture – and recur to his masterwork *The Philosophy of Money* (Simmel, 1978).

Throughout his mature writings on culture, until the radical break which he makes in 'The conflict,' Simmel's fundamental description of modernity is constituted by the tension between objective and subjective culture. Working within the parameters of a naturalized Hegelian dialectic, he defines man as a being who objectifies life in cultural forms, such as technology, science, art, philosophy and religion, which then demand that life conform to their constraints and standards. Under ideal conditions the form-giving activity of human life is able to appropriate its objectified creations to fill out and enhance individual subjectivity; that is, the objective culture of things serves the subjective culture of personal development. In 'The crisis' Simmel gives one of his best accounts of the normative grounds of his cultural theory, arguing that 'improvement of the soul' is culturally achieved indirectly 'by way of the intellectual achievements of the species, the products of its history: knowledge, life-styles, art, the state, a man's profession and experience of life – these constitute the path of culture by which the subjective spirit returns to itself in a higher, improved state' (Simmel, 1976a: 253). The foundation of Simmel's cultural theory, then, is a triadic relation of 'form creation–objectivized form–form appreciation,' which functions ideally as a self-reinforcing process through which human products come back to their creators to enrich their lives. Simmel's descriptive analyses and his criticisms of culture all trade off his normative ideal, showing the various ways in which the reciprocal relation between the three moments of the fundamental dialectic is broken in modern life.

Had Simmel followed in Hegel's footsteps he would have endeavored to show how the idealized dialectic of culture was the actual form of historical development, but his deepest insight into human life was that the three terms of the relation were inherently unbalanced. 'The crisis' culminates Simmel's tragic sense of culture by bringing together his major arguments about how the objective culture of modernity fails to serve the development of the individual's personality. His radical claim is that the form-giving activity tends to perfect its objective creations indefinitely through differentiating them into autonomous cultural realms, which then are developed according to their own inherent norms, and through generating ever more intensive and extensive means to fulfill those norms. Meanwhile, finite individual subjectivity remains bound within its natural limits and becomes progressively incapable of assimilating and appropriating the vast array of cultural objects for its own perfection, and increasingly lost within the jungle of means to the point at which it even loses sight of its native goal. The crisis of an impoverished subjectivity confronting an overwhelming objectivity is further exacerbated by the demands for service that each realm of objective culture makes upon the individual spirit. Objective culture, rather than serving the individual as it is supposed to in the normative order, becomes the oppressive master of subjectivity in the actual order of historical development. According to Simmel there is no exit from this tragic predicament, which is grounded in the relation between the indefinite perfectibility of objective culture and the inherent limits of individual subjectivity: the highly developed objective culture is in a state of 'chronic crisis.'

The crisis of culture is enacted in a wrenching conflict within the individual between the demands of objective culture and the struggle of the self for its own expression of its life. The typical reaction of subjectivity to chronic crisis is defensive and protective; that is, to withdraw into a blasé attitude and to withhold commitment to objective forms. The forms become exhausted of any meaning that they might once have had for individual life and various pathologies appear such as the equation of technological with cultural progress, overt covetousness and craving for pleasure, and a desire for money that far exceeds the desire for the things it can buy. Subjectivity trivializes itself as a defense mechanism against the demands of the objective spirit, suffering from a sense of futility rather than caring for its own enrichment. But it also initiates more positive resistances such as war, which provides an overriding end of group survival for life, and modernism, which in 'The crisis' is a struggle for subjective culture in an age of exhausted forms. War, for Simmel, is a temporary recovery of vitality and seriousness in the persistent context of futility, and in the midst of its devastation it may reveal to people how their values have been inverted by their resentment against the overbearing demands of a fragmented objective culture. Modernism, in contrast, is the extreme pathology of peacetime life, the self-contradicted resistance of impoverished subjectivity, the flaring up of an endemic cultural disease.

Although Simmel does not use the term 'modernism' he identifies 'a number of contemporary cultural phenomena' which would later be grouped under that term. Indeed, he may be considered as one of the first to discover the affinity between the various tendencies in diverse spheres of culture that self-consciously attempt to rupture received conventions and to give free play to immanent creative process. In 'The crisis' he interprets such phenomena as futurist art, post-Christian religiosity and post-metaphysical philosophy as responses to an environment of inherited cultural forms which were 'eroded and lacking in self-assurance.' Modernism here is the kind of creativity that occurs when there is 'a passionate desire for the expression of life, for which traditional forms are inadequate, but for which no new forms have been devised, and which therefore seeks pure expression in a negation of form, or in forms that are almost provocatively abstruse' (Simmel, 1976a: 257). The modernist impulse is described here negatively as a spirit in a cultural interregnum that has lost allegiance to old models but that is incapable of creating new ones. In light of its deprivation it falls back upon itself and seeks to present itself 'formless and naked.' But such an effort, according to Simmel, is doomed to failure because the inner life can only be expressed 'in forms which have their own laws, purpose and stability arising from a degree of autonomy independent of the spiritual dynamics which created them' (Simmel, 1976a: 257). Expressionism, which tries to objectify psychological processes directly, ends in 'a chaos of fragmentary vestiges of form as a substitute for a form which is unified.' Futurism, which is Simmel's touchstone in 'The crisis,' has created 'prisons,' not 'pure expression.'

Post-Christian religiosity, which is best exemplified by a 'formless mysticism' through which the soul attempts to stand 'naked' before its God or to be 'its own inmost metaphysical life not moulded by any forms of faith whatever' is also traced by Simmel to an 'historical moment when inner life can no longer be accommodated in the forms it has occupied hitherto, and because it is unable to create other, adequate forms, concludes that it must exist without any form at all' (Simmel, 1976a: 259). Simmel places the new piety, which would later resonate in the movement of process theology, against the backdrop of pre-war culture, a 'peaceful age of gradual transitions, of hybrid forms, of that pleasant twilit zone where one can indulge alternately even in mutually exclusive attitudes' (Simmel, 1986a: 258). He believes that the War has ended that era of trivialized faith and ushered in a time which 'demands from each and every man a decision as to where he ultimately stands.' Anticipating Heidegger's (1962) notion of 'resolute choice' in *Being and Time*, Simmel hopes that the 'resoluteness' that the Germans have shown in the war effort 'will also penetrate to this inmost area of decision.' Here Simmel adopts a decidedly existentialist outlook, speaking of a 'radical eruption of man's religious depths.' He is moving along the line of Karl Jaspers' *Existenz* and Paul Tillich's 'ultimate concern,' breaking out of the idea of religion as a cultural form without falling prey to 'formless mysticism.' With his notion of radical choice he is on the brink of discovering the forms of personal existence; Heidegger's 'existentials' and Jasper's 'ultimate situations,' both of which were forged in the effort to renew culture in the wake of its collapse by revealing intimately real forms.

The idea that modernism is a sign of what Heidegger called the interregnum between gods, that it bespeaks the impotent yearning for new forms, carries over into Simmel's discussion of post-metaphysical philosophy. Anticipating Heidegger, Simmel suggests that the system of philosophy which has been 'elaborated since classical antiquity' is 'beginning to become an empty shell.' Ideal antinomies such as free will and determinism, and absolute and relative, 'no longer permit a clear decision to allocate any dubious case definitely to the one concept or the other' (Simmel, 1976a: 260). There is a 'demand for an as yet indefinable third possibility,' because 'our resources for mastering reality by giving it intellectual expression are no longer adequate to their task.' The 'philosophical instinct' quests for 'new forms, which as yet announce their arcane presence only as intuition or perplexity, desire or clumsy gropings.' In the inter-war period there would be an effort throughout the West to engender those new forms. Ludwig Wittgenstein would find in ordinary language the matrix out of which philosophical abstractions escaped, Heidegger and later existential phenomenologists would coordinate the classical antinomies in the category of being-in-the-world, and the late Heidegger would make the daring attempt to break through metaphysics altogether to the thought of Being itself. None of those efforts has proven adequate to the traditional task of philosophy, which, for Simmel, is to make reality intelligible, but they show that the very problem he identified during the War would become the center of philosophical reflection after it was over.

The discussion of modernism in 'The crisis' is framed within the primal understandings of the exhaustion of received cultural forms and of the deprivation of subjective culture. Modernism, as a failed mediation between form-creating activity and form appreciation, occupies a gap between a past and a possible future culture, both of which provide a modicum of satisfaction to the subjective demand for coherent personal development. Although the essay concludes with an assertion that the 'chronic crisis' of highly developed objective culture cannot be reversed in the long run Simmel still nurses a hope that the tendency of such a culture to 'disintegrate into futility and paradox' will be recurrently arrested by 'the fundamental dynamic unity of life' (Simmel, 1976a: 265). He senses that the 'concept of *life* now seems to permeate a multitude of spheres and to have begun to give, as it were, a more unified rhythm to their heartbeat' (Simmel, 1976a: 263). Simmel here endows the form-giving activity of life with its own meaningful integrity, its own inherent pre-intellectual and self-preservation and self-renewing direction. The crisis of culture is the exhaustion of form and its pathological manifestations are the currents of modernism which attempt to dispense with form only because they are unable to create it. Indeed, in 'The crisis' life and form are held in tension with each other in a 'process of interaction' – they are not antithetical forces, but are defined reciprocally in terms of the polarity flux and fixed, each one a necessary moment in the totality of the life process. The real antithesis here, as it is through all of Simmel's work from *The Philosophy of Money* until 'The conflict of modern culture,' is between objective culture (objectivized form) and subjective culture (form appreciation). Life itself, as form-giving activity, is not problematized and, thus, can be dogmatized, can remain a repository of hope for spontaneous renewal, encircling the tragic opposition between the two cultures. In 'The conflict,' however, the ground shifts altogether and Simmel problematizes the relation of form-giving activity to objectivized form, abandoning the last vestiges of his metaphysical optimism and opening the door to postmodernist perspectives on culture. He abandons the waiting game of the interregnum and enters the age of radically contradicted life.

The rebellion of life

Georg Simmel was the leading philosopher of life in Germany in his generation, performing the function of assimilating the idealist tradition into the ground of lived experience as it is seized directly from within by a conscious finite self. Like his French contemporary, Henry Bergson, with whom he is often compared, he philosophized from a vision of life's structure which he achieved by a reflective review of the various human activities, guided by his intuition of life's process. Far from taking the pose of the detached ego who floats above life observing it indifferently or of the *flaneur* who mingles in society but can take it or leave it, he experienced to the depth all of the conflicts of his time. He was acutely aware of the multiplicity and relativity of forms, but he took each one of them seriously, pondering its internal meaning and its relations to the others. He did not commit himself to the perfection of any special form as a Weberian vocation, but concerned himself with the problematicity of form itself: he was, on the contemplative side, a cultural theorist, and, on the active side, a cultural critic. He was a man of forms, not of form; a man of many qualities, not a man without them. He understood and was loyal to a moral ideal of a culture in which human beings express their lives in objects which return to them to fortify their personal development, but he did not believe that this ideal was capable of realization. Rather, in his review of life as a whole he discovered irremediable paradoxes, ironies and contradictions.

Simmel's vision of the dialectic of 'form creation–objectivized form–form appreciation' governed his entire mature intellectual development, but he placed emphasis on different tensions within that dialectic over time. Through the middle period of his career (1900–1910), he was concerned with the conflict between objectivized form and form appreciation, arguing that the objective culture of things had outrun the ability of individuals to incorporate it into a satisfying subjective culture of personal enrichment. He did not attend during this period to the moment of form-giving life, leaving it as an unanalyzed ground and taking for granted the 'chronic crisis' of the highly developed objective modern culture. In his late writings, however, a decisive shift in his focus occurs which culminates in 'The conflict of modern culture.' Whereas in the preceding phase of his thought objectivized form was the protagonist overwhelming form appreciation, which adopted a multitude of compensatory and defensive measures to maintain some semblance of integrity, in his thought during the War period the form-giving activity of life itself becomes the protagonist, seeking to deconstruct objectivized form; to capture it, assert sovereignty over it, and assimilate it into itself. Concern with subjective culture drops out of his thinking, as though it had become anachronistic, and the creative spirit confronts its products without the mediation of the appreciation of culture: creative life seeks to become the self-sufficient appreciator of itself, of its own creativity.

Simmel began 'The crisis of culture' by defining culture subjectively as 'the improvement of the soul' attained indirectly through 'the intellectual achievements of the species.' The ground shifts decisively in 'The conflict,' which he initiates with the reflection that 'we speak of culture when the creative dynamism of life produces certain artefacts which provide it with forms of expression and actualization, and which in their turn absorb the constant flow of life, giving it form and content, scope and order' (Simmel, 1976b: 223). Culture is here primarily a product of creative life, not an object of appreciative life. In light of this new focus, the site of the conflict of culture moves to an antagonism between creativity and its creations. According to Simmel, form-giving life produces objectivized forms which 'have their own logic and laws, their own significance and resilience arising from a certain degree of detachment and independence *vis-à-vis* the spiritual dynamism which gave them life' (Simmel, 1976b: 223). The independence of objectivized form from the life which creates it is the root of cultural theory. The forms created by the life process stand over against it, demanding that the process contain itself within them. Life as creative activity, however, immediately departs from them and seeks to engender new forms in which to express itself. Objectivized form necessarily tends to become hostile to life, which constitutes itself as cultural history by ceaselessly creating and abandoning a succession of forms, none of which ever fully satisfies its restless and multifarious drive for self-expression.

The history of spiritual life, which is cultural history, does not have, for Simmel, a formal unity or meaning, but it does reach an intelligible crisis in the twentieth century. Until the present era, the conflict of culture has been fought out by the replacement of one form of meaning by another, each one commanding obedience as an objective imperative and then ceding to others after a struggle. But during the nineteenth century a unique and far-reaching eruption occurred in modern culture: life began to take itself as its own object of meaning, first in the thought of such philosophers as Schopenhauer and Nietzsche (cf. Simmel, 1986), and then in every region of culture; that is, life at last understood itself as the generator of all of the forms to which it had pledged obedience, and could no longer tolerate subservience to objectivized form which it knew to be its own product. By the twentieth century, cultural movements were in process that not only sought to replace exhausted forms with new ones, but that rebelled against the submission to any objective demand: 'We are at present experiencing this new phase of the age-old struggle, which is no longer the struggle of a new, life-imbued form against an old, lifeless one, but the struggle against form itself, against the very principle of form' (Simmel, 1976b: 225). Simmel here breaks through the confines of the 'cultural pessimism' of much of his generation. He no longer interprets modern history through the exhaustion of form but has discovered the rebellion of life, toward which he experiences a deep ambivalence. Indeed, Simmel's cultural theory in 'The conflict' is an expression of that ambivalence.

Just as his contemporary Unamuno (1954) was the agonist of Christianity, Simmel is the agonist of modern culture. His agony cuts as deeply as can be possibly imagined. His great sensitivity enabled or, perhaps, condemned him to experience the spiritual currents of his time more profoundly than his contemporaries did, and his brilliant intellect allowed or even coerced him to express those currents with acute clarity. He was the premier German philosopher of life in his generation; that is, he did more than most others to propagate the rebellion of life, yet he understood that the fate of life was to submit itself, even if only temporarily, to its own products. An uncompromising will to truth prevented him from seeking comfort in the aestheticism of dwelling in the exhausted forms, but he also had to acknowledge the special or, as he called it, 'peculiar,' quality of form, its demand to constrain life. So, he could not embrace the modernist rebellion against the principle of form, its normative autonomy. And, further, he could not, like Emile Durkheim, take normative constraint for granted as constitutive of actual culture because, somehow, it was not. In his thought, just as in Unamuno's, lucidity bred agony and paradox, from which he could not escape, but which he could express by a strategic distancing in the form of cultural history and criticism.

As Simmel turns in 'The conflict' to a fresh interpretation of the currents of modernism which he had analyzed in 'The crisis' he breaks through to the set of ideas that are associated with the contemporary rubric of 'deconstruction.' His criticism is not itself deconstructionist – it is a pure descriptive analysis – but it details how the modernist movements are themselves deconstructions of their objects or, better, of the objectivity of their objects. The essence of modernism is the deconstruction or de-objectivization of objectivized form; the attempt to assimilate form to the process which generates it and to keep it there, immanent to the process, so that it can never gain sufficient independence to constrain creative expression. In general, modernist deconstruction proceeds by the two-step process of rejecting the objectivity of form and then of striving to make form an immanent function of life. Simmel's ambivalence shows through in his description of the impulse to make form subservient to form-giving life. In his discussions of expressionist art, pragmatic and vitalist philosophy, and post-Christian piety he is careful to affirm their intelligibility in terms of their positive vitality, but he is equally concerned to show the problematicity of their rebellion against the principle of form. His interpretation is an articulation, an objectivization, of his ambivalence as a philosopher of life, a step, therefore, beyond the modernist pretension and into a postmodernist acceptance of broken form, failed mediation, and a subjectivity decentered by the irreconcilable motives that constitute it. As he wrote in concluding 'The crisis,' cultural conflict is 'consciously or not, the crisis of our own soul.'

Simmel's ambivalence appears clearly in his interpretation of expressionist art, which, unlike his treatment of it in 'The crisis,' is sensitive and even approving when it is contrasted to impressionism, which retains the immediately perceived datum as an objective model. Expressionism performs its deconstruction of objectivized forms of art by taking seriously 'the insight that a cause and its effect can have wholly dissimilar external manifestations, that the dynamic relationship between them is purely internal and need not produce any visual affinity' (Simmel, 1976b: 230). The expressionist artist 'replaces the "model" by the "occasion," ' translating the impulse awakened in him by a datum into a representation rather than attempting to communicate the significance of the datum for itself. Although the product of expressionist art is necessarily a form it does not have the conventional work of art's 'significance in itself,' which requires 'creative life merely as the basis of its actualization.' Instead, the expressionist's form is an 'unavoidable extraneous appendage' of the form-giving process: form is present, but it has been deconstructed, deprived of independence from creativity and, there-fore, of regulatory authority over it – it is a by-product of the function of expressivity. The positivity of vital impulse here gains a triumph, but at a severe cost: 'Life, anxious only to express itself, has, as it were, jealously withheld . . . meaning from its product' (Simmel, 1976b: 230).

The same pattern appears in such currents of post-metaphysical philos-ophy as pragmatism and vitalism. In this phase of his discussion Simmel replaces his reflection in 'The crisis' on the exhaustion of classical metaphysi-cal categories with a positive account of the deconstruction of what Jacques Derrida (1974) calls the 'metaphysics of presence,' the description of a realm of objective truth which the knower must acknowledge and seek to discover. Pragmatism, according to Simmel, denies 'the independence of truth' by interpreting the object of knowledge not as a descriptor of an autonomous reality but as an imagined idea which is called true if it supports vital demands and false if it does not. The pragmatic philosopher carries out the same sort of procedure of de-objectivization as the expressionist artist, holding that 'our ideas are dependent on our mental make-up, they are by no means a mechanical reflection of the reality with which our practical life is interwoven' (Simmel, 1976b: 234). There is, then, 'no independent, pre-existent truth which is merely later incorporated, as it were, into the stream of life in order to guide its course.' Instead, life seeks to guide itself through an imagination disciplined by the consequences of its hypotheses: it reasserts 'its sovereignty over a sphere which hitherto appeared to be separate and independent of it.' Here Simmel does not even enter a reservation about the modernist impulse to deconstruct objectivized form and to engender forms which are fully immanent functions of its own vital dynamic. Indeed, his own philosophical doctrine of the objectification of life into form was a contribu-tion to modernism, differing from the pragmatic interpretation mainly in its insistence on the 'peculiar' autonomous imperative of form and not on any independent realm of truth.

Simmel concludes his interpretation of modernist tendencies with a reflec-tion on post-Christian piety, which also displays a deconstructionalist impulse, this time aimed at any articles or doctrines of faith which would command the believer's assent. Here the deconstruction proceeds even more radically than it did in the cases of expressionism and pragmatism, to the point at which life would 'itself produce the sense of absolute value which, in the past, appeared to be derived from the specific forms of religious life, the particular articles of faith in which it had crystallized' (Simmel, 1976b: 238). Religious modernism seeks to make faith an 'intransi-tive concept'; it is life seeking to produce out of itself 'that unique inner blend of humility and exaltation, tension and peace, vulnerability and consecration, which we can describe in no other way than as religious' (Simmel, 1976b: 238). Simmel shrinks from the implication of this tendency, which is simply narcissism, the self-worship of life. At the only point in 'The conflict' at which he retreats to the interregnum thinking of 'The crisis' he doubts 'whether a fundamental religious need does not inevitably require an object . . ., whether this is not merely an interlude of an ideal nature which can never become reality, the symptom of a situation where existing religious forms are being repudiated by the inner religious life, which is, however, unable to replace them with new ones' (Simmel, 1976b: 239). Religious modernism poses such a challenge to Simmel because for him, as for Unamuno, a sentiment of life is at the core of religion and there have always been mystics who have rejected its objectification into imagery and doctrine. A mysticism of life, the final and radical outcome of modernist deconstruction, would substitute immanent feeling for transcendent meaning, putting into question the necessity of Simmel's dialectical vision of the inevitable tension between life and form, the need for life to confront itself as other to itself. It is just that tension which is questioned and problematized by certain postmodern thinkers who recur to Nietzsche (Allison, 1985). The conflict in modern culture persists today, perhaps even more intensely than when Simmel wrote.

Simmel ends 'The conflict' equivocally and far more soberly than he did 'The crisis.' No longer does he repose any trust in a 'unified dynamic' of life to heal even temporarily the modern agony, which is not a struggle between two forms of culture but of life against what is deemed to be its own inherent structure, an attempt of life to deconstruct itself. In 'The crisis' he had suggested the most 'perilous' project: 'to salvage the values of the former life and carry them over into the new life' (Simmel, 1976a: 260). At the end of 'The conflict' he observes that 'the link between the past and the future hardly ever seems so completely shattered as at present, apparently leaving only intrinsically formless life to bridge the gap' (Simmel, 1976b: 241). But then he adds that 'it is equally certain that the movement is towards the typical evolution of culture, the creation of new forms appropriate to present energies.' That has not happened in the generations since his death. Indeed, those generations have witnessed ever renewed attempts of life to enslave form. One need only think of the totalitarian rejections of the independence of law and their milder counterparts in the industrialized democracies to grasp the expansion of the rebellion against autonomous and demanding form, or of mass entertainment in which life seeks an undemanding appreciation of itself through the replication of its vanity. The rebellion of life has become far more extensive since Simmel's time. Indeed, one might conclude that autonomous form is not a need of the vital spirit but one of its greatest goods, which must be self-consciously affirmed if it is to exist at all.

References

Allison, David B. (ed.) (1985) *The New Nietzsche: Contemporary Styles of Interpretation.* Cambridge, Mass.: MIT Press.

Derrida, Jacques (1974) *Of Grammatology.* Tr. G.C. Spivak. Baltimore: Johns Hopkins University Press.

Frisby, David (1981) *Sociological Impressionism: A Reassessment of Georg Simmel's Social Theory*. London: Heinemann.

Heidigger, Martin (1962) *Being and Time* (1927). New York: Harper & Row.

Lawrence, Peter (1976) *Georg Simmel: Sociologist and European*. New York: Barnes & Noble.

Levine, Donald (1971) *Georg Simmel: On Individuality and Social Forms*. Chicago: University of Chicago Press.

Simmel, Georg (1971) 'The metropolis and mental life' (1903), in Donald Levine, *Georg Simmel: On Individuality and Social Forms*. Chicago: University of Chicago Press. pp. 324–39.

Simmel, Georg (1976a) 'The crisis of culture' (1917) in Peter Lawrence, *Georg Simmel: Sociologist and European*. New York: Barnes & Noble. pp. 253–66.

Simmel, Georg (1976b) 'The conflict of modern culture' (1918), in Peter Lawrence, *Georg Simmel: Sociologist and European*. New York: Barnes & Noble. pp. 223–42.

Simmel, Georg (1978) *The Philosophy of Money* (1900). Tr. Tom Bottomore and David Frisby. London: Routledge & Kegan Paul.

Stauth, Georg and Turner, Bryan S. (1988) *Nietzsche's Dance*. Oxford: Basil Blackwell.

Unamuno, Miguel de (1954) *The Tragic Sense of Life*. New York: Dover.

PART THREE

CRITICAL THEORY AND THE MODERN PROJECT

7

HABERMAS AND THE COMPLETION OF 'THE PROJECT OF MODERNITY'

David Ashley

I

In recent years, critical, neo-marxist traditions in social theory have come under attack from what has been labeled a new 'neo-conservative' school of French theoreticians. During the 1980s, the members of this 'postmodernist' school, including Jean Baudrillard (1983a, 1983b, 1983c, 1983d, 1987, 1988a), Jean-François Lyotard (1984a, 1987, 1988a) and Arthur Kroker, Marilouise Kroker and David Cook (1989), have suggested that historical transformations characteristic of late modernism have progressively undermined the very possibilities of grounding both critical theory and what used to be regarded as the fount of theory: knowing, reasoning individuals.[1] Joining Michel Foucault (1973, 1980), who, beginning in the 1960s, helped to undermine some of modernism's pretensions by successfully launching a sophisticated attack on the modern rationalist reconstruction of Enlightenment thought, today other French nihilists (for example, Deleuze and Guattari, 1977, 1987) have taken the lessons of post-structuralism to what might be regarded as logical, if sometimes bizarre, conclusions.[2]

Theorists of postmodernism essentially are concerned with the destabilization of classically modern signifiers and the overall destruction of symbolic orders. In this context, perhaps the most important contemporary theorist of postmodernism is Baudrillard, whose challenge both to traditional and critical theory centers on his analysis of the disappearing bourgeois individual and his identification of 'floating' modes of signification that depart radically from those constitutive of high modernity. Starting with his relativization of historical materialism in *For a Critique of the Political Economy of the Sign*, and *The Mirror of Production*, Baudrillard has argued, with

increasing vehemence and – some would suggest – with growing malevo-
lence, that the referential 'finalities' of modernism (such as, use-value,
exchange-value, society, the transcendental self, etc.) can no longer apply.
In his more recent work he has declared that

> If being nihilist is to take, to the unendurable limit of the hegemonic system, this
> radical act of derision and violence, this challenge which the system is summoned
> to respond to by its own death, then I am a terrorist and a nihilist in theory as
> others are through arms. (Baudrillard, 1984: 39)

Jürgen Habermas (1981a, 1983, 1987a), a 'second-generation' critical
theorist, has been one of the sharpest critics of what he believes are the
degenerative and reactionary paths taken by French intellectuals (and, now,
by Baudrillard's German followers) since the disappointments of 1968.[3]
Habermas presents himself as a guardian of 'the project of modernity'
(epitomized for him by the goals of the Enlightenment). Unlike Foucault,
whom he labels an 'irrationalist' and Baudrillard, categorized as a 'neo-
conservative,' Habermas believes our present age can be revitalized and set
back on its proper course with those intellectual tools first developed during
the eighteenth century. According to Habermas (1987a: 302), 'The New
Critique of Reason' promulgated by Foucault, Baudrillard, Lyotard,
Deleuze and others 'suppresses that almost 200-year-old counterdiscourse
inherent in modernity itself,' which he feels duty-bound to recall. Yet,
Habermas does not deny the seductiveness of these theorists' writings: he
acknowledges the corrosive impact of Baudrillard's vitriolic and contemp-
tuous treatment of mass communication in contemporary society, and he
also concedes that perhaps 'Derrida and a capering deconstructivism give
the only appropriate answer to [the] surrealism' of 'de-differentiated,' 'de-
reified' 'mass culture' (Habermas, 1985b: 97). Similarly, Habermas is hardly
unfamiliar with the issues surrounding Lyotard's (1984a, 1987) 'postmodernist' analyses of the complexities of functional (lifeworld) differentiation or
of the heterogeneity and heteronomy of extant language games. To some
extent, then, the dispute between Habermas and the new nihilists (who
include both the late Foucault and more recent postmodernist theorists like
Baudrillard) centers on issues of common interest and identifies empirical
trends about which there is some agreement – though, perhaps, strong
disagreement too, about how far it is possible to generalize from the
observation of these trends.

Situated awkwardly, and untenably, between the neo-conservative, neo-
Parsonian, neofunctionalists and the post-structuralists, though moving
ever more closer to the worldview of the neofunctionalists, Habermas, in
grand theoretical style, has attempted to draw together these discrete
threads in the complex tapestry of his own system. He agrees with the new
Parsonians that problems of functional differentiation and integration are
fundamental for the sociological understanding of modernity. At the same
time, he has absorbed, and learned from, the post-structuralist critique of
traditional theory.[4] Unlike the neofunctionalists, though, Habermas wishes

to be politically engaged. Rejecting Baudrillard's attempt to bid farewell to the dialectic of enlightenment, he is prepared to believe that moral communities, social solidarities (and sociology) still can ground individuals bound by normative evaluations for which, ultimately, they must be held responsible. While he concedes that philosophy must surrender 'its claim to be the sole representative in matters of rationality,' Habermas (1985a: 196) holds that it is still possible to believe in *procedural* 'finalities' and to clarify 'the presuppositions of the rationality of processes of reaching understanding, which may be presumed to be universal because they are unavoidable.'

Habermas's position as the leading social theorist of his day thus is apparently secured by the ambitious project he has defined for himself. In this essay, I shall be concerned especially with those issues to which Habermas, the neofunctionalists, and the postmodernists are joined. It could be argued that US neofunctionalism and French postmodernism represent neoconservatism in the ascendency on both sides of the Atlantic. Habermas's struggle to show how the project of modernity could be completed is often cited as the most promising attempt to give a critical alternative to such contemporary modes of (neo-)conservative acquiescence in this as the best of all possible worlds.

The 1980s, however, has not been a happy decade for critics of the status quo. Recently, in the United States, the remains of the Eisenhower-era conservative and idealist, Talcott Parsons, laid to rest two decades ago, have been deftly retrieved by the neofunctionalists, aided by old supporters of structural functionalism still extant within the sociological establishment. Few leftists seemed to be able to muster the energy necessary to try to put structural functionalism back into its box a second time. The disinterment of Parsons occurred – not entirely coincidentally – during a period in which unhistory and unreason have been put back where they belong: at the center of US politics. In the USA, the successful rehabilitation of dominant intellectual concerns of the early 1950s signalled the re-establishment of cultural conservatism as a respectable intellectual option in the social sciences; it also indicated that the possibility of joining theory with critique, or with meaningful modes of political organization, could, once more, safely be jettisoned. In France, during this same decade, Foucault seemed to cast a dark shadow over the ruins of the Enlightenment. And like some demented fourth-century philosopher, unhinged by the imminent demise of a classical era of reason, Baudrillard capers around the self-immolation of a whole epoch. Meanwhile, though using heroic measures, Adorno's heir attempts to keep our era of modernity alive.

Although, to some extent, the disagreements between 'rationalists,' like Habermas, and 'irrationalists' of all colors reduce to circular and empty attempts to ground the domain assumptions that make theorizing possible in the first place, comparisons of the relative scope and power of competing 'rationalist' or 'irrationalist' research programs can be instructive.[5] For instance, while Foucault neatly sidestepped any involvement with what Habermas would regard as an emancipatory program, it does not follow that he turned his back on the possibility of critical thought (see, for instance, Foucault, 1982a). I believe a convincing argument can be made that Foucault deals more adequately with the possibility of effective critique in late modern society than does Habermas.

The dialogue between Habermas and critics of modernity concerns, at least partially, disagreements about historical trends and empirical contingencies. In dealing with nihilists like Foucault, and postmodernist nihilists like Baudrillard, Habermas has to come to terms with the possibility that a now perverse history might have dissolved the chances of realizing those formal validity claims identified by him as immanent in bourgeois (modern) society. In what follows I shall look briefly at Habermas's reaction to Foucault (and vice versa). Second, I shall examine the challenge Baudrillard and other postmodernists mount against Habermas.

II

if it is just a matter of mobilizing counterpower, of strategic battles and wily confrontations, why should we muster any resistance at all against this all-pervasive power circulating in the bloodstream of the body of modern society, instead of just adapting ourselves to it? . . . why fight at all? 'Why is struggle preferable to submission? Why ought domination to be resisted? Only with the introduction of normative notions of some kind could Foucault begin to answer this question . . .' (Habermas, 1987a: 283–4, quoting Fraser, 1981: 283)

Habermas has roundly condemned Foucault and is dismissive about his 'genealogical historiography,' which limits the meaning of transubjective validity claims to the power effects they have. While Foucault claims that his analysis of power does not exclude the possibility of revolt and counterpower, Habermas (1987a: 279) counters that such a theory of power is a dead end, for 'if it is correct, it must destroy the foundations of the research inspired by it as well.' From Habermas's point of view, both Foucault's 'biopower' and Baudrillard's 'ecstatic communication' apprehend and reflect the institutionalization of nonrationalist tendencies in late modernism. He believes that these two theorists are utterly unable to come to terms with potentialities for reason still immanent within modernism.

Nevertheless, there is broad agreement between Habermas and Foucault about how – and in what sense – modernity has overreached itself. For both men, the modernist philosophy of consciousness, or philosophy of the subject, led to subject-centered reason and 'a structurally overloaded subject (a finite subject transcending itself into the infinite)' (Habermas, 1987a: 261; see also Foucault, 1973: 303–43). For Habermas, this overloaded subject reflects the inability of the modern, overwhelmed individual to sort out qualitatively distinct validity claims associated with differentiated life spheres (as represented in Table 7.1). According to Habermas, the 'pathologies' of modernism stem from the underdevelopment of the *lifeworld* (the system of intersubjective communicative action) compared with the more

Table 7.1   *The grounding of rationality complexes embodied in differentiated life spheres*

Life spheres	Functional for	Orientation toward	Rationality complexes	Validity tests grounded by
Science	System integration	External nature	Cognitive Instrumentalist	(1) Truth of propositions (2) Effectiveness of action
Morality	System integration and lifeworld	Society	Moral-Practical	Consensus about the rightness of action
Art	Lifeworld	Internal nature	Aesthetic-practical	Shared understanding about aesthetic expression
Language	System integration and lifeworld	Linguistic productions	Reflective	Comprehensibility or well-formedness of symbolic constructs

complete and thoroughgoing rationalization of the social *system* (which is viewed by Habermas in terms of functional differentiation and the instrumental problems associated with the objective maintenance of social order).[6]

The philosophy of the subject, believed by Habermas to be a wrong metaphysical turn in the history of philosophy, holds that the individual rationally can take up two possible relationships toward 'the world of imaginable and manipulable objects': (1) 'cognitive relations regulated by the *truth* of judgments'; and (2) 'practical relationships regulated by the *success* of actions' (cognitive-instrumentalism in Table 7.1) (Habermas, 1987a: 274). Habermas's theory of societal rationalization and modernity breaks with the philosophy of the subject by adopting the paradigm of mutual understanding. It turns toward the lifeworld and an analysis of formal procedural principles of *communicative* rationality as these evolve within differentiated, but heteronomous, spheres of communicative action.

Habermas believes that the persistence of subject-centered reason, together with modernism's swamping of the subject, threatens to overcome historical forms of methodical lifestyle rationalism and to lead to a collapse of the *principii individuationis*. Ultimately, this collapse undermines the very basis for the existence of rational, relatively self-contained individuals and fosters a regressive Dionysian and ecstatic impulse toward 'a painful de-differentiation, a de-delimitation of the individual, a merging with amorphous nature within and without' (Habermas, 1987a: 94):

> this complicated structure of a subjective reason that is socially divided and thereby torn away from nature is peculiarly de-differentiated . . . it is directly the vital forces of a split-off and repressed subjective nature, it is the sorts of phenomena rediscovered by Romanticism – dreams, fantasies, madness, orgiastic excitement, ecstasy – it is the aesthetic, body-centered experiences of a decentered subjectivity that function as the placeholders for the other of reason. (Habermas, 1987a: 306)

This is a slap at Foucault, as well as at Baudrillard, but the former was hardly unaware of this tendency in modernism. *Both* Foucault and Habermas recognized that the modernist will to knowledge, and ever more knowledge, is fueled by the frustration that emanates from the institutionalization of partial, open-ended and unconsummated efforts at self-thematization in what – to use Habermas's terms – is a fragmented, hopelessly complex, yet unrationalized lifeworld.[7]

Habermas and Foucault both concluded that subject-centered reason is 'the *product of division and usurpation*, indeed of a social process, in the course of which a subordinated moment assumes the place of the whole, without having the power to assimilate the structure of the whole' (Habermas, 1987a: 315). Habermas maintains that the modernist, *diremptive* model of reason should seek to show how cognitive-instrumental, moral-practical and aesthetic-practical rationality complexes can actually converge in 'solidary social practice.' He believes that, since Hegel, the fundamental problem facing Western philosophy has been the need for modernity to stabilize itself on the basis of the very divisions it had wrought (Habermas, 1987a: 16ff.). There are no prior exemplars to show us how this might be possible. Yet, for the Frankfurt Schooler, Foucault's *exclusion* model turns its back on the possibilities of rationalizing diremption. Instead of institutionalizing and reconciling modes of self-reflection within differentially mediated systems of communicative action, the exclusion model reduces communicative action to 'bare power.' According to Habermas, this response to modernism is facile: as reason is unmediated it reduces to subjectivity.

Habermas accuses Foucault of 'presentism,' 'relativism' and 'cryptonormativism.' He suggests that Foucault is unable to explain how 'persistent local struggles,' 'confrontations mediated by the body' and 'the ebb and flow of an anonymous process of subjugation' are 'consolidated into institutionalized power' (Habermas, 1987a: 287). Consequently, he argues, Foucault's theory of power lacks any sociological depth. Although Foucault hoped 'to lead his research out of the circle in which the human sciences are hopelessly caught,' Habermas declares that, in the end, Foucault 'cannot lead to a way out of the philosophy of the subject' because his theory 'has been taken from the repertoire of [this philosophy] itself' (Habermas, 1987a: 274). Habermas concludes that, as a result of his errors, Foucault is guilty of an 'unholy subjectivism.'

According to Habermas, Foucault's *legerdemain* was to invert the cybernetic control that obtains between the two kinds of relationships that, according to the philosophy of the subject, the individual can have toward the world. Rather than making the success of actions subject to the truth of judgments (an arrangement with which Habermas could at least be comfortable) Foucault makes truth dependent upon success. This, Habermas asserts, does not weaken Foucault's commitment to the philosophy of consciousness. By transforming 'power's truth-dependency into the power-dependency of truth,' Foucault liquidates competently acting and judging subjects. But, in so doing, he resolves neither the antinomies of modernism nor the alienative stranding of the subject. Habermas's judgment on Foucault is that 'no one can escape the strategic conceptual restraints of the philosophy of the subject merely by performing operations of reversal upon its basic concepts' (Habermas, 1987a: 274).

While Nietzsche's romantic flight from modernity's overloading of the subject did embrace a rhetoric of de-differentiation, a de-delimitation of the subject and the break-up of individuation through art, Foucault was less of a romanticist and escape artist. His empirical and historical concern with power led naturally to the investigation of how the body, with its pleasures, pains, sensations, secrets and emotions, is caught within a never-ending network of domination, and control. Foucault believed that strategic movement within power complexes can be mediated by the body itself and that, at least in part, the collapse of the *principii individuationis* can reduce to a struggle for domination over such bodies. But this concern with biopower is not subjectivist or 'presentistic': it stems from Foucault's interest in seventeenth- and eighteenth-century forms of domination that exercised themselves through 'social production and social service'. As power became a matter 'of obtaining productive service from individuals in their concrete lives . . . power had to be able to gain access to the bodies of individuals' (Foucault, 1980: 125).

Foucault's theory of power is considerably more concrete and historically specific than the level of analysis displayed in *The Theory of Communicative Action*. Furthermore, Habermas notwithstanding, Foucault's genealogical historiography does not simply reduce to the notion that individual subjects obtain power over objects in terms of cognitive-instrumentalist orientations (Habermas, 1987a: 274). Instead of being entrapped by the philosophy of the subject, Foucault demonstrated how the subject is produced by power. Rather than seeking a romantic ('de-differentiated') solution to the anarchy of modernism, Foucault attempted to ground possible modes of reason in those conditions in terms of which particular kinds of historical individuals could become conscious in the first place. As Foucault, himself, stated, his work did not so much endeavor to analyze 'the phenomena of power' as try 'to create a history of the different modes by which, in our culture, human beings are made subjects' (Foucault, 1982b: 208).

Foucault held that Habermas's theory of communicative action is, at its base, 'utopian.' He believed that Habermas was 'blind to the fact that relations of power are not something bad in themselves.' Habermas's faith in the possibility of communication among humans 'without obstacles, without constraint and without coercive effects' seemed hopelessly naive to Foucault (1987: 129). Unlike Habermas, Foucault did not strain to create the effect of producing a general theory that would explain how all power becomes legitimate. Furthermore, for Foucault, there are no transcendent grounds for truth. Looking for such grounds in 'universal processes of reaching understanding' is a waste of time because – even from a proceduralist standpoint – there are no such universal processes.[8] Foucault can be criticized for turning his back on the paradigm of 'critical theory.' Nevertheless, it is Habermas, rather than Foucault, who became most enmired in the epistemologies and ontologies of modernism. To use an unattractive word, if anyone is 'presentistic' it is the Frankfurt Schooler.

III

The argument that, in attempting to complete 'the project of modernity,' Habermas accepted too readily the presuppositions and historical particularities of modernism could be said to cut both ways. On one side it can be said that Habermas fails to attain sufficient critical distance from that which he seeks to transcend. But, on the other, it can be argued that, for someone with Habermas's left-progressive agenda, the attempt to discover the rationality immanent in modernity is the only possible route to follow. In any case, Habermas's plan to rationalize diremption – that is, division and fragmentation within the lifeworld – is meant to be *the* completion of modernity. Consequently, it is worth reminding ourselves what 'modernity' represents, as a preparatory step to asking why its completion should represent a standard of universalism and emancipatory closure. Habermas's interest in universalistic proceduralism is, itself, definitively modernist; yet, the question remains of whether or not this interest can be projected *ad infinitum* into the future.

As Habermas himself has pointed out, beginning with the early bourgeois period, modernist modes of domination characteristically have come about through system differentiation and through the rationalization of media-steered interactions. Such instrumentalist media, like money and power, steer interactions and interconnect them in increasingly complex communicative networks without it being necessary for anyone to take responsibility for them (Habermas, 1987b: 263). As a result of such absolute alienation from the lifeworld, these media seem 'nature-like'; that is, they appear to legitimate themselves.

In *Legitimation Crisis* (probably his best work) Habermas explains how the bourgeois class attained dominance in the period of early modernism. According to this early work, the class power of the bourgeoisie was rooted in the successful application of 'a strategic-utilitarian morality' compatible with a 'Protestant' or a 'formalistic ethic.' This morality, *when tied to the sphere of social labor*, enabled commodity relations to displace already existing social relations, and to do so without political authorization from above. In Habermas's own words: 'Bourgeois ideologies can assume a universalistic structure and appeal to generalizable interests because the property order has shed its political form and been converted into a relation of production that, it seems, can legitimate itself' (Habermas, 1975: 22).

No one could deny the historical and relative 'truth' of bourgeois economics, which has proven to be an indispensable tool for planners and administrators. Yet, as Habermas would be the first to acknowledge, commodity mystification was first generalized as an ideological weapon to be used against a subordinate class. In *Legitimation Crisis*, then, Habermas seemed to suggest that the requirements of class hegemony determine 'truth.' Thus his own analysis of the historical and ideological roots of bourgeois hegemony would seem to provide a rather compelling illustration of the 'power-dependency of truth,' rather than the 'truth-dependency of power.'

Foucault's rejection of the idea that reason in modernity could exhibit an empty proceduralism in part reflected his recognition of the error of opposing ' "ideal" criticism' to ' "real" transformation' (Foucault, 1982a: 33). (Thus the 'irrationalist' Foucault paid greater heed to the *Theses on Feuerbach* than does the 'Marxist' Habermas!) Furthermore, it could be argued that Foucault's thinking is more universalistic, in that it is less subject to modernist restrictions on thought, than is Habermas's. Above all, Foucault seeks to understand modernity from within. Responding to Habermas's dutiful obeisance to the '*counter*discourse' of modernity, Foucault might well have pointed out that to accept Hegel's program in the first place (that is, to accept the principle that philosophy must stabilize itself on the basis of the very divisions it has wrought) is to imprison and restrict thought within the very system of diremption which then would determine the resulting hopeless and unending search for a way out.[9]

If Foucault is right, 'truth' is a thing of this world, and each society, or mode of domination, has its own 'regime of truth.' According to Foucault (1980: 109–33), knowledge cannot be produced independently of its use. This means that each type of social formation must establish those 'mechanisms and instances which enable one to distinguish true and false statements,' together with 'the techniques and procedures accorded value in the acquisition of truth' and 'the status of those who are charged with saying what counts as true' (Foucault, 1980: 131). Foucault and Habermas both understood that it is precisely the relationships among subjects that appear self-legitimating which seem most true – and, at the same time, are most ideologically determining. But, unlike Habermas, Foucault never lost sight of the fact that, under 'the project of modernity,' the yearning for a truth that is demonstrably non-historicist, formalistic and depoliticized was fostered and given direction by hegemonic power: a power that, historically, was rooted in the first class to claim universality: the *bourgeoisie*.

Foucault lacked Habermas's transcendent, Kantian perspective. Whereas Habermas presumes the possibility of a transcendental subject that is grounded by its universalisms, Foucault believed we should not assume the subject is capable of transcending, or seeing beyond, the practices it has institutionalized *and which have grounded it*. For Foucault (1982a: 33), then, criticism consists in seeing how our 'liberties,' 'practices,' and 'nonreflective modes of thought' become self-evident for us. 'To criticize is to render the too-easy gesture difficult'; to change the world is to alter the material conditions that make thought possible. The limit of 'human freedom' is reflected in the limits of our capacity to alter the substratum which determines us. This substratum is incorrigibly materialist in that it includes the use and discipline of the body, the organization of work, the development of technology, etc., as well as thought itself. Our freedom as self-reflective beings is not discovered through the analysis of some empty Kantian domain of transcendental unity, which, in any case, exists only to serve power by helping to reproduce certain social relations of production. In the *bourgeois* world order, one-sided universality served hegemony, and nothing else. In this context, to look for 'unavoidable' 'processes of reaching understanding' in the abstract properties of language is not material critique but an invitation to philosophical idealism.

IV

In [the] constellation, which persists from Nietzsche to Heidegger and Foucault, there arises a readiness for excitement without any proper object; in its wake, subcultures are formed which simultaneously allay and keep alive their excitement in the face of future truths (of which they have been notified in an unspecified way) by means of cultic actions without any cultic object. This scurrilous game with religiously and aesthetically toned ecstasy finds an audience especially in circles of intellectuals who are prepared to make their *sacrificium intellectus* on the altar of their need for orientation. (Habermas, 1987a: 309–10)[10]

As we have seen, Habermas (1987a: 295–6) believes that the exhaustion of the philosophy of consciousness can be overcome only by the paradigm of 'mutual understanding among subjects capable of speech and action.' His model of *communicative* rationality posits a 'common lifeworld' which provides 'an intuitively known, unproblematic, and unanalyzable, holistic background ... it both forms a *context* and furnishes *resources* for the process of mutual understanding' (Habermas, 1987a: 298). The 'attitude of participants in linguistically mediated interaction' provides a context of mediation in terms of which the transcendental doubling of the relation of self or the doubling of self-thematization need no longer apply.[11]

The reproduction of social systems requires that, within the lifeworld, motivational complexes are rooted in cultural practice, social solidarities are meaningfully reproduced, and individuals are effectively socialized as grounded subjects. Habermas acquiesces in Weber's well-known thesis that, under capitalism, the lifeworld increasingly has been 'colonized' and re-structured by the system imperatives of money and power. This initially occurred as early capitalism successfully uncoupled the subsystem of commodity production and exchange both from the lifeworld and from the political-administrative subsystem. A differentiated economic subsystem, that increasingly took over social integrative (that is, lifeworld) tasks, was then subjected to a cognitive-instrumentalist rationalization (described at length in *Das Kapital*). This rationalization of the lifeworld was freed from moral-practical, evaluative, expressive or reflective considerations, thus enabling commodity production and exchange to 'colonize' communitarian and intersubjective domains of action. Habermas (1987a: 349) points out that, while both Weber and Marx understood this process in modernism, only Marx grasped how the 'norm-free sociality' of commodity relations opposed 'imperatives based on system maintenance to the rational imperatives of the lifeworld.' In fact 'Marx was the first to analyze this conflict between system imperatives and lifeworld imperatives in the form of a dialectic of dead labor [that is, abstract labor] and living labor [that is, labor as part of the lifeworld].'

Habermas believes that an understanding of the rationalization of systems of communicative interaction is possible only if an empirical and historical analysis of the concrete *interpenetration* of system and lifeworld takes place. Structural functionalism (and neofunctionalism) acknowledge the interdependence of system (the economy and polity) and lifeworld (societal community and culture). Yet, while Parsons himself understood that the rationalization of *system* integration, and increases in power (that is, domination) depended upon differentiation and individuation, he was unable to grasp the possibilities within modernism of rationalizing the lifeworld through a process of 'decolonization.' Structural functionalists and neofunctionalists invariably have assigned a passive, acquiescing role to the *deformed* domain of lifeworld interaction. Indirectly, then, they have lent themselves to a shoring up of the social-welfare-state compromise and to support for a particular and historical mode of domination.[12]

Habermas (1987b: 304ff.) strongly rejects the idea that the rationalization of the *lifeworld* can be reduced to disenchantment and cognitive-instrumentalism. He believes that Weber failed to grasp that the 'pathological side effects of modernism,' (such as loss of meaning, anomie, psychopathologies, etc.) were the result of cognitivist-instrumentalist modes of rationality surging beyond the bounds of the system requirements of state and economy and achieving dominance in what should be communicatively structured areas of life. Accordingly, Weber failed to understand that these pathologies could be neutralized by the 'postconventional moral and legal representations' of moral-practical and aesthetic-practical rationalities required by our contemporary age.

As shown in Table 7.1, Habermas wants us to accept that it is possible to extend rational control over moral and aesthetic domains using logics of control that are appropriate to these differentiated life spheres. If the symbolic reproduction of the lifeworld and its material reproduction are internally interdependent, *system* developments represent new opportunities for rationalizing communicative interaction. Yet, the possibility of theoretically grasping that capitalist modernization has enhanced a communicative potential for reason has been ignored by the neofunctionalists and denied by the postmodernists. For Habermas, social theory should seek to complete the project of modernity by developing universalistic modes of proceduralism within the lifeworld.

While Foucault scoffed at such a program, claiming that Habermas was too uncritical about the sweeping ideological claims of the Enlightenment, Baudrillard (1983b: 17–18) is more willing to hold open the possibility that at least during 'the golden age of *bourgeois* representative systems (constitutionality: eighteenth-century England, the United States of America, the France of *bourgeois* revolutions, the Europe of 1848)' the political scene became a place 'where a truth of space and of representation was inscribed' through the evocation of a meaningful (non-ironic, non-cynical) signified: 'the people,' 'the will of the people,' etc. Baudrillard concedes that during the high bourgeois epoch Habermas's public spheres of communicative action might actually have constituted a 'social' space. For Baudrillard (1983b: 67), the 'social' is a simulacrum, which grounds self-reflective social individuals. Modernity is that epoch that describes the apogee of the social, and sociology came into existence in order to 'consecrate' the social's 'obviousness and agelessness.'

Yet, according to Baudrillard (1983b: 19) 'the only referent which still functions is that of the silent majority.' Because the masses no longer belong to the order of representation, the 'social' is now unrepresentable. In postmodern social formations, mass and media are indistinguishable; no distinction is made between the simulation and representation of the mass. For example, polling is more important today than it has ever been, not because it measures what citizens think and enhances 'democracy' but because opinion polls help define and fashion appropriate issues around which commodities and images will be constructed for mass consumption. (In this light, it becomes quite understandable why polling is *equally* important in the 'political' and commercial domains of will-formation.) Scientific polling tells us that 'forty-seven per cent of our respondents believe that Cher has had reconstructive surgery'; 'twenty-nine per cent believe that the Democratic nominee for President will take a "tougher" line on defense than his Republican opponent'; 'sixty-seven per cent believe that child pornography is a serious problem in Ohio.' These 'findings' implosively represent nothing but their own newsworthiness. We could conclude that they alienate social being if, and only if, we could believe that the social possessed an 'authentic essence,' with 'its own needs, its own will, its own values, its finalities' (Baudrillard, 1985: 578). Baudrillard (1985: 582) believes that no such 'authentic essence' is representable and, therefore, no such alienation can occur: 'The people have become *public*. They even allow themselves the luxury of enjoying day to day, as in a home cinema, the fluctuations of their own opinion in the daily reading of the opinion polls.'

The principle of 'hyperreality' (the conflation of simulation with representation) is most obviously applicable in the area of economy. For Baudrillard (1983b: 27) the transition between modernity and postmodernity occurs at the point when the production of *consumers*, the production of *demand*, becomes 'infinitely more costly than that of goods.' In the highly developed countries 'it is the production of demand for meaning which has become crucial for the system.' As capitalism matures, the structure of the sign reasserts itself over the commodity as sign and the meaning (value) of objects sold is increasingly distanced from the 'real,' objective referent of material production and distribution. Thus the 'value' of an object desired by consumers cannot simply be reduced to, or measured by, the exchange value the object represents. As consumer capitalism overripens, the cycle of production and consumption is less rigorously rationalized by those workers and producers who count pennies according to the logic of unequal exchange described by Marx. As semiurgy replaces production, the world increasingly becomes hyperreal and posits a realm of infinite and imploded possibilities, replacing the cold, sober, disenchanted domain of Western rationalism.

Tracing the historical roots of this transformation in semiology, Baudrillard (1983a: 83ff.) points out that the destructuring of the feudal order by the bourgeoisie 'led to the emergence of open competition on the level of distinctive signs.' The feudal world was constituted by a strong, symbolic, 'cruel' order where signs entailed reciprocal obligations among castes, clans, or persons. Echoing Habermas's observations in *Legitimation Crisis*, Baudrillard (1983a: 84–5) notes that the bourgeois world order unleashed the *arbitrary* sign, which 'begins when, instead of linking two persons in an unbreakable reciprocity, the signifier starts referring back to the disenchanted universe of the signified, common denominator of the real world toward which no one has any obligation.' Therefore the bourgeois epoch signals the 'end of the *obliged* sign' and the 'reign of the emancipated sign,' of which all classes will partake equally.

The bourgeois revolution thus laid the groundwork for a postmodern era of nihilism. Dialectically within Western rationalism is the explosion, and thus the *end*, of meaningful value-orientations. Like a cancer, Western rationalism progressively displaces traditional, communitarian, *settled* lifeworlds. But modern disenchantment results not merely, as Weber had it, from the spread of cognitive-instrumentalism into the domain of the lifeworld. Modernity has a more radical agenda: the severance of the sign from any definitive socially signified and, hence, its emancipation from caste, clan, group, class or collectivity. Weber, however, did grasp that, ultimately, modernism's dark side would be manifested in the destruction of meaning. Modern, 'overloaded' individuals, desperately trying to maintain rootedness and integrity within diremption, ultimately are pushed to the point where there is little reason *not* to believe that all value-orientations are equally well-founded. Therefore, increasingly, choice becomes meaningless. According to Baudrillard (1984: 38–9) we must now come to terms with the second revolution, 'that of the 20th Century, of postmodernity, which is the immense process of the destruction of meaning equal to the earlier destruction of appearances. Whoever lives by meaning dies by meaning.'

V

Overall, then, there is broad agreement among Marx, Weber, Habermas and Baudrillard about how the modern, disenchanted universe of meaning was self-constituted. There is disagreement between Marxists and Weberians about whether these modernist developments are explicable in terms of an historic mode of class hegemony or whether they can best be understood as indicative of the logic of general processes of rationalization within the world process. There is a fundamental disagreement between Baudrillard and Habermas about whether 'the project of modernity' is moribund and collapsing upon itself, or whether it can be revitalized. Foucault questions the appropriateness of trying to understand modernity in its own, limited terms. Habermas criticizes Weber for equating the advance of modernity and rationalization with cognitive-instrumentalist tendencies that, once in place, would inevitably lead to progressive disenchantment and alienation. He believes that a rejuvenation of the lifeworld is not incompatible with the yet-to-be-completed project of modernity. Baudrillard rejects such optimism; he cautions us that to undermine bourgeois society by undermining the material substratum upon which it is predicated is to dissolve that type of social formation for which individuated, reasoning individuals possibly could be functional. Thus, even if Habermas is right in arguing that, theoretically, humans could gain control over the rationalizing, diremptive tendencies of modernization, ironically, this chance of control is lost as soon as the practical conditions for its realization are attained.

By grounding theories of societal rationalization within the evolving potentialities of modernism, Habermas makes himself extremely vulnerable to nihilistic postmodernists like Baudrillard, who also link modernism with rationalism of a sort, but who then go on to argue that the existential, *modernist* basis for a rationalization of diremption no longer exists. Habermas argues that the 'social-welfare-state compromise' of late capitalism repoliticized relations of production in response to crises resulting from the anarchy of the market and that, as the definition of what is politically feasible is enlarged, new progressivist options were unleashed.[13] Yielding not an inch to his detractors he declares that:

> Money and power can neither buy nor compel solidarity and meaning. In brief, the result of the process of disillusionment is a new state of consciousness in which the social-welfare-state project becomes reflexive to a certain extent and aims at taming not just the capitalist economy, but the state itself. (Habermas, 1987a: 363)

Yet, Habermas acknowledges that legitimation crises that are likely to result from the dismantlement of a nature-like economy (that is, an economy that had placed itself beyond critique) will be *staved off* by an emphasis on civic privatism and consumerism. Both Habermas and Baudrillard acknowledge that the 'silent majorities' will play a major role in making up legitimation deficits. But, for Baudrillard (1983b: 22) there is no longer even a dialectic of dead and living labor; as we have seen, the masses '*can no longer be alienated . . .*' There is, therefore, no longer a social signified in reference to which an emancipatory dialogue could emerge.

Habermas implicitly attempts to refute the arguments of postmodernists like Baudrillard by maintaining that the undoubted passivity of the masses reflects class compromise and not the abolishment of those types of social formations for which the *principii individuationis* could be useful. For

Habermas, Baudrillard's vision of mass society represents a reactionary and anti-rationalist capitulation to the ugly underside of modernism. Yet, at its root, the *principii individuationis* is rooted in that 'strategic-utilitarian morality' characteristic of the disenchanted universe of the bourgeoisie. This morality was used as a class weapon under early modernism. It does not follow that it will be so used under the changed conditions of late capitalism, when, in any case, the bourgeoisie are no longer a revolutionary force. The ideologically well-structured superego of early capitalist modes of social formation could well be highly dysfunctional for the needs of cultural reproduction in late capitalism. Postmodernity is predicated upon the fragmentation and dispersal of strong ego and superego structures. The postmodern 'individual' is not forged by repression but manufactured by control over those commercially rationalized images most likely to be cathected by a resurgent id.

Baudrillard (1983a, 1983b, 1988a) believes that the end of bourgeois modes of representation is simultaneously (1) the end of modernity; (2) the end of the (bourgeois) social order; and (3) the end of representation itself, that is, the end of the commodity as pointing to something 'real' or objective: the world of material production and distribution. If, under consumer capitalism, the sign is no longer based in the need to rationalize commodity production and (unequal) exchange, those critiques of modernism that have accepted the presuppositions of modernity (like Marxism-Leninism) begin to lose their relevance. Marxism makes constant reference to its metanarrative: a transcendental commitment to reason and progress – which helps explain why it has had such a hold over Habermas. But, as Baudrillard acknowledged in his early work, the central weakness of Marxism was always the failure to see the *collusion* that links its mode of representation to the mode of material production brought into existence by the bourgeoisie (see Baudrillard, 1975: 17–51).

In short, Baudrillard relativizes Habermas's theory of communicative action. He concedes that Marx and the early Habermas were probably right in showing that, in the early modern stage, political economy was the social signified that gave *meaning* to a political signifier. Bourgeois democracy and discursive will-formation require an infrastructure of nature-like property relations concerning which, and in terms of which, reasoned debate can occur. In spite of vacuous claims concerning 'human dignity,' 'the rights of man,' 'freedom of expression,' etc., in capitalist societies 'reasoned' debate is highly circumscribed and cognitively-instrumentally based in the reproduction of that substratum which is, of necessity, *beyond* discursive deliberation: that of property 'rights.'

At the end of the twentieth century, such reasoned debate has hardly disappeared completely. It is commonly found, for instance, behind legal opinion and in bureaucratic legislation. But Baudrillard's challenge to Habermas centers on his claim that, in the long run, mass culture and mass society work to undermine and to dissolve rationalization. Minimally, rationalization requires the subject to have a self-reflective understanding of its objects of attention. Yet, under postmodernity, where are the (social) forces which individuate? Marx, Weber and Freud theorized about individuals who define themselves in relation to a struggle with, or recognition of, a classically defined 'social.' But, in post-Reagan America, could such entities flourish, let alone prevail?

For Baudrillard, the end of modernity and the dissolution of bourgeois forms of mutual understanding and communicative action augur the end of the social, as well as the death of Western rationalism. Postmodernity certainly does not point to the development of discursive will-formation, nor does it lead to new forms of 'communicative competence.' Living, as he thinks he does, in the shadow of the end of his epoch, unlike Habermas, Baudrillard can see no possibility that extant reservoirs of reasoned debate somehow will be joined with democratic discursive will-formation in the lifeworld as a whole.[14] Although he might have done no more than call into question some of Habermas's 'too easy' progressivist assumptions about modernity's capacity to resist its own mechanisms of self-destruction, this alone would signify Baudrillard's importance as a theorist. The thrust of *his* project, in comparison to Habermas's, raises the intriguing possibility that, in retrospect, it might turn out that – all along – he has successfully managed to play Marx to Habermas's Spencer.

Notes

1 There has been considerable discussion of Baudrillard's work recently. Many of his later writings have been translated into English by *Semiotext(e)*. Since 1985, articles about Baudrillard have appeared in *Sociological Theory, Telos, October, Artforum, Theory Culture and Society, On the Beach, Impulse, Thesis Eleven, New Literary History* and *Cultural Critique*, among other journals. Recently, the *Canadian Journal of Political and Social Theory* devoted a whole issue to 'French Fantasies: Baudrillard and Foucault' (11 (3), 1987).

2 The neofunctionalist attempt to return to the *Weltanschauung* of the voluntarist and cultural idealist Talcott Parsons has to sidestep the radical post-structuralist critique of traditional theory. For an example of neofunctionalist thinking, see Alexander (1980–83) and (1985). For a pointed critique of this attempt to rehabilitate Parsons, see Sica (1983).

3 Baudrillard's German followers have been particularly receptive to his dark apocalyptic and eschatological vision (see Baudrillard, 1983c). They are especially taken with Baudrillard's description of the Bomb as the 'ultimate signifier.' For a discussion of this tendency, see Scherpe, 1987.

4 For the Nietzschean postmodernists, theory can provide no rational justification for individuals to make normative choices. Pumped up as a new 'master sociologist' by the Parsonian old guard, it is hardly coincidental that what Alexander shares with these postmodernists is the lack of interest in joining theory with applied critique. Both the postmodernists and the neofunctionalists can only watch helplessly as social welfarism breaks apart and the anarchy of the market reasserts itself, as technological innovation is '*intentionally* tied to an armaments spiral that has gone out of control' (Habermas, 1987b: 356), as a reactionary and brutal foreign policy is inflicted on the peasantry of the Third World, and as political life, itself, dissolves into the technical possibility of presenting 'political' leaders to the outside world as 'fictive realities' (Habermas 1985b: 82–3, 97). See also Habermas, 1982.

5 Although Habermas lumps him with Baudrillard et al. as an 'irrationalist,' Foucault is not generally classified as 'postmodernist' (although, see Foucault, 1989: 233–55). What joins

Foucault to theorists like Baudrillard and Deleuze is his Nietzschean genealogy. Together with the postmodernists, Foucault (1973: 387) was prepared to contemplate the 'end of the individual': 'man is an invention of recent date. And one, perhaps, nearing its end.'

6 Habermas discusses these themes exhaustively in the pages of his *magnum opus: The Theory of Communicative Action*, Vols. 1 and 2. It is beyond the scope of this chapter to describe in detail Habermas's theory of communicative rationalization, or to deal with the numerous commentaries and critiques of this theory. Briefly, Habermas sees 'modernization' as a process of *rationalization* and *differentiation*. 'Modernity' means that self-regulating social *systems*, which attempt to maintain their integrity in the face of a wide range of environmental and internal variation, become increasingly differentiated. Within these systems, (1) cultural orientations tend to become cognitive-instrumentalist, (2) roles become more specific, and (3) individuals increasingly become more fragmented and atomized. Second, under 'modernization,' the *lifeworld*, which comprises a system of communicative (intersubjectively grounded) action, becomes increasingly rationalized. Rationalization of the lifeworld involves (1) 'the increased reflexivity of culture,' or the 'enhancement of critical consciousness'; (2) the generalization of values and norms, or the enhancement of 'autonomous will-formation'; and (3) 'the heightened individuation of socialized subjects.'

For Habermas, the differentiation of system and social integration accelerates a further differentiation of the 'life spheres' of (1) science, (2) morality, and (3) art. Thus, Habermas argues that modern communicative rationality is multidimensional: it involves (1) 'the relation of the knowing subject to a world of events or facts' (entailing cognitive-instrumental communication); (2) 'the relation to a social world of an acting, practical subject entwined in interaction with others' (entailing a moral-practical communication); and (3) 'the relation of a suffering and passionate subject ... to its own internal nature, to its subjectivity and the subjectivity of others' (entailing aesthetic- and evaluative-practical communication) (Habermas, 1981b: 16).

Habermas believes that the opportunities for a modernist (or postmodernist) rationalization of communicative interaction lie: (1) in a further differentiation of system and lifeworld; (2) in a further differentiation of the autonomous spheres of cognitive-instrumentalism, moral-practical argumentation, aesthetic-practical understanding, and pure reflection, and of the forms of argumentation and validity tests associated with these life spheres. Differentiation is linked to the possibilities of rationalizing systems of communicative interaction, in that the forms of argumentation associated with life spheres increasingly will be compelled to answer *only* to the validity tests *appropriate* to that particular rationality complex. Similarly, the successful rationalization of the lifeworld requires that it not be distorted and deformed by the system media of money and power.

7 Habermas, citing Foucault's critique of the human sciences in *The Order of Things*, declares that the modernist 'overloading' or 'doubling' of the subject has led to three sets of oppositions (1987a: 261–5; see below). The first doubling is Kantian: the subject is both an empirical object in a world full of objects and also 'a transcendental subject over against the world as a whole, which it constitutes as the totality of the objects of possible experience.' This sets up an unending, irresolvable dialectic between the transcendental and the empirical. By reason of this double status, the knowing subject seeks to reconcile transcendental synthesis with the observation of an empirical process governed by natural laws. Habermas suggests that such attempts at reconciliation reach from Hegel to Merleau-Ponty. This existential dilemma explains the 'flip-flop' process observable in the human sciences over the last two centuries between the search for 'complete self-knowledge' and 'positivism.'

According to a similar mechanism, the second dilemma of reconciling that which is 'extraterritorial,' or objectively opaque, with the 'unthought and hidden foundation of the performing subjectivity' posits utopic fantasies about the possibilities of complete *self*-transparency. These ultimately 'flip over into nihilistic despair and radical skepticism.' The third dilemma involves reconciling the 'originally creative' subject with the historical subject, alienated from its point of origin. (Thus, for the postmodernists – and for Habermas – there can be no Odyssean homecoming to a life wrested from myth.)

Oppositions	*Act of mediated self-positing*
(1) Between the transcendental and the empirical	A process of *self-knowledge*
(2) Between the act of becoming reflectively aware and the reflectively unsurpassable and irretrievable	A process of growing *reflective awareness*
(3) Between the a priori perfect of an 'always already' prior origin and the advent-like future of the still-to-come return of the origin	A process of *self-formation*

8 This denial of an overarching *epistēmē* obviously links Foucault with those theorists who are more overtly and self-consciously 'postmodernist,' such as Baudrillard and Lyotard.

9 Deleuze and Guattari (1977: 151) argue that capitalist politics thrive on the divisions wrought by capitalism:

> social machines make a habit of feeding on the contradictions they give rise to, on the crises they provoke, on the anxieties they *engender*, and on the internal oppositions they regenerate. Capitalism has learned this, and has ceased doubting itself . . . And the more it breaks down, the more it schizophrenizes, the better it works in the American way.

10 Habermas, 1987a: 309–10. Is Habermas's response to his critics always fully reasonable? Commenting on Habermas's reactions to 'neo-conservatism' and postmodernist opponents, Arac (1986: xv) argues that 'in making his case, Habermas rapidly dismisses competing political and theoretical positions with an inaccuracy, a failure of understanding, that is shocking in one whose best work so depends on probingly sympathetic critique of others, and whose long-standing ethical norm has been the transcendence of "systematically distorted communication." '

11 Habermas thus wishes us to believe that a rationalized lifeworld that propagates cultural traditions, integrates groups, and socializes individuals, can provide a 'context' and furnish 'resources' for a *quasi-transcendental* process of mutual understanding. This highly problematic attempt to bridge the Scylla of subjectivity and the Charybdis of cognitive objectivism has been reformulated and refined several times by Habermas himself in the course of his writing career, and has been much discussed by his critics. See McCarthy, 1978: 101ff.; Bernstein, 1985: 1–25; and Roderick, 1986: 62–136.

12 Habermas insists that 'the only functional domains that can be differentiated out of the lifeworld by steering media [e.g., "money" and "power"] are those of *material* reproduction' (emphasis added). Therefore, he argues, Parsons erred in trying to generalize from the example of money as a medium of intersystemic exchange. With the possible exception of 'power,' the structural analogies between money and the other media that Parsons identified (such as 'influence,' 'value commitment,' etc.) are too vague and imprecise to merit more than a metaphorical comparison. See Habermas, 1987b: 257–61.

For Habermas, Parsons and the structural-functionalists were one-sidedly concerned with problems of *system* integration. Like Weber, they failed to analyze the lifeworld *in its own terms*, and thus failed to acknowledge its underdevelopment.

13 Apparently, most of these tendencies are to be found on the continent of Europe. Habermas (1987a: 367) displays distinctively Eurocentric views in his most recent work. He inquires: 'Who else but [Old] Europe could draw from *its own* traditions the insight, the energy, the courage of vision . . . to shape our mentality?'

14 In one of his most recent works, Habermas (1987a: 364–7) insists on attributing emancipatory significance to 'autonomous, self-organized public spheres,' 'which are neither bred nor kept by a political system for purposes of creating legitimation.' Although he acknowledges that if such public spheres 'cross the threshold to the formal organization of independent systems' they are likely to be co-opted and threaded into the tapestry of system integration, he still lamely suggests that these spheres could 'develop the prudent combination of power

and intelligent self-restraint that is needed to sensitize the self-steering mechanisms of the state and the economy to the goal-oriented outcomes of radical democratic will-formation.'

Habermas notes the *cultural*-revolutionary traits of many contemporary movements, but limply asks us to believe that there will be almost a naturalistic overcoming of particularism. Little awareness is shown of how movements like, for instance, the 'women's movement' integrally have been tied to the further rationalization of *system* integration and to the needs of late capitalist accumulation.

References

Alexander, J.C. (1980–83) *Theoretical Logic in Sociology* (4 vols). Berkeley: University of California Press.

Alexander, J.C. (ed.) (1985) *Neofunctionalism*. Beverly Hills: Sage.

Arac, J. (ed.) (1986) *Postmodernism and Politics: Theory and history of literature*, vol. 28. Minneapolis: University of Minnesota Press.

Baudrillard, J. (1975) *The Mirror of Production*. Tr. M. Poster. St Louis: Telos Press.

Baudrillard, J. (1981) *For a Critique of the Political Economy of the Sign*. Tr. C. Levin. St Louis: Telos Press Ltd.

Baudrillard, J. (1983a) *Simulations*. Tr. P. Foss, P. Patton, P. Beitchman. New York: Semiotext(e)/Foreign Agent Press.

Baudrillard, J. (1983b) *In the Shadow of the Silent Majorities*. Tr. P. Foss, P. Patton and J. Johnstone. New York: Semiotext(e)/Foreign Agent Press.

Baudrillard, J. (1983c) *Tod der Moderne: Eine Diskussion* (with Michael Rutschky, Ulrich Sonnemann, and Heidrun Hesse). Tübingen: Gerke.

Baudrillard, J. (1983d) *Les stratégies fatales*. Paris: Bernard Grasset.

Baudrillard, J. (1984) 'On nihilism', *On the Beach*, 5: 19–25.

Baudrillard, J. (1985) 'The masses: the implosion of the social in the media,' *New Literary History* 16: 577–89.

Baudrillard, J. (1987) *Forget Foucault*. New York: Semiotext(e)/Foreign Agent Press.

Baudrillard, J. (1988a) *The Ecstasy of Communication*. Tr. B. and C. Schutze. New York: Semiotext(e)/Foreign Agent Press.

Baudrillard, J. (1988b) *America*. Tr. C. Turner. London: Verso.

Bernstein, R. (ed.) (1985) *Habermas and Modernity*. Cambridge, Mass.: MIT Press.

Deleuze, G. and Guattari, F. (1977) *Anti-Oedipus: Capitalism and Schizophrenia*. New York: Viking Press.

Deleuze, G. and Guattari, F. (1987) *A Thousand Plateaus: Capitalism and Schizophrenia*. Tr. B. Massumi. Minneapolis: University of Minnesota Press.

Foucault, M. (1973) *The Order of Things: An Archeology of the Human Sciences*. New York: Pantheon Books.

Foucault, M. (1980) *Power/Knowledge: Selected Interviews and Other Writings, 1972–1977*. Ed. C. Gordon. New York: Pantheon Books.

Foucault, M. (1982a) 'Is it really important to think? An interview with Michel Foucault'. Tr. T. Keenan. *Philosophy and Social Criticism*, 9: 29–40.

Foucault, M. (1982b) 'Afterword: The subject and power', in H.L. Dreyfus and P. Rabinow (eds), *Michel Foucault: Beyond Structuralism and Hermeneutics*. Chicago: University of Chicago Press. pp. 212–34.

Foucault, M. (1984) *The Foucault Reader* (P. Rabinow, ed.). New York: Pantheon Books.

Foucault, M. (1987) 'Interview: The ethic of care for the self as a practice of freedom.' Tr. J.D. Gauthier. *Philosophy and social criticism*, 12: 112–31.

Foucault, M. (1989) *Foucault live (interviews 1966–84)*. Tr. J. Johnstone; Ed. S. Lotringer. New York: Semiotext(e)/Foreign Agent Press.

Fraser, N. (1981) 'Foucault on modern power: Empirical insights and normative confusions', *Praxis International*, 1: 272–87.

Habermas, J.(1975) *Legitimation Crisis*. Tr. T. McCarthy. Boston: Beacon Press.

Habermas, J. (1981a) 'Modernity versus postmodernity', *New German Critique*, 22: 3–11.

Habermas, J. (1981b) 'The dialectics of rationalization: An interview with Jürgen Habermas by Axel Honneth, Ebernard Knödler-Bunte, and Arno Widmann', *Telos*, 49: 5–31.

Habermas, J. (1981c) *The Theory of Communicative Action vol 1: Reason and the Rationalization of Society*. Tr. T. McCarthy. Boston: Beacon Press.

Habermas, J. (1982) 'A reply to my critics', in J.B. Thompson and D. Held (eds), *Habermas: Critical Debates*. Cambridge, Mass.: MIT Press. pp. 219–83.

Habermas, J. (1983) 'Die Kulturkritik der Neoconservativen in den U.S.A. und in der Bundesrepublik: über eine Bewegung von Intellektuellen in zwei politischen Kulturen', *Praxis International*, 2: 339–58.

Habermas, J. (1985a) 'Questions and counterquestions', in R. Bernstein (ed.), *Habermas and Modernity*. Cambridge, Massachusetts: MIT Press. pp. 192–216.

Habermas, J. (1985b) 'A philosophico-political profile', *New Left Review*, 151: 75–105.

Habermas, J. (1987a) *The Philosophical Discourse of Modernity: Twelve Lectures*. Tr. F. Lawrence. Cambridge, Mass.: MIT Press.

Habermas, J. (1987b) *The Theory of Communicative Action, vol. 2: Lifeworld and System: A Critique of Functionalist Reason*. Tr. T. McCarthy. Boston: Beacon Press.

Hoy, D.C. (1988) 'Foucault: modern or postmodern?' in J. Arac (ed.), *After Foucault: Humanistic knowledge, postmodern challenges*. New Brunswick: Rutgers University Press. pp. 12–41.

Kroker, A. and Cook, D. (1986) *The Postmodern Scene: Excremental culture and Hyperaesthetics*. New York: St Martin's Press.

Kroker, A., Kroker, M. and Cook, D. (1989) *The Panic Encyclopedia*. New York: St Martin's Press.

Lyotard, J.F. (1984a) *The Postmodern Condition: A Report on Knowledge*. Tr. G. Bennington and B. Massumi. Minneapolis: University of Minnesota Press.

Lyotard, J.F. (1984b) *Driftworks*. Ed. Roger McKeon. New York: Semiotext(e)/Foreign Agent Press.

Lyotard, J.F. (1987) 'Rules and paradoxes and svelte appendix', *Cultural Critique*, 5: 209–19.

Lyotard, J.F. (1988a) *The Differend: Phrases in Dispute*. Tr. G. Van den Abbeele. Minneapolis: University of Minnesota Press.

Lyotard, J.F. (1988b) 'Interview with Willem von Reijen and Dick Veerman', *Theory, Culture and Society*, 5: 277–309.

McCarthy, T. (1978) *The Critical Theory of Jürgen Habermas*. Cambridge, Mass.: MIT Press.

Roderick, R. (1986) *Habermas and the Foundations of Critical Theory*. London: Macmillan.

Scherpe, K.R. (1987) 'Dramatization and de-dramatization of the "end": The apocalyptic consciousness of modernity and post-modernity', *Cultural Critique*, 5: 95–129.

Sica, A. (1983) 'Parsons Jr', *American Journal of Sociology*, 89: 200–19.

Thompson, J.B. and Held, D. (1982) *Habermas: Critical debates*. Cambridge, Mass.: MIT Press.

8

LYOTARD AND WEBER: POSTMODERN RULES AND NEO-KANTIAN VALUES

Charles Turner

Weber and Lyotard offer accounts of modernity and postmodernity which appear to share a rejection of totalizing philosophies of history. Here I suggest that analyses couched in terms of neo-Kantian 'value-spheres' and Wittgensteinian 'language games' depend upon and promote radically different accounts of culture and subjectivity. While Lyotard's postmodernism is limited to the analysis of purposive-rational action, Weber refuses pluralism, remains sensitive to the enduring power of value-rationality, and acknowledges the constitutive role of tragedy in history.[1]

In his lecture 'Science as a vocation' Max Weber writes:

> 'Scientific' pleading [for 'practical and interested stands'] is meaningless in principle because the various value spheres of the world stand in irreconcilable conflict with each other . . . we realize again today that something can be sacred not only in spite of its not being beautiful, but rather because and in so far as it is not beautiful . . . It is a piece of everyday wisdom that something may be true although it is not beautiful and not holy and not good . . . these are only the most elementary cases of the struggle between the gods of the various orders and values. (1948: 147–8; translation altered)

Sixty years later, in his 'report on knowledge', *The Postmodern Condition*, Jean-François Lyotard writes:

> Science possesses no general metalanguage in which other languages can be transcribed and evaluated . . . There is no reason to think that it would be possible to determine metaprescriptives common to all . . . language games or that a revisable consensus like the one in force at a given moment in the scientific community could embrace the totality of metaprescriptions regulating the totality of statements circulating in the social collectivity. (1984: 64–5)

On first reading, these statements appear similar. Despite doubts about whether intellectual history possesses a metalanguage in which they might be transcribed and evaluated, both seem to be descriptions of a pluralistic universe in which value-spheres or language games are mutually irreducible. If this is so, then what Lyotard calls 'postmodernity' is cognitively nothing new, merely the latest move in a 'war against totality' which has been taking place since well before Weber.

But this conclusion ignores two facts. Firstly, there is a difference between the intellectual tools with which Lyotard and Weber fashion their analyses. The bulk of this chapter will be devoted to this difference. Secondly, whereas Lyotard – at least in *The Postmodern Condition* – uses 'language games' to analyse what he has already designated as an 'epoch', Weber remained ambivalent towards such a concept. Unlike Lyotard and his chief contemporary opponent Habermas, Weber, particularly in the 'early' essays in the *Wissenschaftslehre*, was suspicious of the concept of an epoch, which he regarded as the product of an unscientific need for a 'feeling of totality', and implied that the neo-Kantian account of value-spheres grounded a general theory of culture. On the other hand, he has a tendency to present his own 'philosophy' as a response to historical circumstance – 'today' something can be true without being beautiful or good. And at times, he accepts that the very concepts of 'Kultur' and the 'Kulturmensch' which ground his *Kulturwissenschaft* are secularist concepts. (Though even if this is true, this would make the *Wissenschaftslehre* less a theory of modernity than modernity's theoretical self-expression.) Establishing a clear relation between an argument from history and from principle would require another essay. But the tension between them will be implicit in this discussion.

The essay which lends itself most readily to comparison with *The Postmodern Condition* is the 'Zwischenbetrachtung' in the *Collected Essays in the Sociology of Religion*. The first point to be made about this essay is that it is not a 'report on knowledge'. Most of it is devoted to the perspective of a universalist religious ethics of brotherhood, and examines 'man's relations to the various spheres of values' from this point of view. It argues that the rationalization of these relations has 'pressed towards making conscious the internal and lawful autonomy of the individual spheres' (1948: 328). Weber treats the tensions between religion and economics, religion and politics, religion and art, religion and sexuality, and religion and what he calls 'the intellectual sphere' in terms of the way in which a universalist ethics, or better, an individual who holds to such an ethics, so to speak, 'runs up against' the 'world' and is thereby faced with the choice of maintaining its purity or acting upon the world while being subject to ethical compromise. In so doing Weber is careful not to treat the 'world' as an historical constant, as a given which can either be affirmed or denied, accepted or rejected, fled or mastered, but which remains essentially the same. The concept of 'worldliness', on which much of his account of modernity hangs, is intelligible only in relation to a Christian concept of otherworldliness which is the privileged member of the pair.[2] But the otherworldliness upon which a universalist religious ethics depends excites Weber's interest because it possesses the formal property of *any* ethic whose aim is to provide grounds for the 'unity of culture', a unity in which conflicts between value spheres would dissolve, or, in Weber's terms, 'could be held to be *aufgehoben*' (1948: 323; translation altered). And Weber makes clear in the first page of the essay that it is not his intention to argue that the immanent logics of the various value-spheres constitute an argument against the assertion of their unity. As an empirical scientist it is his duty to eschew such arguments – empirical science cannot criticize 'the speculative view of life'. His object is the conditions of human action, one of which *may* be precisely the assertion that conflicts between value-spheres *can* be dissolved, another of which *is* that this assertion is at most a regulative ideal. Despite this, Weber accepts a rather weak secularization thesis according to which the objective capacity of religious, transcendentally anchored ethics to 'hold the world together' has been undermined. On the other hand, his account makes it clear that he does not regard the tensions between a universalist ethics and the 'world' as a peculiarly modern phenomenon. The difference between the pre-modern and the modern is too obscure to allow anything other than a series of distinctions of degree. Weber's procedure is to identify for each cultural sphere an animating principle – what Windelband called a normal consciousness – and on the basis of this to define each sphere in the most rationally consistent way possible. By driving the logic of each sphere to its limits, by 'rationalizing' it, he maximizes the tensions between religious ethics and any of these spheres.

If the connection between 'modernity' and 'rationalization' has any sense, it lies in the fact that for Weber, the undermining of a religiously grounded account of the unity of culture sharpens the animating principles of economics, politics, art, sexuality, and science; that is, produces a series of secular value rationalizations. But the consequence of this is not that the collapse of a Christian world-view, or the death of God, brings with it a mere cultural pluralism in which the activity germane to a particular sphere of value follows the logic immanent to that sphere. If this were the case, the 'struggle' to which Weber refers in the opening quote would make little sense. On the contrary, Weber's concern is directed to the manner in which individual value-spheres can become the sites for the construction of universalist claims, that is, foundations for the unity of culture. The old gods which ascend from their graves do not rest content with the government of a particular province of culture. They are to provide criteria by which the whole of cultural reality might be justified. With the alleged collapse of religious forms of speculative knowledge, the animating principles of individual spheres themselves take on a speculative character. This gives rise to rival anthropologies and world-views, in which reality can only be legitimated as the type of phenomenon peculiar to those domains.

The historical context for Weber's analysis is the emergence of a number of such *Weltanschauungen*, or to adopt, uncritically, Lyotard's terminology, grand narratives. Thus, reality can only be justified as: an aesthetic phenomenon for the George circle; as a sexual phenomenon for the Freudian Otto Gross; as an economic phenomenon for Marxism and ideologies of the market; as a causal mechanism for scientistic positivism; and (by way of anticipation) as a political phenomenon for Weber's wayward student Carl Schmitt. And just as Christianity ties its universalist claims to the problem of individual salvation, so these ideologies carry with them the idea of utopian (but secular) self-realization, be it self-realization through art, sexuality, labour, or politics.

The special significance of scientific rationalism in this account is twofold. Firstly, it is religion's most powerful rival in the battle to provide a coherent account of how the world hangs together. To the (dualistic) idea that the orderliness of the 'world' is anchored 'transcendentally', in an otherworldly realm, it opposes the (monistic) idea that the source of the world's coherence is immanent to the world. To the idea of the world as a *meaningful* totality whose phenomena are reducible to a single centre it opposes the idea of the world as a *causal* mechanism whose phenomena are reducible to the laws which govern them. Secondly, the rhetoric of scientism allows economism, eroticism, and even aestheticism to clothe themselves in rationalistic terminology, whenever the (frequent) need arises. Weber was acutely aware of the paradoxical way in which a *principled* objection to rationalism by any form of irrationalism – including, by implication, many varieties of postmodernism – could promote attempts to tap the power of the irrational which exhibited the very rationalism they were meant to oppose.[3] The idea that the liberating potential of the unconscious might depend upon a science of the unconscious is only the most obvious example of such a paradox.

The fact that the relationship between the animating principles of different spheres is antagonistic rather than pluralistic is reflected in the 'departmental patriotism' of the human sciences, against which Weber fought constantly. These sciences ground themselves in universalist 'scientistic' rhetorics, and thereby claim, implicitly, that their object domains are not constituted perspectivally, but constitute the most 'real' reality.

The question of the difference between Weber's and Lyotard's analyses appears at first to be a methodological one. Weber's analysis of value-spheres is derived from neo-Kantian value philosophy, Lyotard's analysis of language games from the later Wittgenstein. A language games approach in the spirit of Wittgenstein would assert the existence of a variety of linguistic *practices* and the absence of any overarching metalanguage. A value-spheres approach also asserts the absence of such a metalanguage but the presence in *each* sphere of a normative standard. (Recall that the 'good' is merely one 'normative' standard alongside the true and the beautiful.) If there is a difference between Wittgenstein and neo-Kantianism it would seem to lie in the difference between the analytic status of 'rules' and 'values'. Whereas rules are inextricably bound up with or immanent to the linguistic practices they constitute, values for neo-Kantianism have a validity wholly independent of the existence of the empirical reality they order in constituting an object domain. Rather than defining the properties of utterance – no rules, no game; no game, no utterance – Wittgenstein seems to suggest that rules are expressions of a usage which is always already 'there'. As he puts it, 'there is a way of grasping a rule which is *not* an *interpretation*, but which is exhibited in what we call "obeying the rule" and "going against it" in actual cases' (1953: para. 201). A discussion of the precise status of 'rules' in Wittgenstein is beyond the scope of this chapter. I merely wish to register an ambiguity in Lyotard's Wittgensteinian 'method'. At times it appears to depend upon an overinterpretation of 'rule-following'. Thus he argues that categories of utterance can be 'defined in terms of the rules specifying their properties and the uses to which they can be put' (1984: 10). And on the last page but one of *The Postmodern Condition* he combines this hard version of rule-following with an observation about the 'postmodern development' of the pragmatics of science, which brings a 'decisive "fact" to the fore: even discussions of denotative statements need to have rules. Rules are not denotative but prescriptive utterances, which we are better off calling metaprescriptive utterances to avoid confusion (they prescribe what the moves of language games must be in order to be admissible)' (1984: 65). Rules here specify what can count as a move in the first place. Thus, Lyotard seems to have rediscovered Weber's version of neo-Kantian value-philosophy and simply expressed it in a postmodern idiom.

If Lyotard's language game approach is really Weber's neo-Kantianism in another guise, are we to lump their social philosophies together and see them as common opponents of one of their staunchest rationalist critics, Jürgen Habermas? For it might be argued that Weber is a theorist for whom 'modernity' signifies a multiplication of the means by which local narratives can be elevated to the status of grand narratives, but whose (pluralist) attitude to this given state of affairs is to assert the undesirability of such elevation; while Lyotard is a theorist for whom 'postmodernity' signifies the objective impossibility of that elevation, and whose attitude is to accept it. As he puts it, the mourning process which followed the collapse of the idea of totality 'has been completed. There is no need to start all over again' (1984: 41). Weber and Lyotard are certainly both committed to the impossibility of the rationalist project Habermas identifies with 'modernity'. For both there is little possibility of a mediation between value spheres or language games. To ask for anything more than this is to ask for a metadiscourse which is at worst impossible and at best a mere postulate. Weber and Lyotard believe that, in an age of 'specialization', the 'cultivated man' with the capacity to move effortlessly between spheres is either an anachronism or a sham. Both attempt to find a 'third way' between Habermas's academicism, which requires an account of cultural and experiential unity, and what Lyotard calls eclecticism. And superficially, their attempts look similar. Both deny that the 'splintering' they identify has to lead to barbarity. Both seem to advocate a principled resignation in the face of the non-existence of the unity of culture. Both argue that science – and by implication any other cultural domain – 'plays its own game' (Lyotard, 1984: 40).

And yet it is in these more affirmative moments that Weber and Lyotard part company, and the difference between the practical implications of a neo-Kantian and a Wittgensteinian theory of culture manifests itself. The difference between them is no mere reflection of a transition from a philosophy of consciousness to a philosophy of language, upon which Habermas in particular places so much stress. For although a philosophy of language might be held to be attempting the same 'moves' as those attempted by a philosophy of consciousness,[4] this conflation ignores the fact that while Weber always accords 'values' a transcendental status, when Lyotard discusses the pragmatics of discourse he reverts to an account of rule-following and rule-breaking in which rules no longer provide the criteria for judgement in advance of any move in a particular language game, but are instead the formulation of the result of moves which have already been made. This distinction is best illustrated by a consideration of 'what follows' from the (practical) impossibility of grand narratives.

For Weber, the individual's compensation for the absence of a grand narrative is the possibility of pursuing a specialized 'vocation', of devoting oneself to one activity with objectivity and commitment. The difference between an activity which is a vocation and one which merely 'runs on as an event in nature' is the difference between an activity which has a 'cultural value' and one which is pursued according to its 'inherent logic'; that is, simply according to the rules of the game of which it is a part. This difference was formulated most precisely by Simmel in his essay on the tragedy of culture, and the *Zwischenbetrachtung* bears all the hallmarks of its influence. The tragedy of culture is that the products of human activity develop according to logics of their own, and thereby confront and threaten the very beings who produced them. The claim behind the distinction between cultural value and objective logic is that, while the pursuit of any human activity can either be the product of a commitment to an ultimate value or the exhibition of a technical competence in the domain of activity in question, only an activity pursued on the basis of a cultural value, as a means of *mediating* between the self and the orders of life within which it acts, can promote the development of the personality. Although Weber does not share Simmel's *Bildungsideal*, his own theory of personality does depend upon the cultural value/intrinsic logic distinction. The concept of a 'personality', already provided for in the essay on Knies and the problem of irrationality, entails a relation to certain values which an individual *takes to be* immutable and 'which are forged into purposes and thereby translated into rational-teleological action' (1975: 192). The dignity of human beings consists in pursuing an activity according to its inherent logic – this is unavoidable – but out of a real commitment to the values without which that activity is unintelligible. Without the *capacity* for *Wertrationalität* there is no personal *Zweckrationalität*, only the *Zweckrationalität* of objective rules. This conceptual and ethical hierarchy is expressed in the order in which *Wert-* and *Zweckrationalität* are introduced in *Economy and Society*. The 'subject' for Weber is constituted as a *valuing* subject, and not merely as a *procedurally correct* subject, as a cultural being with the capacity to adopt a position towards the world, not simply as one who knows how to go on.

For Lyotard, what saves people from the barbarity which supposedly follows the collapse of a grand narrative 'is their knowledge that legitimation can only spring from their own linguistic practice and communicational interaction' (1984: 41). But I take this to mean that legitimation follows from a knowledge of the rules germane to a particular language game and of the means of altering the boundaries within which those rules operate. What Lyotard calls metaprescriptives are not values in Weber's sense. The rules of

'communicational interaction' contain no reference to the personal commitment of interlocutors or antagonists. Lyotard's subject is a *procedural*, not a
valuing subject.

The difference between Weber's values and Lyotard's rules is reflected in
the difference between their accounts of science, which are only superficially
the same. While Weber insists on the 'eternal youth' of science, meaning the
inevitable transience of scientific truths, Lyotard talks of 'postmodern
science as the search for instabilities' (1984: 53) and of 'legitimation by
paralogy' (1984: 60), by which he means that the end of scientific dialogue is
the acceptance of different metaprescriptives. By attempting to specify the
'end' of scientific dialogue Lyotard simply mirrors Habermas's claim that
that 'end' is normative consensus. For one, an act of judgement precedes the
rules of judgement, for the other rules of judgement precede an act of
judgement.[5] But the difference between them and Weber is that for Weber
science is a vocation, by which he meant that science depends upon not only
specific alterable discursive rules, but on a will to truth, on an inner need for
truth which makes science a form of faith. Weber accepted Nietzsche's
characterization of science as an ascetic ideal, and held to that ideal to his
famous last words – 'Die Wahr ist die Wahrheit' – even while accepting – and
hoping – that his own truths would eventually be surpassed. The presuppositions of scientific dialogue were twofold: the value of a truth assumed to be
eternal, and the inherent logic according to which truth would be infinitely
surpassed. Thus he writes:

> the inner *belief*, which we all have in some form, in the metaempirical validity of
> ultimate and highest value ideas, in which we anchor the meaning of our existence
> does not exclude, but includes, the incessant changeableness of the concrete
> viewpoints from which reality gets its significance. (1949: 111; translation altered)

And in the next paragraph, as if in anticipation of Lyotard's concept of
paralogy, he adds:

> All this should not be misunderstood to mean that the essential task of a social
> science should be a continual hunt for new viewpoints and conceptual construc-
> tions. (1949: 111)

By contrast, Lyotard's interpretation of science cannot address the
question which haunts Weber's every utterance – why bother to do science in
the first place? His concept of paralogy contains no sense of the ineradicable
tension between the will to truth and scientific procedure, between the
heroism of the scholar, whose intoxication – *Rausch* – is inexplicable to the
outsider, and the institutionalization of scholarship – a tension which would
confer real meaning and pathos on his idea of 'the pragmatics of science' –
and therefore no sense of the *tragic* character of human commitment.

I want to conclude by recalling a remark made by Richard Rorty in his
paper on the Habermas–Lyotard debate. He notes the rather tedious nature
of the reductionist and anti-reductionist struggles which follow the asserted
separation of science, morality and art, and argues that a philosopher of the
'modern sort' must be equally unwilling to allow these spheres to coexist

uncompetitively or to reduce any two spheres to the remaining one. Rorty himself cannot fill that role. Neither he nor Habermas nor Lyotard appreciate that this unwillingness depends upon an understanding of the tragedy of choice. For it is hard to imagine a competitive relation between value-spheres, or between the concrete ideals for which human beings strive, which does not refer implicitly to the very reductionism Rorty dismisses as tedious. This reductionism – which is actually a form of theoretical and political impotence – can only be avoided through a Weberian understanding of the dual nature of tragedy: of the fact that human dignity, the dignity of 'personalities', resides in holding firmly to one's own convictions while recognizing the existence of hundreds of other convictions, which are held as firmly by others as ours are by us; and that precisely because of this, and because of the intrinsic logic to which any activity is subject, our ultimate values are destined never to be actualized. This Weberian move away from an (ironic) 'totalizing perspective' refuses to substitute for an ethical 'totality' a series of postmodern partial standpoints. For a standpoint worth adopting is one which, even in the face of its impossibility, in the face of the world's 'baseness', never abandons its secret desire to be the only one worth adopting. Without this desire, this 'Here I stand I can do no other', which Weber theorized as value-rationality, there can be no tragedy, only the comforting and bureaucratic purposive-rationality of game-playing. In 1952, Weber's friend and devotee Karl Jaspers wrote a little book called *Tragedy is Not Enough*. It seems that for many pluralist postmodernists, tragedy is too much.

Notes

1 Since I do not address the question of Lyotard's post *Postmodern Condition* move away from the language of language games towards questions of justice and judgement, my comparison between Weber and Lyotard may appear superficial. In particular, Lyotard's more recent concern with the precise nature of the relationship between prescriptive and descriptive statements might be held to absolve him of charges of simple pluralism. Despite this, and a 'seriousness' as great as Habermas's, my point remains that Lyotard lacks Weber's essentially tragic vision of historical action. Perhaps his (Kantian) interest in the 'Idea of Humanity' is an even greater testament to this than is the earlier language game analysis.

2 For the most illuminating treatment of this danger see Blumenberg, 1983.

3 1948: 143. This is one of the most pertinent examples of the paradox of unintended consequences. For Weber, of course, all consequences were unintended, all action subject to this paradox. It is in his attempt to confer ethical status upon an attention to consequences that he expresses his greatest distance from Kantianism, for which the ethical content of an action resides in intention alone.

4 Habermas both wants to argue that philosophy can no longer claim to be self-validating, that empirical science is necessary if the hazardous contingencies of existence are to be overcome, and at the same time avoids a 'descent' to the level of concrete empirical research. Which leads one to suspect that his social theory is really the attempt to do speculative philosophy by other means.

5 On this point see Caygill, 1988. Caygill proposes a radical Hegelianism as a 'way out' of the Kantian aporia of judgement in which he argues that Lyotard and Habermas are both embedded. Perhaps a Weberian attempt to think through tragedy is another.

References

Blumenberg, H. (1983) *The Legitimacy of the Modern Age*. London: MIT Press.
Caygill, H. (1988) 'Postmodernism and judgement', *Economy and Society*, 17.
Lyotard, J.-F. (1984) *The Postmodern Condition*. Manchester: Manchester University Press.
Nietzsche, F. (1967) *The Genealogy of Morals*. New York: Vintage Books.
Rorty, R. (1984) 'Habermas and Lyotard on postmodernity', *Praxis International*, 4 (1).
Schmitt, C. (1976) *The Concept of the Political*. New Brunswick, NJ: Rutgers University Press.
Simmel, G. (1968) *The Conflict of Modern Culture and Other Essays*. New York: Teachers' College Press.
Weber, M. (1948) *From Max Weber*. London: Routledge & Kegan Paul.
Weber, M. (1949) *The Methodology of the Social Sciences*. New York: Free Press.
Weber, M. (1975) *Roscher and Knies*. New York: Free Press.
Wittgenstein, L. (1953) *Philosophical Investigations*. Oxford: Basil Blackwell.

9

TOWARDS A REINTERPRETATION OF MODERNITY IN AN AGE OF POSTMODERNITY

Adam B. Seligman

In this chapter I address the interrelated themes of reason, equality and social ordering. The first two are, in essence, touchstones of the modern world vision, through which its particular conceptions of society are constituted. It is, moreover, the very concomitance posited between these terms that serves as one of the foci of the postmodern critique of the 'project of modernity'. To fully appreciate both the inherent aporias of the modern world view, as well as the problematic nature of any alternative, it is therefore necessary to clarify the relationship between these three terms. We must analyse the manner in which modern assumptions on the universality of reason and the autonomy of the individual subject serve as constitutive components of the social vision of modern civilization.

In the following it is argued that one way to achieve this is through analysis of the changing conceptions of the universal and the particular as these were transformed by both the soteriological doctrines of ascetic-Protestantism and, later, by secularization. This transformation threw in stark relief the problems of social representation in modern society. The following is a brief outline of the major points I develop below: I argue that (1) the debate between modernity and postmodernity is essentially a debate between reason and nihilism; (2) in its more sociological aspects, this debate revolves around the issues of hierarchy versus equality, value rationality (*Wertrationalität*) versus instrumental rationality (*Zweckrationalität*), and holistic (inclusive) models of social ordering versus individualistic (exclusive) ones; (3) as derivative (both historically and analytically) of the progress of secularization and the loss of a transcendent matrix to social life, this debate can most fruitfully be understood in terms of the changing categorization of the universal and the particular; (4) from this perspective, the very fundamental premises of modernity, based on the universality of reason and autonomy of the individual ego, led to a collapse of the distinction or difference between the universal and the particular, and to the inability to represent the universal and particular as distinct and separate categories; and (5) this problem of representing difference (between the universal–social and the particular–individual) stands at the core of the modern predicament. It was, however, addressed in fundamentally different ways in the era of classical modernity than it is by the more contemporary philosophies of postmodernity. Ultimately, the conflicting social visions of modernity and postmodernity rest on their respective models of how society represents itself. The specific manner in which modern society is represented cannot, however, be understood without reference to its fundamental assumptions on the equality of citizens and the workings of reason.

The debate over reason and modernity

In the modern, post-Hegelian era the concepts of reason and equality have been viewed as, if not synonymous then at least complementary. The notion of reason as embedded in the State and expressed in the equality of citizens has been a (philosophically) given axiom since the French Revolution. It was on this basis that Immanuel Kant greeted the French Revolution and never fully removed his support for it, even during the Terror. It was the historical force of this idea that inspired Hegel's *Phenomenology of Spirit* (1807), with the 'forces of reason' knocking, as it were, on the gates of Jena. It was the desire to work through the logic of this connection beyond its abstracted ahistoricity that motivated the young Marx to his work of self-clarification in the *German Ideology* (1844–45). Finally, by the end of the century it was the realization of the necessary connection between reason – as the absence of particular criteria for judgement and action – and the nature of modern life that led Max Weber to the iron cage of an *entzauberte* world.

In a similar vein, addressing what was essentially the same problem but from a different perspective, is the work of Émile Durkheim. In his writings he was less concerned with reason *per se* than with the social implications of formal equality. Durkheim was, after all, interested in what held modern society together. In a world of increased social division of labor, defined by an individualistic ethic, what, he asked was the source of social solidarity. In answering this question, Durkheim broke with the theoretical paradigm he had developed in the *Division of Labor* (1933), and in *The Elementary Forms of Religious Life* (1915) posited the notion of collective representations, not as a common subjectivity of ideas, but as a shared normative orientation to the phenomena of social life (Parsons, 1968: 389). In this move the modern discipline of sociology was founded and the nature of morality defined sociologically. For our own purposes Durkheim's move was central, for he laid the basis of the integration of the domain assumptions of modernity with those of sociology; that is, the universality of the individual ego based on the categorical, a priori, structure of knowledge (Durkheim, 1974; Parsons, 1978: 213–32).

It is, however, precisely these assumptions on the universality of the individual ego and with them of the universality of reason which are at the heart of the postmodern critique of modernity. Thus, the recent philosophical perspectives developed by Lyotard attempt to posit normative attributes precisely to the bracketing out, indeed to the very impossibility of constructing, a universal discourse of reason. The human world is constructed of 'simples' which are named (and not described); they are the building blocks of this 'prelogical' universe (Lyotard, 1988: 37) and thus preclude any logical assertion of truth value.

Drawing on the traditions of phenomenological 'ontology' (Heidegger, 1962) as well as such disciplines as ordinary language philosophy (Austin, 1970), the postmodern position challenges traditional belief in the accessibility of the 'good' to the workings of reason. All stress the limits of language (reason) and its essential inability to articulate the *summum bonum*. The 'good' cannot be articulated and so cannot be subject to a discourse of reason. This nihilistic posture stemming ultimately from Nietzsche is then at the root of 'the postmodern condition' bereft of a transcendental matrix.

The core of the postmodern position can be presented in two central and related themes: (1) an attack on the existence of universals (which are either vigorously denied, or, in the Wittgensteinian mode, posited beyond language and reasonable discourse); and (2) an attack on the philosophy of the subject (best illustrated by Foucault's (1973: 387) by now famous quip that 'man is an invention of recent date and one perhaps nearing its end'). This position is, of course, in marked contrast to that of modernity with its focus on the individual subject and belief in the accessibility of the 'good' and the 'true' (universals) to the workings of reason. To better appreciate the seemingly intractable problems raised by the contemporary, postmodern critique of modernity, we must go beyond abstract debate over these issues and view them more sociologically, as different modes of social ordering.[1]

The problem of the relation between the particular and the universal is indeed no less a sociological than a philosophical concern. Since the work of Troeltsch (1960) and Weber (1978) on the different social orientations of sects and Church, sociologists have been keenly attuned to the role of the particular and the universal as ordering principles of social life. They become central as one of the pairs of pattern-variables by which Parsons (1962: 77, 81–82, 90) categorized all system needs. These perspectives have been supplemented more recently by the work of Louis Dumont (1982: 1–27; 1986) who has compared 'homo hierarchicus' to 'homo aequalis' – compared, that is, holistic (universal) social structures to individualistic ones.

The destructuring of the Cartesian ego (subject) has, as it were, been at the heart of the postmodern agenda and it is in no small degree the search for a response to this challenge that has motivated the (overall historicist) attempts of sociologists, anthropologists and historians to account for the development of the Western notion of the individual (Carrithers et al., 1985; Heller et al., 1986).

This concern with the individual in the matrix of social relations is but another attempt to think the particular (in this case the individual unit) in its relation to the universal (social) framework. It is but another reflection of that philosophical-cum-sociological problem of particular and universal that is at the centre of the current debate over modernity.

Reason, the universal and the terms of social ordering

What must be grasped is the relation of these problems to that of reason – conceived of as the progressive working through of universalist assumptions. Central in this connection is the 'elective affinity' between *Wertrationalität* and hierarchic principles of ordering on the one hand, and between *Zweckrationalität* and equality on the other. Indeed we can go one step further and present two models of ordering. The one founded on ultimate values, which would be a *Wertrationalität* and embody hierarchic assumptions of order (for social action would be evaluated according to its realization of these principles) – as, for example, in Thomas Aquinas's *Summa* – and would present something akin to Dumont's 'holistic' model of society; that is, all-embracing. On the other hand, we can see a social formation (as in modernity) lacking in ultimate values (without a transcendental matrix of *Wertrationalität*) whose governing principle is equality (of reason) and which would be seen as an individualistic society. The two models, presented schematically, would look something like this:

Hierarchy	Equality
Wertrationalität	*Zweckrationalität*
Holistic	Individualistic

Surely on first sight this schematization strikes us as an exaggeration? Whereas the first is somehow acceptable – at least as far as the connection between hierarchy and holism is concerned – in the second set the problem of the place of reason becomes ever so much more blatant. True, empirically there is a realization that modern *entzauberte* society – rooted in equality and individualism – is also characterized by *Zweckrationalität* and the loss of transcendent values. Yet the positing of the relation between the different terms as necessary and in a sense inherent, is glaring in its nihilistic implications and so chafes at our consciousness.

Yet another problem with these dichotomous pairs is derivative of the concomitance between hierarchy/holism and equality/individualism. Again, while hierarchy is inclusive, containing discrete, individual or aggregate units in their idiosyncratic identity, is the corollary also true? Equality would seem either to conflate individual units into one (if A=B how can we distinguish between them?) or to exclude those not given to such a reduction.[2] Yet, historically, were equalitarian societies in fact exclusive?

To begin, both types of societies are inclusive of members and exclusive of non-members (this is albeit a tautology). However, if we think in terms of the Catholic Church, we recall that one is born into the Church; and even in the New World, mass conversions (of those not killed) were also the rule. Moreover, the Church, through its sacramental doctrine, was a potentially universal and inclusive framework (as illustrated by the first millennium and a half of Christianity). Protestant sects, which would be paradigmatic of individualism and rationality, were, on the other hand, rooted in exclusivity and particularism. One was not born into a sect, but had to undergo an internal transformation – the experience of grace – to attain membership. The universality it espoused was one of particular subjects, each rooted in the experience of (universal) grace. Its institutionalization (and hence universalization), however, resulted in the loss of its transcendental referent. Thus, the process of institutionalization implied *eo ipso* a universalization of tenets, and hence a degree of inclusion.

The problem at hand cannot therefore be one of simple inclusion or exclusion. On one (tautological) level, both must be exclusive (or else the very term of membership becomes meaningless). On another, more substantive level, we have seen that we are not really dealing with inclusion or exclusion *per se*, but rather with the terms of inclusion. In this sense we are, in fact, dealing with three terms: self–society–transcendental matrix; and of course the nature of the relations between the three terms. Individualistic Protestantism rules out one of the terms – society – and leaves the relations as: transcendental matrix–individual. 'Holistic' Catholicism unites all three in a dialectic relation.

From this perspective, for Protestantism to be institutionalized – universalized – it had to change its terms of inclusion. In its original formulation the 'inclusionary' term of the social was, after all, 'defined out', leaving only the individual and the transcendent. The loss of transcendence, secularization and ultimately *Entzauberung*, were thus inherent to the institutionalization of Protestantism, as the transcendent referent was replaced with an immanent one, rooted in the human realm (that is, the individual conscience).

The problem of equality and hierarchy is thus related, through the institutionalization of Protestantism, to the radical, immanent historicity of post-Hegelian European thought. A world denuded of transcendence is devoid as well of an ultimate principle of hierarchic ordering. It also leaves us without a common third term of relation – of a relation in and through which *A* and *B* (social actors) can define their communality. The necessity of the third term, through which a transcendentally construed subjectivity can itself be constituted, has been pointed out by, among others, Habermas (1974: 51), who notes that 'To the degree that mystical world-views hold sway over cognition and orientations for action, a clear demarcation of a domain of subjectivity is apparently not possible'. In archaic societies, Habermas continues, individuals cannot 'rely on a formal concept of the ego that could secure his own identity in the face of a subjectivity that has become independent and fluid' (ibid.).

Approaching from an historical or developmental perspective, we must therefore distinguish between what have been termed 'Axial' and 'pre-Axial' civilizations.[3] 'Axial civilizations' refers to those civilizations which emerged, and became institutionalized, in the period between 500 BCE and AD 600 and in which there emerged

a conception of a basic tension between the transcendental and the mundane orders, a conception which differed greatly from that of a close parallelism between these two orders or their mutual embedment which was prevalent in so-called pagan religions. (Eisenstadt, 1982: 294)

In pre-Axial societies the terms of social communality were defined in relation to the totemic, which precluded the development of a subjective individual identity. In Axial civilizations, on the other hand, a transcendentally defined 'Other' provided that constitutive third term through which the notion of the individual could develop. In modernity, the third term became that of an immanent historical self-generating, future-directed ideal of human perfection. In postmodernity, however, there is only a Nietzschean abyss. The 'deconstruction' of the individual subject is but the logical outcome of the lack of a third term through which subjectivity can be constituted.

What, however, of the second term – that is, of the realm of the social, of interpersonal action? How is the loss of transcendence felt in the realm of social ordering – in the principles or world-visions governing such ordering? Again we are back to equality/individualism – whose only transcendence is that of a morality 'immanent in [but] transcending' (Durkheim, 1974: 54) the individual. The similarity of this formulation with Weber's on the charisma of reason (stemming from sectarian Protestantism) is striking – an internalized reason on the one hand and an internalized morality on the other – as foundations for social life. Here, the governing notion of sociality is in the transcendentally constituted subject. Rooted in the Kantian notion of the ego and entering sociological discourse through Durkheim it is, in Niklas Luhmanns's (1982: 5) words, 'the very otherness of the other . . . which does not simply make sociality necessary and desirable, but actually makes it possible for the first time'.

But this leaves unanswered the problem of the *summum bonum*. For the good, defined in terms of the absolutely other, becomes subject ultimately to an immanent historicism based on an absolute subjectivity. It is indeed in an attempt to overcome this subjectivity that Hegel posits the *I* as the identity of the universal and the singular. Thus Habermas has shown in his interpretation of Hegel's (1803–4, 1805–6) *Jena Philosophy of Spirit* precisely the attempt to reformulate a universal – if not transcendental – moral basis for intersubjective action. The success or failure of this programme is that of Habermas himself in his attempt to resuscitate the early Hegelian vision in his notion of communicative action.

At present we are left with what are in essence pretty well known perspectives, which define the debate over modernity. The outstanding problem remains that of the necessary connection between instrumental reason and equality/individualism. In other words, (1) must individualistic societies be characterized by an equalitarian orientation, and (2) does this imply, by necessity, the lack of a *Wertrationalität* and of universal values upon which a morality rooted in the *ganz Anderen* is predicated?

The essence of individualism is in the transcendental subject, or framed more theologically, in the direct relation of the individual to God. Men and women are, in this reading, constituted by their individual relation to the transcendent source of meaning and order. This idea, inherent to early Christianity, developed through the soteriological doctrines of ascetic-Protestantism. It continued in the devotional movements of the late seventeenth century and in the privatization of grace beyond the boundaries of a community of saints – leading in the eighteenth century to our notions of the individual as possessing metaphysical and moral value (Mauss, 1985: 20–2). As long as the individual is conceived of in these terms – and we can in fact 'think' no other (if not in the secularized version of this notion) – there must always be an equalitarian element in the governing notion of relations between transcendentally constituted individuals.

The answer to the second question, however, while a bit more difficult, is crucial. For the whole project of modernity stands or falls with its ability to articulate an ethical absolute. To attempt an answer to this question we must therefore briefly sketch out the nature of relations between the particular and the universal as these developed in classical modernity.

The particular and the universal

The loss of difference

In the relation as described above (that is, those constitutive of the modern subject), the particular and the universal stand in a uniquely unmediated relation to one another. More specifically, there exists no third term through which the distinction between them is mediated. As this distinction is in a sense constitutive of personality, all relations between individuals must have an aspect of (at least formal) equality to them. When the transcendental element is removed (with the progress of secularization), the problems imposed by equality become even more salient (as they become immanently historical and essentially political). We remain, however, with the problematic nature of the relationship between the particular and the universal and development of instrumental reason. This can be conceptualized in the following terms:

In the pre-modern era the universal was conceived of transcendentally. That is to say, it was radically separated from humanity by the 'Axial' or 'transcendental chasm'. The particular in this case took the form of the individual. (It could also be the collective, but even in those civilizations where the collective orientation was strong, such as in Judaism and Islam, the individual was present.)[4]

On first sight, in modern societies, the universal would seem to be the social whole. In this case, one could well assume that here too the particular could be constituted as the individual. In point of fact, however, the modern notion of society is not conceived of in these terms. Rather, society itself as universal is so only as a derivative of the individual; that is, of the growing recognition of the individual as subject and society as the amalgamation of these 'universally' constituted subjects.

What becomes a universal in the individualism ethic is thus the individual him/herself. That the particular becomes the universal is the reigning ethic of individualistic societies – hence equality (of individuals/particulars).

Hence also *Zweckrationalität* as the sum of quantifiable particulars reduced to their common denominator. But in a social formation governed by *Zweckrationalität* there is no ultimate standard beyond the technical competence of exchange (symbolic or material) between individuals *qua* universal entities.

Thus far we have drawn a parallel between a universalized subject (particular) and the lack of transcendence; that is (turning it around), of an immanent historicism defining/containing/developing together with the dissolution of the distinction between the universal and the particular. As the universal is conflated with the individual, the alterity and dissonance between the two moments is lost. This development was parallel to the loss of soteriological tension with (1) secularization, and (2) the devolution of the ideal of progress. Yet it is important to bear in mind that these are two analytically distinct moments. While obviously related to the same dialectic, they are nevertheless separate. Secularization and the failure of progress are changes at the level of historical or cultural phenomena. So too, the loss of the transcendental tension is but the analytic 'label' for these changes. To speak, however, of the loss of distinction between the universal and the particular is to move beyond the phenomenological forms to a transformation in what may be termed the ordering premises, or cognitive codes themselves.[5]

Viewing the loss of transcendence from this perspective – as the loss of distinction between particular and universal – we have a new way to approach the problem of equality and reason (or rather *Zweckrationalität*). For the relation between universal and particular is now transformed into the relations between (universal) subjects – each ontologically self-contained and existing in a state of 'metaphysical' equality. (The mutual exclusion between them is precisely what Weber noted as existing between social groups in the United States, which he nevertheless saw as existing within an inclusive framework (Weber, 1985: 1–12).)

Theoretically we can view the interaction of these subjects in two quite contrasting modes, either (1) as lacking a common universal or transcendental 'Other' and so characterized by *Zweckrationalität* and existing in an *entzauberte* world of the iron cage; or as (2) accepting the universal (if not transcendental) subjectivity of one another and orientating social action towards that goal. (Habermas's programme of course seeks to root intersubjective action in a universal but *not* transcendental matrix of communicative reason.)

The argument we have been following so far has been based on the first perspective (1). The second perspective (2) can be adduced, however, to draw a totally different conclusion. But if we do adopt what may be termed here a Durkheimian (or Kantian) perspective, we are left with explaining an *entzauberte* world. It is therefore not really sufficient, at the theoretical level, as an explanation of modernity. That is, it provides – in the work of philosophers like Habermas – a prescriptive formula for reconstituting social interaction, but it is less than adequate at the descriptive level for explaining the tensions of modern life. This is so precisely because (in the latter argument, however construed) any demarcation between universalism and particularism is lost. To reiterate, what I am saying is that it is not the loss of transcendence itself that is at the heart of the seemingly unconquerable problem of postmodernity – of immanent reason, historicism, loss of subjectivity, etc. Rather it is the concomitant loss of any ability to represent the universal and the particular as distinct and separate categories that is at the core of the modern predicament. This problem was, as noted above, one that Hegel, *pace* Habermas, attempted to resolve by reformulating the very terms of reason itself.

From mediation to representation

This rephrasing of the problem in terms of the representation of the universal and the particular provides us, however, with a new and important focus in our analysis of modernity and (in the following) of the postmodern condition as well. For, as we have seen, what is at issue, beyond the existence of a universal as distinct from the particular, is the very ability to constitute a relation between them through representation. From this perspective, defined by the issue of representation, of how society is represented to its members, new insights can be gained into the contrasting dynamics of modernity and postmodernity respectively.

The issue of societal representation is first and foremost one of the symbolization of society, as a universal, or, as described above, as an amalgam of particulars. The necessity of distinguishing between both modes is, moreover, central to any understanding of modernity and so to the ability to contrast it to the more contemporary phenomena of postmodernity. As a prelude to just such a contrast let us first consider Max Weber's (1978: 556) famous characterization of the unique religious features of ascetic-Protestantism:

> It demands of the believer not celibacy, as in the case of the monk, but the elimination of all erotic pleasure or desire; not poverty, but the elimination of all idle enjoyment of unearned wealth and income, and the avoidance of all feudalistic, life-loving ostentation of wealth; not the ascetic death-in-life of the cloister, but an alert, rationally controlled conduct of life and the avoidance of all surrender to the beauty of the world, to art, or to one's own moods and emotions. The clear and uniform goal of this asceticism was the disciplining and methodical organization of conduct. Its typical representative was the 'man of vocation' or 'professional' and its specific result was the rational, functional organization of social relations.

On one level we see here yet another example – perhaps the prototypical one – of universalized particularity noted above. The (universal) values of celibacy, poverty and a devotional life, in essence of *imitatio Deo*, are incorporated into the particular, becoming constitutive of each believer's *Lebenswelt*. The universal is collapsed into the particular. In this collapse the relations between the particulars become those of exclusion as the universal totality becomes the particular. This is precisely that move 'from

Tribal Brotherhood to Universal Otherhood' charted by Benjamin Nelson
(1969). At a different level, this is reminiscent of Hegel's insights into the
loss of the 'absolute morality of the Greek *polis*' as it was transformed into
the 'formal legal relations of the Roman universal monarchy' (Habermas,
1974: 132–3). With this move 'the spirit of substantial universality, which
has died and split up into the atoms of many absolute isolated individuals,
has decayed to become the formalism of law' (ibid.). This is precisely the
problem of an abstracted universality which has lost its tension with the
concrete (particularity).

The identity of universal and particular (characteristic of modernity) is
therefore far different from the universal's *re-presentation* in the particular
which had characterized medieval Christendom. The result is an exclusion
of (as well as between) particulars based on *identity* as opposed to an
inclusion (of/between particulars) based on *representation*.

Sociologically, we are thus dealing with two quite contradictory modes of
society 'thinking' or 'positing' itself. In one, society is a *metaphor* for the
universal, in the other society *is* the universal. However, this second,
modern formulation becomes tautological. And as Niklas Luhmann (1988:
34) has pointed out:

> Tautologies are distinctions that do not distinguish. They explicitly negate that
> what they distinguish really makes a difference. Tautologies thus block obser-
> vations. They are always based on a dual observation scheme: something is what it
> is. This statement, however, negates the posited duality and asserts an identity.
> Tautologies thus negate what makes them possible in the first place, and, there-
> fore, the negation itself becomes meaningless.

They block not only observation. In this case, what is blocked is the specific
ability to formulate the relation of the individual to the collective in terms
other than that of an instrumental reason mediating between exclusive,
universalized and particular individuals.

From a sociological perspective, there is, however, one critical flaw in this
argument – its failure to explain the continuity of ethically based solidarity
except through a theory of remainders (continuity of primordial identities or
others, secular and/or religious, not totally devalued through reason). In this
sense, the tautology argument is the mirror image of the Kantian one noted
above. That argument, we recall, could not adequately explain the disenchanted world, this fails to explain the continuity to ethical solidarity. Both
leave us with Hegel's night in which all cows are black.

One way out of this impasse would be to acknowledge that, while the
distinction between universal and particular has here been lost, some modes
of representation (of breaking down tautological identities) continue: both
(descriptively) allowing the continuity of ethical solidarity and (prescripti-
vely) providing a means for reconstituting it *grosso modo*. This would shed a
new light on Habermas's intersubjective communicative action. The point
then is not in the existence of a universal–particular dichotomy, but in the
very existence of a difference which can be constituted through representation, including that of the individual in the social, and which does not need

of necessity a transcendental matrix. It is then precisely the difference inherent to representation and made possible by society's representation of the individual (recall, universality rooted in particular subjects not in society as such) that has allowed for the continuity of ethical solidarity in the modern era.[6]

From this perspective we can now return to the sociological aspects of the debate over modernity, postmodernity and reason. The issue therefore is, as we have seen, not so much the loss of a *Wertrationalität* or of a transcendental (ultimate) matrix for instrumental action, but is rather the issue of representation. The question of the postmodern condition thus becomes the question of the self-reflection of society. Is the positing of society in the late twentieth century fundamentally different from that of 'modernity'? Whereas the classic modern vision posited society as the representation of universal individuals, has this changed in the present era?

Sociological inquiry into this question must explore two possibilities. The first would indeed seek to delineate the changing conception of society; that is, a redefinition of the role of society in terms of its individual members. The second would have to inquire into the roots of this change in the very essence of the liberal-market orientation. That is, in the conception of the public realm as a neutral arena where individual interests are played out. For if the public arena is indeed conceived simply in terms of this neutral space, then the phenomenon of postmodernity is nothing but the working out of the inherent dynamic of modernity. If, however, as indicated earlier there was, in the classic liberal doctrine, a 'transcendent' significance to society then postmodernism signifies a fundamental change which must be explained.

Representation in modernity and postmodernity

There would seem to be a number of ways to achieve an understanding of classic-modern notions of representation (of the particular/individual in the universal/social), all rooted in the political theory of the eighteenth and nineteenth centuries. Given the importance of the debate between Habermas and his critics – over his attempt to renew an Enlightenment project of reason – the thought of Hegel is especially pertinent to our theme. However, Hegel's notions of ethical solidarity find a strong resonance in the earlier tradition of the Scottish Enlightenment (of 'natural sympathy' and 'sociability'), as well as in the thought of such disparate thinkers as Burke and Rousseau.

Striking from today's perspective is the classic-modernist recognition of society (conceived of as civil society, including what Habermas has termed the public sphere) as invested with value. The phenomenon of property exchange which takes place in the market is itself imbued with a value that subsequent Marxist and utilitarian theories have, in different ways, obfuscated. In Hegel's writings on the state and law (1952: 4–57) it becomes clear that the individual need for recognition (and hence existence) is attained through the recognition of property. Indeed, for Hegel, property – in the realm of civil society – takes the place of love – in the realm of the family (1952: 105–55; 1983: 99–118). Through both (as different moments in the actualization of the spirit) a universal will is constructed through recognition, and as Hegel (1952: 118) observed at the end of part I of the Jena lectures: 'The will of the individual is the universal will – and the universal will is the individual. It is the totality of ethical life [*Sittlichkeit*] in general, immediate, yet [as] Right.' It is thus, according to Hegel, precisely through the mutual recognition involved in property exchange that the individual as self-consciousness (*für sich*) is constructed, which is the closest we can come to an ethical realm in a world defined by the mutual exchange between different entities (as opposed to the ideal self of the Greek *polis*, undifferentiated from community) (Bernstein, 1984: 14–39). In this latter-day world, the realm of ethics is constructed in and only in the mutual recognition which defined civil society.

Strangely congruent with this notion is the idea found in Adam Smith's (1759) *The Theory of Moral Sentiments*, which argues that the moral basis of individual existence is the need for recognition and consideration on the part of others. 'To be observed, to be attended to, to be taken notice of with sympathy, complacency and approbation' are for Smith (1982: 50) the driving force of 'all the toil and bustle of the world . . . the end of avarice and ambition, of the pursuit of wealth'. Thus, and as tellingly pointed out by A.O. Hirschman (1977: 109), economic activity itself is rooted, in *The Theory of Moral Sentiments*, in the non-economic needs for sympathy and appreciation. It is, for Adam Smith (1982), our interest in 'being the object of attention and approbation' that leads to the complex activity which defines economic life. What is common to both perspectives, albeit in different ways, is the idea of the arena of exchange (of civil society) as rooted in a sphere of values predicated on the mutuality of individual recognition.

In terms of our problematic what both attitudes would indicate is an approach to the public realm – to the sphere of commodity exchange – as something well beyond the neutral arena where the 'universally particular' (owner of commodities) act out their individual interests. Rather, both approaches, albeit with different stresses, maintain that interaction itself as the ethical matrix of individual existence. The element of representation is maintained, not solely in the objectified self of property, but in the very act of exchange in which, in Hegel's terms, the individual and universal wills unite.

This unity of wills in a shared public realm with its own autonomous status is of course strikingly similar to Rousseau's notion of 'general will' existing beyond private or particular wills (Book II, Ch. 3). And though it is true that Rousseau posited the individual conscience as resting at the core of social life, scholars from Durkheim (1965) to Shklar (1969) have realized the strong ambiguity in Rousseau's thought which stresses as well 'the individual as dependent on society, which far transcends the multiplicity of individual wills' (Durkheim, 1965: 103).

Finally, we would do well to recall that Burke's traditionalism was premised on the shared ethical ideals of a whole body of people as being superior to the subjective opinions of the particulars – which represent, at best, abstract reason (Suter, 1971: 57–9). Burke's traditionalism, which legitimized reason in temporal terms of continuity with the past, should not blind us to the organicist assumptions he shared with Hegel and indeed with all attempts to root individual existence in a shared community of ethical life. What was *Sittlichkeit* for Hegel, was for Burke, laws and manners (Suter, 1971: 65).

Indeed, it is precisely the temporal aspect that divides Burke from Marx in their antithetical attempts to unite public and private realms – to unite man as citizen with man in civil society. For Marx, such unity was only in the future, for Burke it was inherent in the existing order. While it is precisely this difference which defines the difference of conservative from revolutionary theory, they are both rooted in a shared vision of what constitutes particular existence. Both share the idea of Rousseau's contract in which *l'homme* is dissolved into *le citoyen*.

The self-same validation of the individual in and through the universal which we found in the realm of exchange was, according to Habermas, at the essence of the legal-normative structure as well. Thus he points out that:

> The criteria of generality and abstractness that characterizes legal norms had to have a peculiar obviousness for privatized individuals who, by communicating with each other in the public sphere of the world of letters, confirm each other's subjectivity as it emerges from their sphere. . . . These rules, because they are universally valid, secure a space for the individuated person; because they are objective, they secure a space for what is most subjective; because they are abstract, for what is most concrete. (MS: 77)

However, and crucial for the whole notion of representation in this period, is the development of instrumental reason – which stood at its core. For whether in the realm of commodity exchange, or of legal sanctions, it is precisely the generalized, formal and abstract nature of the rules governing intercommunicative action that afford the particular its universal status (in the meeting of particular wills). This then, is the paradox at the core of modern civilization – an ethical solidarity achieved through the universalization of abstract reason.

What this entailed for the notion of representation is again a transposition of its terms. For in Catholic-hierarchic-holistic (and feudal) society we saw a unity represented as diversity. As Niklas Luhmann (1987: 105) said of hierarchy, which he termed a 'discovery of genius',

> The unity of the system is the difference of ranks, with a double significance: it gives each part a rank, and so lets the part participate by means of the difference. And it uses the same difference to represent itself in the supreme rank at the summit of the system. It is unity as difference, as difference permits the representation of the unity of the system through the *maior et sanior pars*. Hierarchy is the paradox resolved, paradoxically reflected in itself, as it were, and which thereby becomes interconnectable.

In modernity, however, we are faced with precisely the opposite – instead of unity represented as difference, we have difference represented as unity.

With this in mind we can now return to our earlier query on the nature of the public (universal; the German word *Allgemeine* comprises both these meanings) representation of the private in classic modernist theories. On the one hand, it is clear that the arena of civil society, of law and exchange, was not viewed as simply a neutral space of interaction. It was, rather, that arena where the particular was itself constituted and so shared in the attributes of some ethical – or transcendent (not transcendental) validation. On the other hand, the very establishment of this ethical space was based on abstract, instrumental reason, orientated towards the (ultimately self-referential) parts rather than to the whole. In fact Habermas's whole analysis of *The Structural Transformation of the Public Sphere* in the nineteenth century traces precisely this awareness (expressed albeit in class terms) of the reduction of the public sphere to an arena of private interests, incapable of representing the whole (*das Allgemeine*).

What then of what has been termed postmodernism? Is it qualitatively different from modernity – or solely (as the Frankfurt School would put it) a progressive working through of the logic of instrumental reason? While not parting from the fundamental insights of Critical Theory on the nature of instrumental reason, we would do well to broaden the analysis and open some new perspectives on the phenomenon of representation in the contemporary world. In this vein I propose to view the postmodern as an attempt to transcend and reconstruct a mode of representation through a new dialectic of public and private.

While this is undoubtedly only one small aspect of that amalgam of phenomena that have been termed (if not rigorously defined) as postmodern, it is especially appropriate for our purposes. As we have been dealing throughout with the terms of the universal and the particular and the related problems of representation (itself a focus of postmodernist critique), the changing definitions of the public and private would seem the proper place to broaden somewhat our understanding of the difference between society's representation of itself in modernity and postmodernity.

One of the slogans of the 1960s protest movements was 'the person is political'. Flying in the face of traditional politics (of both liberal and socialist intervention), this attitude has been increasingly prominent in institutional politics of the 1980s. It has been manifest in such phenomena as the growth of new political movements oriented to demands not hitherto considered political in nature; in the practice of such movements involving non-institutional and non-conventional means of political participation and in fact in a protracted struggle in different institutional realms (health care, welfare entitlements; the definition of the 'domain' of women in society) over the very definition of the boundaries of public and private, and indeed of the person *per se* (Maier, 1987; Pateman, 1988; Luhmann, 1987).

One of the interesting arenas where the logic informing these struggles is manifest is in the changing language of 'rights'. Rights are no longer framed in terms of citizen or civil rights, but of human rights.[7] Moreover, a brief look at today's newspaper, a half-hour listening to the radio and a walk around campus reveal that among these rights are: 'the right to wear fur', 'the right to good health', 'the right to bear AK-47 assault rifles', 'women's reproductive rights' and of course 'animal rights'. Indeed, the ecology movement can be seen as imbuing natural phenomena, the oceans, whales, trees, etc., with 'rights'.

Now, on first sight these examples would seem to be relegating to oceans, whales, trees and kitty-cats the status of citizens. However, here I believe the articulation of rights in terms of human rights (rather than citizen rights) is central. For it is not that kitty-cats become citizens – but rather that the realm of shared public space, within which the citizen is constituted, has itself disappeared. What has taken its place is the most abstract of generalities (again instrumental reason/*Zweckrationalität*) within which individuals exist in public only as generalized universals (humans, animals, etc.).[8] It is precisely in these terms that we are to understand the 'right to wear fur' or even 'women's reproductive rights'. None of these is a citizen right. They are, rather, private passions and interests projected into the public arena in terms of rights.[9]

There is an important lesson to be learned from this in terms of the dynamics of representation. For while the traditional critical reading would see the devolution of the public sphere as entailing a concomitant destructuring of the private (and this is Habermas's thesis in the work cited above), the opposite process is also at work. In lieu of the public, the private is projected into the public arena, is made public, in an attempt to reconstitute itself through its representation in that sphere.

This is the dynamic underlying that peculiarly American phenomenon of making private (and what in other societies would be deemed trivial) matters, public concerns.[10] In the USA, that most postmodern of all societies, the private is invested with a public nature in an attempt to constitute its value in the face of what is conceived to be a neutral public arena. Into this 'void' the private is projected in an attempt to constitute presence. Thus, whether dealing with the drinking or fornication of a public official or the rules regulating smoking in restaurants, the private is given a public presence (and value) unique in contemporary societies. Past analyses of this characteristic feature of American life have sought to explain it in the 'religious' nature of the American polity. While they have not been incorrect in this, they have missed one important point. For it is precisely due to its 'Protestant' nature that America is the most postmodern of all societies. That is to say, in the USA, more than anywhere else, the underlying dynamic we have been tracing – of universalized particulars, existing in a state of 'metaphysical equality' and united only by the logic of rational exchange – is to be found. It is no wonder then that America, of all places, has been the most receptive to the postmodernist argument. As there, more than anywhere else, the fundamental premises of social existence are those of the apotheosis of the particular.

Whether this attempt will succeed or not is of course an open question. The historical exigencies of power and the control of markets and resources make any attempt to generalize such a mode of representation very fragile and unstable. Furthermore, its threat of collapse into a self-referential system supported by power is an ever present threat and danger. (Though of course Marxists, from one perspective, and Lyotard from another, would claim, no less dangerous than the bourgeois attempt at representation through civil society.) Whatever the nature of its long-term effects, we can offer, at this point, two tentative perspectives: (1) that the nature of social representation in the contemporary postmodern world is markedly different from that of classic, modern society; but that (2) attempts to provide such representation of both public and private life continue, despite the lack of any ultimate or transcendental referent.

Finally, we would do well to recall that the problem posed by the public representation of the private, the particular represented as universal, are, as pointed out by Niklas Luhmann (1987: 101–8), those of any self-referential system, ultimately of a part supporting the whole. This problem is at the heart of the postmodern system of representation, of which the case of the public and private has served as but an example. Whether it is also an historically viable project remains to be seen. However, the current crisis in rationality, with its intimations of a *weiderentzauberte* world, point to some of the problems involved in this project.[11] In the social realm, with which we have been concerned, we must bear in mind that a *weiderentzauberte* world bears with it, not the possibility of a renewed universal and transcendental matrix of otherhood, but, more probably, of a new form of 'magical' manipulation of the (social) cosmos. This would, in the worst of cases, threaten even that *zweckrational* orientation which stands at the core of the social world of both modernity and postmodernity *tout court*.

Notes

I would like to thank Johannes Mohr, Terry Evens, Charles Axelrod and Uri Ram for their careful reading and very helpful suggestions on earlier versions of this chapter.

1 The most sustained attempt to address the philosophical issues raised by the proponents of postmodernity can be found in Jürgen Habermas's *The Philosophical Discourse of Modernity* (1987b). See as well the recent volume of *Praxis International* (1989) which devotes most of one issue to an analysis of this debate.

2 This theme has been dealt with extensively, if controversially, in Louis Dumont's recent *Essays on Individualism* (1986), especially in pp. 104–82, 223–68.

3 On the sociological conceptualization and use of the term 'Axial Age Civilization' see the work of S.N. Eisenstadt (1982, 1986).

4 As the subject of this essay is the nature of representation in modernity and postmodernity we are concerned with the logic of Western development and will not enter into the developmental characteristics of the non-monotheistic, but Axial, civilizations (of Buddhism, Confucianism and Hinduism).

5 If we take the perspective of an unfolding rationality in the West as articulated by Weber and further developed by Schluchter (1984) and Habermas (1987a), we have here an interesting additional perspective. That is to say, reason, in progressively demystifying the

world and becoming instrumental reason, loses (or perhaps transforms) the nodal points of its referents. The tension between the particular and universal (which for example stood at the core of the medieval doctrine of correspondences) becomes the tension/problem of subject–object, born with the Cartesian ego.

6 Indeed, the importance of re-presentation (*Vorstellung*) in maintaining an ethically based solidarity and so the very conditions of human (social) existence is rooted in the perduring dialectic of reason and desire. As Stanley Rosen (1969: 206–13) has made clear the 'self-transcending character of desire [is] its rational nature'. Speech (which is reason) is necessary to provide desire 'with a sufficient *distance* [sic] from things, within which it may begin to practice the discrimination, restraint or evaluation upon which satisfaction depends'. It is therefore precisely the mediation of representation (of desire in reason) which makes existence possible. In our terms it is a similar representation (of the individual-as-universal within society) which makes social existence possible.

7 When the issue of 'rights' were phrased in the seventeenth century (and before Hobbes) in terms of human rights, this referred back to their grounding in the classic natural law tradition which rested on the notion of transcendental matrix. On this tradition see the illuminating work of R. Tuck (1981). In the transformation of natural rights theories from Hobbes via Rousseau, Kant and Fichte to Hegel, the 'natural' grounding of rights was transformed and the term, while remaining in use, was voided of its previous philosophic content (Reidel, 1971: 146).

8 Again, such a conception stood at the root of one tradition of classical natural law with its notions of *ius naturale* bound to a transcendental referent. Without such a generalized and universal other, however, any similarity with the contemporary status of the individual is lacking.

9 The use of the title of A.O. Hirschman's (1977) famous study *The Passions and the Interests* in this sentence is intentional.

10 I am grateful to John Meyer for bringing this trait of American life, as well as its analytic importance to the thesis presented here, to my attention. Needless to add, he bears no responsibility for the interpretation offered above.

11 For some relevant analyses of current work on the problems of rationality see M. Hollis and S. Lukes, 1982.

References

Austin, J.L. (1970) *Philosophical Papers*. London: Oxford University Press.

Bernstein, J.M. (1984) 'From self-consciousness to community: act and recognition in the master–slave relationship', in Z.A. Pelczynski (ed.), *The State and Civil Society: Studies in Hegel's Political Philosophy*. Cambridge: Cambridge University Press. pp. 14–39.

Carrithers, M. et al. (eds) (1985) *The Category of the Person*. Cambridge: Cambridge University Press.

Dumont, L. (1982) 'A modified view of our origins: The Christian beginnings of modern individualism', *Religion*, 12: 1–27.

Dumont, L. (1986) *Essays on Individualism: Modern Ideology in Anthropological Perspective*. Chicago: University of Chicago Press.

Durkheim, E. (1915) *The Elementary Forms of Religious Life*. Tr. Swain. London: Allen and Unwin.

Durkheim, E. (1933) *The Division of Labor in Society*. Tr. Simpson. New York: Free Press.

Durkheim, E. (1965) *Montesquieu and Rousseau: Forerunners of sociology*. Ann Arbor: Michigan University Press.

Durkheim, E. (1974) *Sociology and Philosophy*. New York: Free Press.

Eisenstadt, S.N. (1982) 'The Axial Age – the emergence of transcendental visions and the rise of clerics', *European Journal of Sociology*, 23: 294–314.

Eisenstadt, S.N. (ed.) (1986) *The Origins and Development of Axial Age Civilizations*. Albany: SUNY Press.

Foucault, M. (1973) *The Order of Things*. NY: Vintage Press.

Habermas, J. (1974) *Theory and Practice*. Boston: Beacon.

Habermas, J. (1987a) *The Theory of Communicative Action*. Tr. T. McCarthy. Vol. 1. Boston: Beacon Press.

Habermas, J. (1987b) *The Philosophical Discourse of Modernity: Twelve lectures*. Cambridge Mass.: MIT Press.

Habermas, J. (MS) *The Structural Transformation of the Private Sphere*. Manuscript, tr. Thomas Burger.

Hegel, G.W.F. (1952) *The Philosophy of Right*. Tr. T. Knox. Oxford: Oxford University Press.

Hegel, G.W.F. (1977) *Phenomenology of Spirit*. Tr. A.V. Miller. Oxford: Oxford University Press.

Heidegger, M. (1962) *Being and Time*. Tr. J. Macquarrie and E. Robinson. Oxford: Basil Blackwell.

Heller, T. et al. (eds) (1986) *Reconstructing Individualism*. Stanford: Stanford University Press.

Hirschman, A.O. (1977) *The Passions and the Interests*. Princeton, Princeton University Press.

Hollis, M. and Lukes, S. (eds) (1982) *Rationality and Relativism*. Cambridge, Mass.: MIT Press.

Levinas, E. (1978) *Existence and Existents*. Hague: E.J. Brill.

Levinas, E. (1981) *Otherwise than Being or Beyond Essence* (trans. A. Lingis). Boston: Martinus Nijhoff.

Luhmann, N. (1982) *The Differentiation of Society*. New York: Columbia University Press.

Luhmann, N. (1985) 'The Individuality of the individual: historical meaning and contemporary problems', in Heller et al., 1985: 312–25.

Luhmann, N. (1987) 'The representation of society within society', *Current Sociology*, 35(2):101–8.

Luhmann, N. (1988) 'Tautology and paradox in the self-representation of society', *Sociological Theory*, 6(1).

Lyotard, J.-F. (1988) *The Differend: Phrases in Dispute*. Minneapolis: University of Minnesota Press.

Maier, C. (ed.) (1987) *Changing Boundaries of the Political: Essays on the Evolving Balance between the State and Society, Public and Private*. Cambridge: Cambridge University Press.

Marx, K. and Engels, F. (1976) *The German Ideology*. Collected Works, Vol. 5, 1844–45. London: Lawrence and Wishart.

Mauss, M. (1985) 'A Category of the human mind: the notion of person, the notion of self', in Carrithers et al., 1985: 1–25.

Nelson, B. (1969) *The Idea of Usury*. Chicago: University of Chicago Press.

Parsons, T. (1962) *Towards a General Theory of Social Action*. New York: Harper and Row.

Parsons, T. (1968) *The Structure of Social Action*. New York: The Free Press.

Parsons, T. (1978) 'Durkheim on religion revisited', in T. Parsons, *Action Theory and the Human Condition*. New York: The Free Press. pp. 213–32.

Pateman, C. (1988) 'The fraternal social contract', in J. Keane (ed.), *Civil Society and the State*. London: Verso Press. pp. 101–28.

Pelczynski, Z.A. (ed.) (1971) *The State and Civil Society in Hegel*. Oxford: Oxford University Press.

Reidel, M. (1971) 'Nature and freedom in Hegel's philosophy of Right', in Z.A. Pelczynski, 1971: 136–50.

Rosen, S. (1969) *Nihilism*. New Haven: Yale University Press.

Rousseau, J.J. (1967) *The Social Contract*. Ed. L. Crocker. New York: Washington Square Press.

Schluchter, W. (1984) *The Development of Western Rationalism*. Berkeley: University of California Press.

Shklar, J. (1969) *Men and Citizens: A Study of Rousseau's Social Theory*. Cambridge: Cambridge University Press.

Smith, A. (1982) *The Theory of Moral Sentiments*. Ed. D.D. Raphael and A.L. MacFie; based on 1759 edition. Indianapolis: Liberty Classics.

Suter, J.F. (1971) 'Burke, Hegel and the French Revolution', in Z.A. Pelczynski (ed.) *Hegel's Political Philosophy*. Cambridge: Cambridge University Press. pp. 52–72.

Troeltsch, E. (1960) *The Social Teachings of the Christian Churches*. Chicago: University of Chicago Press.

Tuck, R. (1981) *Natural Rights Theories: Their Origin and Development*. Cambridge: Cambridge University Press.

Weber, M. (1978) *Economy and Society*. Berkeley: University of California Press.

Weber, M. (1985) 'Churches and sects in North America' (tr. and introduced by C. Loader and J. Alexander), *Sociological Theory*, 1(3): 1–12.

PART FOUR

POLITICS, WOMEN AND POSTMODERNITY

10

WOMEN BETWEEN FUNDAMENTALISM AND MODERNITY

Ayşegül Baykan

In various countries today, the religious-fundamentalist movements are making their presence known in many ways, mostly through a struggle against secular institutions and the constitutions which guarantee them. The modes of discourse originating from the traditional notions of religious morality, family, class, and sexual differences have been re-emerging at the political level and the Islamic fundamentalist movement, even in secular countries like Turkey, is appealing to the old custom of separating the domain of sexes with an emphasis on traditional clothing, education, etc. The observance of religious rules by women within the public domain, such as in schools or at work, has become a common practice. Furthermore, these movements are occasionally advocated by professional women, as demands for individual rights and free thought, who deny the anti-modernist, anti-secularist implications involved. In the heart of these developments lie issues of great importance: social transformation, global political movements, and the place and rights of women in the society.

My aim in this chapter is to show that it would be a mistake, both theoretically and methodologically, to take these beliefs and practices as a continuation of a historically fixed set of traditions and culture, as if they are structurally identical with the past practices and beliefs. In actuality, they are elements of the present time, emphasizing the specificity of particular societies, but, at the same time, being sustained by the global political, ideological and economic movements (Robertson and Lechner, 1985).

Looking at Turkey from a historical perspective, we see the segmented society of the Ottoman Empire becoming a nation-state. The result, however, has not been a totality that is uniform in its cultural self-representation. Instead, there has been a coexistence of, and a dialectical relation between, the two world-views, life styles and political and ideological structures that have defined themselves as either 'traditional' or as 'modern'. This, however, does not imply that a dualistic society has emerged, a modern and a traditional, each self contained in itself with respect to economic, political, and institutional structures, respectively conveyed by a lack or presence of differentiation and rationalization.

In other words, the 'traditional' society, which is constantly making of itself, has neither stayed the same nor gone through an evolution from the traditional to the modern, but has found a healthy environment to produce its economic, political and ideological character within the process of modernization and urbanization, without necessarily accepting 'modernism' as such. It is creating metropolises of a 'traditional' character and is articulating itself to the dominant political regimes and hegemony, while consuming the products of development either in the form of consumption of goods or services such as schooling and modern communications.

Complementing this, the 'modern' society is finding itself on the defensive on all fronts. It is no longer legitimated by a discourse of a universalist image of progress prescribed by the European Enlightenment. The world of progress which created an alternative for the existing definitions of women and challenged the system of power and inequality of the paternalistic world has been uprooted. Today for many the women's issue, left to the domain of tradition and culture, is not seen as a necessary dimension of modernization. That is, recent developments have shown that modernization and women gaining rights are not necessary corollaries. It should not be expected from modernity to bring about a total transformation, in the teleological, evolutionist, historicist, 'it is unavoidable' sense, for every member of the female gender. It must rather be seen within its ideological dimension, and the self-defined modern women must struggle for their democratic rights in all institutions of the society.

Theoretical background

According to Marshall Berman (1983), modern life has many components. Industrialization, urbanization, nation-states, bureaucratic structures, population growth, new systems of communication, new forms of power and class structures, and a world capitalist market are some of the indices on his list. Called 'modernization' the indicated life is in 'a state of perpetual becoming'. Berman also expounds 'modernism' as 'an amazing variety of visions and ideas that aim to make men and women the subjects as well as the objects of modernization, to give them the power to change the world that is changing them, to make their way through the maelstrom and make it their own' (Berman, 1983: 16). The senses and ideas of modernization and modernism have emerged in the nineteenth century where people experienced the realities of 'this inner dichotomy, this sense of *living in two worlds simultaneously*' (Berman, 1983: 17; my italics).

Another concept that needs to be decoded is 'modernity'. According to David Frisby (1986) in the nineteenth century modernity signified what was 'new' in modern life experiences. The emphasis was on its transitory nature, its contingency, its arbitrariness, and on its sense of opposition to unilinear time. It was about the modes of experiencing social life and its cultural representations, but not an explication of a social totality. Frisby argues that it is this approach to modernity that distinguished Simmel from Weber.

Contrary to their predecessors, the twentieth century theories of modernization in sociology take 'the modern society they delineate as being a fixed end state (development or "progress" only existing up to the present)' (Frisby, 1986: 13). An investigation of modernization focuses on the social totality and on its structural and institutional levels as a whole. Specific aspects of modernity thus disappear behind this totalizing investigation which divides societies, or social entities into either traditional or modern fixed states.

> With pessimistic hindsight, it has been fashionable in much modern sociological discourse to read all these polarities as if they were grounded in a philosophy of history thesis as to the inevitable transition from one to the other in such a way that the source of their dynamic – be it functional differentiation, rationalization, etc. – not merely produced only negative consequences but obscured the complexities of the 'present' societies and any countervailing tendencies operating within them. (Frisby, 1986: 13)

Like Frisby, Berman also contends that there is a difference between the nineteenth and the present century of sociological thinking. In the former the aim was to come to grips with the contradictions and the polarities of modern life's experiences.

> Their twentieth-century successors have lurched far more toward rigid polarities and flat totalizations. Modernity is either embraced with a blind and uncritical enthusiasm, or else condemned with a neo-Olympian remoteness and contempt; in either case, it is conceived as a closed monolith, incapable of being shaped or changed by modern men. Open visions of modern life have been supplanted by closed ones, Both/And by Either/Or. (Berman, 1983: 24)

In the case of non-Western societies modernization as an 'end state' has become synonymous with Westernization. Not only traditions as such, but also specifically the East and Islam are construed in their particularistic and static dimensions. These dimensions are then placed in opposition to the European ones characterized as rational and politically and socially differentiated. The theory offers no alternative for understanding change in any way other than Westernization and moving to that stage in the universal history of secularism and differentiation.

At any given time, in any society, there are various conflicts between alternative power structures. Today, given these conflicts and resulting forces for social change, one side of the conflict identifies itself as the one that advocates historical continuity. It stands to represent the 'traditional' society and opposes a 'modern' one which may be regarded as either corrupt, alienating, imperialist, Western, or as any other symbol for the 'other'.

> However, in so far as there is such reference to an historic past, the peculiarity of 'invented' traditions is that the continuity with it is largely factitious. In short, they are responses to novel situations which make the form of reference to old situations, or which establish their own past by quasi-obligatory repetition. (Hobsbawm and Ringer, 1984: 2)

According to Hobsbawm, the main characteristic of an invented tradition is its claim to invariance. The past, tradition, religious beliefs, and cultural practices are all imposed as fixed and formalized. In this context, the idea of a woman and her role in the society is articulated in reference to this past.

The rate of participation in the work force, average levels of education and income, and civil rights are some of the indices used to analyze the relative position of women in a given society. By assigning a score to these indices sociologists place the society somewhere between the polar opposites of traditional and modern. For most of the Middle Eastern countries, traditional society is automatically defined as an Islamic one. Analytically, studies of Islamic societies have been based upon Orientalist approaches. In these, Islam is taken as transcendental and historically and geographically unchanging. Islam itself, not any of the political, historical, geographical or economic dynamics, characterizes the nature of the state and the society. It also becomes the only predicate for women. That is, the Orientalist studies of genders take as their object of study 'Islamic' men and women (Lazreg, 1988). In this way the theory takes subjection of women as a given and as an unchanging definition of what actually needs to be explained in terms of time, place, politics, economics and religion.

In another perspective the adjectives 'traditional' and 'underdeveloped' are co-referential. The traditional position of women becomes synonymous to a situation of economic underdevelopment. Development would erase economic backwardness, resulting in equality between genders. The problem with this 'economic survivalist' approach is that the specificity of the historical control mechanisms of the patriarchal systems become neglected (Hatem, 1986). This view is also teleological since it maintains a unilinear and totalizing approach to history and society.

Analytically, this chapter follows a culturalist approach. In this perspective 'culture' ceases to be a non-materialist category, such as 'values', 'beliefs', 'norms' and/or 'psychological dispositions'. In other words, cultur-ally-symbolically significant realms of life are analysed as separate thematics while they are also grounded within the domain of economy and power relations. The cultural, historical genealogies of people are read without a place within a larger narrative explaining how everything is ordered in a universally valid theoretical system which subjects them to a teleological necessity or causation.

In this perspective the fundamentalist movement is seen as quite material in its institutionality. Contained in the language of its ideological discourse are its aims of restructuring and reconstructing the society according to some given referents, such as culture, family, veiling of women, or nationalism. It is also pragmatically oriented. In referring to tradition, the aim is to reorder this worldly domain with an anti-secularist, anti-Westernist system. As claimed earlier, tradition and culture do not exclusively imply the realities of a fixed time and place of the past, but they are elements of cultural self-representations of today's new right. This new right does not stand opposed to modernization but is strongly against modernism.

Given this, how do we explain the fundamentalists' negative position towards modern women and their positive acceptance of economic and political modernization? It can be argued that secularism has separated this-worldly material life from the other-worldly domain concerned with religious beliefs, spiritual needs and existential questions. Recent years have shown that secularism has not diminished the interest in the sacred. This is in accord with the view that modernism as an alternative ideology, being about images of men and women or fragmented experiences of life, is not a necessary dimension of modernization.

But there remain serious problems. On one hand, in reference to attitudes towards women, the limits between the sacred and the profane become totally blurred. The religious representation of women becomes a cultural representation that has material consequences for power, politics, economics and all the other aspects of life. On the other hand, Islamic rules regulate even the minute details of everyday conduct and appearance, thus making it difficult to place Islamic religion solely in the domain of the sacred. Theoretically, these problems lead us to think of the fundamentalist movement not only in its religious dimensions but as a larger cultural program for a conservative world that includes the power systems of paternalistic structures and their political and economic dimensions.

For example, Jowkar (1988) states that in the Mediterranean region, the dominant ideology separating men and women is the ideology of honor and shame, which is applied differently to each gender. She argues that

> no religious dogma by itself can account for the origin of sexual double standards. However, sexist institutionalized religious doctrines are fertile ground for the legitimation of tenacious sexual hypocrisy . . ., the ideology of honor and shame is in close accordance with physical segregation of the economic activities of the sexes; they mutually reinforce each other. (Jowkar, 1988: 50–1)

Modernization and the formation of nation-states have also been used to imply the emergence of civil societies. Ideally, both men and women would appear in market relations, class divisions, and in bureaucratic state machineries as citizens. But the social reality in societies that do not fit the conceptual definitions of modern or traditional is somewhat different. A hierarchy has occurred in 'clientelistic vertical ties' that integrates issues of family and honor to modern machineries of the state and the market:

> The chain of clientelistic politics achieves a strategic nexus where the state machinery is unable to reciprocate services to its citizens, and where the general

alienation of the masses from the processes of political decision making and economic regulation of wealth is an endemic feature of the society. Providing a linkage between the smallest villages and the centers of political and economic power, clientelism . . . entails a personalistic ideology that binds and justifies various forms of political ties and favoritism. Family fame and honor are idioms and moral lexicons by which political and economic favoritism in their vertical and horizontal manifestations are justified. (Jowkar, 1988: 54–5)

This ideology may not be supported, but is also not challenged by an educational system that has become the least specialized and the most standardized, according to Gellner (1983). The pre-industrial or the pre-nation-state eras did not have cohesiveness and homogeneity between the ruling classes and the peasantry, as the political units were not defined culturally (cultural domain being in the control of the clericy), but today nationalism has made the unity of culture and polity possible. In a sense, universal education has turned everybody into a cleric, as Gellner argues. This is not only because of the teachings of the educational institutions, but because of their functional role in bringing about cultural cohesiveness.

Gellner's idea of the unity between polity and culture is an interesting one. The Kemalist period, the first period of the Turkish nation-state, may be marked by the centralized state's attempt to bring about forced modernism in order to bring about such a unity for homogenizing the society. Yet the modernists of this period failed to see the difference and the incongruent development between the process of modernization, which included developing centralized state machineries and market structures, urbanization and so forth, and modernism which included new roles for women. The center of the society was united with the periphery but the periphery's 'clientelistic vertical ties' became more instrumental in this than the center's ideology of modernism.

The interpretation of modernization and a new definition of gender roles

In the late Ottoman period, the preservation of the state was the dominant ideological framework of the Western-minded bureaucrats and the intelligentsia who thought of separating the state from Islamic institutions, but 'realized how much religion counted for the rural and urban masses . . . among the less privileged Islam was still a guide for behavior at the community level as well as the guise under which family structure characteristics, such as patriarchal rule and the subjection of women, were perpetuated' (Mardin, 1977: 286). While the division between the temporal and the spiritual aspects of the state was being strengthened, there emerged two different cultures, separating careers from ideological and religious affiliations, marriage customs and other traditional aspects of everyday life. The resistance to change developed into a political and ideological struggle for power between the two groups, which in various forms still persists.

A look at the ideology of the Young Turks is necessary to understand their approach to secularism and modernity. It must be recalled that it was in that same time that Europe itself was working on answers to questions of secularism and modernity. While European sociologists were looking for definitions of their own societies, Young Turks were trying to understand the social context of theirs. In short, they were looking for a European model of modernization without becoming European, a way to secularize while keeping a Muslim identity. They redefined the concepts of progress, positivism, secularism, and nationalism in relation to the way they understood the situation of the sultanate, the role of Islam, Ottomanism and issues of cultural policies. The state always remained very important in their thinking (with the exception of Prince Sabahattin). Separating religion from the functioning of the state, they saw it not as the ultimate truth but as the social cement that functioned as the moral system holding the society together (as in Durkheim's theory). Thus, they thought Europeanization and modernization were possible without changing the moral order of the society.

In sociological theory, the problem of individuality is a problem of modernity. In French social theory, particularly in Durkheim, rituals are free from subjective elements and individualistic conceptions. This was an attractive idea for those who wished to keep the rituals of the society while modernizing the frames of minds of individuals. Theorists among the Young Turks agreed that a cultural policy had to be developed either in consonance with, or supplemented by, Europeanization. For example, according to Ziya Gokalp (a student of Durkheim's views), culture by itself was not enough to build a modern nation-state; there had to be a union of civilization and culture. He sought to understand these two elements so that he could reduce Western civilization to its material and scientific developments and combine it with Turkish religion and culture. Gokalp differentiated religion and culture as well. He argued that the Turkish nation or society was possible not only through religion but by all other factors of the collective consciousness, such as by values, language, literature, and customs.

Along these lines, in the early years of the republican era, the emancipation of women was sought. By the Civil Code of 1926 polygamy was abolished and new rights were given to women by which they could seek divorce. 'Women were allowed to vote and be elected, first in the municipalities (April 3, 1930), the village councils of elders (October 26, 1933), and finally in national elections for the Grand National Assembly (December 1934). Women were admitted to the public schools, the civil-service, and the professions on an increasingly equal basis with men' (Shaw and Shaw, 1977: 385). A ban on veiling was proposed in 1935 but no action was taken, although Ataturk saw the practice as barbarous and uncivilized. In some municipalities, there were orders against women's traditional clothing. It is a common practice to cite incidences where soldiers would forcibly remove the veils of women, although there is no evidence to the extent of these happenings. What was actually happening at that time was the forcing of modernism, legitimated on the grounds of civilization which meant progress and reason.

By the time the nation-state was established, the resistance between the center and the provinces of the country had turned into a power struggle for the control of the institutional structures of the state. This struggle was between the periphery, unified under the domain of religion, and the state espousing modernity, nationalism and centrality (Ozbudun, 1976). The provincial towns and rural masses, not having been integrated to the newly developed systems, were foreigners to the abstract political principles of citizenship and democracy; they opted for the communal and/or religious bonding of clientelistic-vertical ties whose notables effectively used the infrastructures built by the center itself. As Mardin puts it, 'an infrastructure of new institutions emerged which functioned outside the state and at a national level' (Mardin, 1977: 293). The growth in the private sector of the economy, education, the market system, were taken advantage of by the periphery in order to capture the machinery of the state (Mardin, 1977: 293). The ideas of nationalism and economic development became a part of the ideological discourse as the principles of 'Westernism' were disassociated more and more from 'modernity' (Toprak, 1984). As pointed out in the previous section, modernization had also been disassociated from the ideology of modernism, the former retained but the latter rejected as only Westernism rather than civilization.

Looking back, attempts to liberate women were more than restrictions against a mode of dress, further education or establishing legal rights. These attempts were the fight between one mode of social and global consciousness and another for the ways in which individuals, classes and the symbolic order of the society were going to be constructed. As has been witnessed in the last decade, similar struggles are still being waged in Turkey and in other parts of the Islamic world. Recent developments once again prove that religious movements are not limited to demands to practice private beliefs, but are political and ideological movements to change the social system.

Today, given the threat of fundamentalism, it has become important to claim and take advantage of the legal and institutional rights that were defined in the thirties, rather than take them for granted. Women in some other Islamic countries are still struggling for those rights. For example, Egypt and Algeria have distanced themselves from the dominant cultural-symbolic systems of their colonizing powers with policies centered on religion, patriarchal family and women. Fortunately, Turkish women do not have to fight for personal laws and legal rights at a time when the fundamentalist movement, with its control of the state structures, is making it difficult to maintain and apply those that are already in effect.

Gender roles in Turkey can be assessed by the dominance of patriarchal systems; fast urbanization within an underdeveloped economy and conservative politics; and the historical presence of a modernist elite who have challenged the dominant values regarding women's place in public life and have made an impact that is hopefully not easily reversible. However, the lack of cohesiveness among women is the most important consequence of these conditions. As in various other dimensions of the society, there are pockets of modernism scattered here and there and traditionalism in other places. While women in their turbans are becoming professionals and are supported by the dominant ideology of the state, modern women are finding themselves locked away from professions and the labour market due to hard economic conditions. Neither unity nor a sense of shared identity materializes, preventing women from becoming a group-for-itself.

Urbanism, fundamentalism and modernism: challenges to women

Today most of the countries outside the Western world are facing problems of rapid urbanization and population growth. For example, in 1923 when the republic was formed, the population of Turkey was about 13 million. In 1945 the population had reached 18.8 million, of which only 18.3 per cent were living in urban areas (in cities with 10,000 or more population) (Shorter and Macura, 1983: 55). By 1980 this figure had reached 45 million. Today, the urban population has risen to 47 per cent of the entire population, according to the World Bank World Development Report of 1980. In about one generation, the urban population has gone from 3.5 million to 25 million.

   This increase in the size of the population and especially that of urban areas has resulted in an increase in the amount of contact between cities of all sizes. In metropolitan centers one can observe with relative ease the structures of social change, the reciprocal relationship between rural transformation and urban industrial growth. However, a major part of the population still lives in towns whose sizes range between those of villages and the major metropolises. This group of town people, with their life styles and the ways in which they have accommodated to the urban life, have contributed to the political and ideological structures and have been defining the new character of the urban centers.

   Looking into the world of this segment of the population contributes to an understanding not only of people's relationship to religious beliefs and practices, but also, most significantly, of the place of women in terms of their gender-role identities. One can easily argue that the most conservative and religious world-views determine the place of women in small towns. But rapid social transformation has brought them in contact with the wider world through various means such as television. Contact with the wives and daughters of professionals and local civil servants has presented to them alternative life styles, and has shown how social prestige and privilege can come through education and big city life. In becoming urban, traditionalists do not reject everything that modernization has to offer. As seen in the increasing numbers of fundamentalist women in higher education, today women's education is becoming more and more acceptable to all segments of the society. Slowly, as modernization is separated from modernism, the contradiction of attributing a positive value to education and knowledge and holding on to traditional gender-roles at the same time disappears.

Meanwhile, 'urban' and 'urban culture' have gained new meanings as people coming from the provincial towns (or just being born to them in large numbers) have largely adapted the urban way of life to theirs rather than vice versa. People now live not only in their communities but in the entire global order. Projecting their position in the world social-political and economic system to their world-views and religious beliefs, they not only create fundamentalism as historical continuity and particularistic identity, but also reflect back on to their existence within this given world order. The modern offerings of that order, such as mass communication, education and transportation, become effectively used vehicles in this process.

Having to live together, the common cultural field of the masses and the modernists, now in total awareness of each other, is created 'as a place of symbolic struggles which has a logic of its own, but which also in certain respects mirrors the political and economic struggles within the economy and the state' (Turner, 1988: 71). The modernists do not stand as a class, defined economically, against the masses, but as a different status group. Hence while fundamentalism becomes the cultural domain of both the ruling hegemonic groups and their clients, those groups left out of the economic gains need to pursue an opposition to the cultural hegemony, now, interestingly, of the masses. In this context, the struggle for modernity and for economic and political rights has to make the issue of women's rights a central focus.

Note

I wish to thank Sam Baskett and Sharon Baştuğ for their careful reading and editing of the text for its English.

References

Berman, M. (1983) *All that is Solid Melts into Air*. London: Verso.
Curtin, L.B. (1982) *Status of Women: A Comparative Analysis of Twenty Developing Countries*. Reports on the World Fertility Survey 5, Population Bureau, Inc., June.
Frisby, D. (1986) *Fragments of Modernity*. Cambridge Mass.: The MIT Press.
Gellner, E. (1983) *Nations and Nationalism*. Ithaca and London: Cornell University Press.
Hobsbawm, E. and Ringer, T. (eds) (1984) *The Invention of Tradition*. Cambridge: Cambridge University Press.
Hatem, M. (1986) 'The enduring alliance of nationalism and patriarchy in Muslim personal status laws: the case of modern Egypt', *Feminist Issues*, Spring: 19–43.
Jowkar, F. (1988) 'Honor and shame: a feminist view from within', *Feminist Issues*, Spring: 45–65.
Lazreg, M. (1988) 'Feminism and difference: the perils of writing as a woman on women in Algeria', *Feminist Studies*, 14(1).
Mardin, S. (1977) 'Religion in modern Turkey', *International Social Science Journal*, 29(2).
Ozbudun, E. (1976) *Social Change and Political Participation in Turkey*. Princeton: Princeton University Press.
Robertson, R. and Lechner, F. (1985) 'Modernization, globalization and the problem of culture in world-systems theory', *Theory, Culture and Society*, 2(3): 103–17.

Shaw, S. and Shaw, E. (1977) *History of the Ottoman Empire and Modern Turkey*. Cambridge: Cambridge University Press.

Shorter, F.C. and Macura, M. (1983) *Turkiye'de Nifus Artisi (1935–1975)*. Ankara: Yurt Yayin Evi. (*Population Increase in Turkey 1935–1975*. Washington DC: National Academy Press, 1982.)

Toprak, B. (1984) 'Politicization of Islam in a secular state: the National Salvation Party in Turkey', in S.A. Arjomand (ed.), *From Nationalism to Revolutionary Islam*. Albany: State University of New York Press.

Turner, B.S. (1988) *Status*. Minneapolis: University of Minnesota Press.

11

WOMEN BETWEEN MODERNITY AND POSTMODERNITY

Lieteke van Vucht Tijssen

Women and citizenship

One of the major goals of the women's movement has always been the acquisition of full citizenship; that is to say, of the same civil, political and social rights as men. It is well known that women at present have succeeded to a considerable extent in realizing this goal, at least at a formal level. Since the beginning of the nineteenth century, the situation of women has changed a great deal. Legally, women are citizens in the same sense as men. They have the vote now; they can go to the same schools and learn the same things as men do; they no longer have to work eighteen hours a day; they do not depend necessarily on a husband for income and status, and women can sign contracts without the consent of their husbands. Yet in many respects the equality between men and women is still a matter of formality. In practice within Western societies (and more visibly in non-Western societies), there still exists a division between the world of women and the world of men. For example, men do not generally share household duties on an equal basis with their wives, and women themselves guard their domains zealously against the intrusion of men. On the labour market, there exists an analogous division of labour. Some sectors such as nursing are almost fully in the hands of women, while others remain the domains of men. Moreover, women's jobs on the whole carry less status and are paid less than those of men. In its turn the segregation of the labour market is rooted in the segregation of school and university education.

In order to realize equal participation, economic and social conditions have to be fulfilled, but these changes are not in themselves sufficient. Equal rights between women and men are not self-evident. They are part of social arrangements, they are rooted in culture and have to be maintained in social interaction. So women must remain politically active if they want to retain what rights they have won and if they want to win more. For that, women need long-term goals embedded in ideals. As Max Weber showed a long time ago, what happens at the cultural and ideological level can be of crucial importance for the subsequent turn of events. Cultural and ideological factors certainly can stimulate or arrest social developments. Thus, ideals about the role of women can assist the emancipation of woman to a full citizenship, but they also can bring it to a halt.

The ideal of equal rights is derived from the ideology of modernity: the philosophy of the Enlightenment. Postmodernism in its turn takes a critical stance against the heritage of the Enlightenment and opposes the grand narratives of modernity. Instead of equality, it emphasizes the idea of difference. The link between postmodernism and feminism is still a weak one, but there are several possible elective affinities between them. The most important is the one with the radical feminist theories which in one way or another use the idea of difference as a political weapon, as for example radical feminist theory initiated by Firestone or French poststructuralism (Knipnis, 1988). Those feminist authors who favour this kind of alliance point to two common denominators: (1) a shared criticism and deconstruction of the philosophy of the Enlightenment and its emphasis on (male) rationality; and (2) a positive evaluation of socio-cultural and cognitive differences (Flax, 1987: 623–6). Another possibility is an alliance between postmodernism and the feminist approach that perceives the differences between men and women and the differences between women themselves, as reasons for a differential treatment (Fraser and Nicholson, 1988). Apart from that, on the level of research there seems to be a link between Baudrillard's brand of postmodernism and the type of research generated by feminist anthropologists working in the interpretive tradition. However, before welcoming one of the possibilities just mentioned too readily, an attempt should be made to assess the consequences of the fusion of the ideas of postmodernism and feminism for the participation of women as full citizens, both on the level of ideas and in practice.

In this chapter I will confront both modernization and postmodernism in terms of their effects for the attainment and realization of citizenship rights by women. Modernization, understood within the tradition of Weber and Durkheim as the simultaneous rationalization of economy, politics, culture and knowledge, is a main long-term trend in Western society. By now it is relatively easy to assess what it has done to women. Although the movement began in the thirties, the popularity of postmodernism is relatively recent. It is therefore much harder to get a clear view of its final impact on the situation of women. Yet, with respect to the most important possibility, an alliance between postmodernism and radical feminism, we have a kind of yardstick. A nineteenth-century counter-trend, which in several ways can be considered to be the forerunner of postmodernism, is the Counter-Enlightenment. This tradition generated a number of ideal images of how to be a woman in modern society. These images determined to a great extent, at first indirectly and later directly, the policy of the largest German women's association: the *Bund Deutsche Frauenvereine* (the BDF). They also influenced the way in which many upper- and middle-class women organized their lives. Both the images offered to women by modernization and by the forerunner of postmodernism, the Counter-Enlightenment, are connected with ideas about citizenship rights for women.

Women and modernity

For women's emancipation to full citizenship, the consequences of modernization have been rather paradoxical. During the nineteenth century, economic developments in every European country had roughly the same consequences for women. The rationalization of the economy and the growth of capitalism stimulated, if not triggered, the segregation of production and housework which is so characteristic of modern society. This trend towards a split between the public and the domestic spheres, together with extremely low wages and land reforms, for example in England, forced lower-class women to enter the labour force in large numbers. Although it was economically unavoidable because of the low income per capita, the participation of female workers in the labour market did not meet with the general approval of men. In many areas, male workers perceived female workers as direct competitors for their own jobs. Thus time and again, they undertook organized action in order to drive women out of the labour force, or at least to push them back into the lower-status and lower-paid jobs. For example, in England and France the attempt, around the middle of the nineteenth century, to hire women as setters was met by much resistance from male setters. In Germany there were even several revolts by men against women, while the tailors' union of Berlin also tried to ban women from gaining access to their trades. In Paris the setters succeeded in passing a law which excluded women officially from this type of work. Where they had less legal success, male workers adopted more informal means of discouragement (such as shouting insults at the women who attempted to enter the gates of the factory). Everywhere men greeted female colleagues with hatred and mistrust (Braun, 1901: 222; Rowbotham, 1973: 59; Frevert, 1988: 92–6).

The reason for this resistance to women entering the labour force was mainly economic. Female workers were prepared to accept far lower wages than men, they often were strike-breakers and they allowed themselves to be overexploited (Braun, 1901: 223). Thus women lowered the general wages and hindered men in their attempt to attain better conditions. However, because employers had already discovered that women (and children) acted as a reserve of cheap labour, men never fully succeeded in driving women out of the labour force. On the contrary, their numbers increased steadily, and in the second half of the century the number of women working in the factories in many European countries was not far below that of men. For example, in 1891 in France, there were 4,990,635 male factory workers to 3,584,518 female ones. In England in the same year, there were 5,368,865 male to 3,113,256 female workers. In Austria, the women even outnumbered the men (4,363,074 men to 5,310,639 women). The only notable exception was Germany, where the number of women remained about half that of men, 9,295,082 men to 5,293,277 women (Braun, 1901: 247). Although unsuccessful in their attempt fully to exclude women, the male workers succeeded in pushing women and foreign workers into the jobs with the lowest wages and the least status. At the same time, there was a growing differentiation of the labour market into specific male and female sectors. Thus, at the end of the century, women occupied a significant position in the production of lace and knitted cloth, in the binding of books, in the fabrication of cotton and in cleaning jobs. On the other hand, men dominated glassblowing, printing, the making of furniture, and the coal and steel industries (Braun, 1901: 261).

It is often alleged that for middle-class women the rationalization of the economy had consequences which were quite opposite to those for lower-class women. While lower-class women were forced out to work, the separation of home and work seemed to drive middle-class women back into the home. In the eighteenth century, most upper-class and upper-middle-class women had been liberated from the necessity to earn their own income. Their main task was to run their households and to be acceptable companions for their husbands. However, already by the end of the century this situation came to an end for many women. The impoverishment of the nobility and the old bourgeoisie, and the increased ratio of single women resulting from the high mortality rate of men involved in wars and revolution, forced many formerly dependent women to earn their own living. Thus, in the second half of the eighteenth century, many women with a privileged background were already obliged to take jobs as governesses, as ladies' maids, as companions or dressmakers (Braun, 1901: 101). The economic and social developments of the nineteenth century only aggravated this situation. In 1851 in England, there were already about two million single women who were forced to earn their own living (Braun, 1901: 112).

While throughout the whole of Europe an increasing number of women were forced to enter the labour market, the nineteenth-century ideals surrounding the role of women in modern Western society were not inspired by their ways of life. Instead the typically modern notions of women's roles were generated by the distinct life-style of the rather small category formed by the married upper- and upper-middle-class women. The rising new middle class took over from the nobility and the old middle class the practice of having their wives as full-time housekeepers and mothers. As this practice became an important status symbol for the men, married middle-class women increasingly attempted to concentrate exclusively on running their homes and educating their children. Indeed, at the beginning of the nineteenth century, running a middle-class home (with all the cooking, washing, ironing, cleaning, bottling of vegetables, drying of meat, baking and supervising of personnel) was a full-time job, even though a lot of the work was carried out by servants. When, in the second half of the century, industrial production rendered most of this domestic work superfluous, middle-class men and women not only held on to the ideal of the full-time housewife and mother, but they cherished it more strongly than before.

At the level of the economy, two separate developments enhanced this specialization of women in domestic life. One development was the substitution of the male wage by a family wage, thus enabling women to stay at home

and take care of the household and children. The other development was the
'democratization of luxury'. In the second half of the nineteenth century the
rise in average income of the middle-class family, combined with the relatively low prices of factory-produced commodities, provided married
middle-class women with new means to furnish and decorate their homes
elaborately. Moreover, the leisure they gained by replacing home-made by
ready-made commodities also allowed them to acquire, to a certain extent,
the erudition and the artistic skills formerly reserved for upper-class women.
For example, around the middle of the century, many bourgeois families
possessed a pianoforte. Daughters received piano and singing lessons, and
sitting rooms were crowded with furniture, with pictures, bric-à-brac and the
like. Yet for many middle-class women, their retreat from the labour-
market did not mean that they could restrict themselves to housekeeping
and raising children. On the contrary (and particularly when their husbands
were self-employed), middle-class women often had to assist their husbands
(Frevert, 1986: 66–8). Thus, in practice, the number of middle-class women
who could afford to behave as a kind of leisure class was rather limited. Yet it
was precisely this small group that functioned as role-models for women in
general, with the result that working for money for a 'real lady' was
considered to be very undesirable (Wilson, 1977: 4).

The tendency to restrain the participation of women in the labour-market
was accompanied by the continuation of the exclusion of women from the
public sphere. Middle-class women attended their own organizations and
meeting places. These activities fitted in with their roles as wives and
mothers, and included work for charities and/or religious organizations
(Frevert, 1988). Yet other public affairs, such as administration, politics,
science and art, remained as before the specific domain of men. An unintended consequence of this gender division of labour, combined with the
parallel rationalization of male work in the public sphere, was the simultaneous 'genderification' of the rational and the emotional capacities of
people. Values such as rationality, objectivity, logical thinking and matter-
of-factedness came to be considered primarily as masculine. At the same
time, the ideology that legitimated the new role of the middle-class women
not only proclaimed women's foremost destination as wives and mothers,
but also stamped them as the keepers of the dimension of human existence
that was ignored in the domain of men: the emotional, the intuitive and the
caring. 'Women provided the nest, the retreat, the temple to which the
bourgeois businessmen could return to rest from the harsh world of
commerce' (Wilson, 1977: 22). Women were to be the angels in the house.
In all European countries the presupposition of this ideology was that these
nurturing capacities were instilled in woman's nature; that is to say, in her
body and therefore also in her mind. Put positively, it was her physical
capacities, and in particular having a womb and being able to bear children,
that made her also mentally fit for all of the caring tasks. Negatively
formulated, her lack of muscular strength and the lower weight of her brain
made her unfit to participate in the world of men (Braun, 1901: 190).

Over time these ideals also came to be shared by many men and women of the lower class, even though there was little chance that the lower classes could realize them. In many ways this idealization of middle-class life was quite understandable. In practice lower-class women were the first category to be confronted with two roles. After long working days in factories or shops, these women also had to clothe and feed husbands and children, often in difficult circumstances (Wilson, 1977: 20; Rowbotham, 1973: 25). Many poor and exhausted working-class women would gladly have changed positions to live the comfortable, relatively carefree and healthy lives of real ladies. Further, as doctors discovered, full-time maternal care proved to be important for the survival of the new-born in the first months of their lives. Thus full-time mothering became even more important for women than it had been before (Frevert, 1988). Many lower-class men (and women) also regretted the loss of their traditional way of life. They feared the independence of their wives and daughters, working under another roof and with other men and then returning home with their own wages. Many men experienced women's working autonomy as a threat to their own authority over their family. Thus an increasing number of lower-class men came to feel that they also should be paid a wage that was enough to keep themselves and their families (Rowbotham, 1973: 5–33). The workers' quest for emancipation in many European countries therefore included a battle for women to be able to stay at home.

Following Weber and Durkheim, modernization as the rationalization of economy, culture, politics and knowledge has been considered to be the main trend in the development of Western society. Passions are not denied, but they have been directed to the province of the personal and subjective, rather than to the social order. There always have been counter-movements, such as the romantics and the decadents in the nineteenth century and the vitalists and surrealists in the twentieth century, that promoted the realm of feeling over that of reason. Yet sociologists have interpreted these movements as outpourings of something that is fundamentally alien to modernity and hence to rationality. Nevertheless, the founding fathers, especially Comte, de Tocqueville, Spencer, Weber, Durkheim and Simmel, were well aware of the problematic status of the non-rational in terms of the upheaval which modernization had brought about in gender relations. They also perceived as an important characteristic of modernization an ongoing differentiation between the tasks of men and those of women. With the notable exception of de Tocqueville and Weber, most of the founding fathers of modernization theory even assumed that women should take the so-called expressive role, while men should fulfil the instrumental one. Thus, Comte saw in women spiritual power and the power of love, which incidentally he valued over the futile superiority of male intelligence which supposedly women lacked. For Durkheim, just as for Comte, modern society would fall apart without this division of tasks between men and women (Lepenies, 1985: 2–48); Kandall, 1988: 49–89, 126–82). Simmel, moreover, held that it was women's destiny to redeem the fragmentation from which men suffer in a highly differentiated society (Simmel, 1985: 159–75). All of them perceived these spiritual and nurturing qualities of women as highly valuable characteristics. These ideas were not accidental or arbitrary manifestations of the ideology of their times. On the contrary, for each of these thinkers, their ideas with respect to women and emotions were intimately linked with their general modernization theory.

Despite the attention paid by the founding fathers to women and modernity, there exists a vast gulf in present social theory between the sociology of modernization on the one hand, and women's studies on the other. This is a pity. It means in the end that theories of modernization do not sufficiently take into account the restructuring of gender relationships as a fundamental characteristic of modernity. Nor have women's studies tried to explain the transformation of the roles of the sexes (and the resistance to this) in terms of theories of modernization. Yet if we take seriously the ideas of the founding fathers relating to women (while putting aside their normative and sexist undertones), it is obvious that they saw modernization also as the separation of spheres of passions and intimacy, on the one hand, and the exercise of rationality, on the other. Seen from this point of view the 'passionalization' of marriage and family life (and to a certain extent art and religion) stands not in opposition to modernization, but is intimately bound up with the processes of rationalization itself. It goes without saying that the strong ideological support for identifying women largely with the emotional side of life stimulated the continuation of the segregation of the domains of men and those of women rather than furthered the equality of both sexes (Frevert, 1986: 228ff.).

Yet for many women, from the point of view of their civil rights, there were plenty of reasons to demand equality between the sexes. Although an increasing number of single women in the course of the nineteenth century were forced to earn their own income, jobs were simply not available. The main possibilities for women lay in teaching, nursing or clerical duties, but even then the demand for jobs was much greater than the opportunities. According to an investigation carried out by the Seine department in France at the end of the century, 8000 candidates had applied for 193 teaching jobs, while the Banque de France could choose among 6000 applicants for five positions (Braun, 1901: 180). It was not simply the single women who had cause for complaint. Married women were equally aggrieved. Although the economic and social positions of middle- and lower-class women were very different, with respect to their civil rights they shared a common fate. All over Europe and the United States in the first half of the nineteenth century, married women and their children were considered legally to be the property of their husbands and fathers. Without the consent of their husbands, women could not go out to work. If women had some money of their own when entering marriage, it became their husband's property and the money they earned had to be handed over to him. Married women in most European countries had no legal status of their own. Furthermore, men could decide about the education and future of the children (Rowbotham,

1973: 55–60). Thus, while the history of citizenship starts for men in the late eighteenth century with the acquisition of basic civil rights – that is, the right to sell their own labour and to dispose of the profits of their own land – modernization for women meant nothing of the kind. Instead, it brought women into a position of greater dependence.

One of the reasons why middle-class women failed to find appropriate jobs, apart from the economic situation, was their lack of education. The transfer of large parts of the educational function from the family to schools, starting in the early nineteenth century, meant that girls had even fewer opportunities to acquire skills. The institutionalization of teaching within schools and universities only improved education for boys. The few attempts to create separate schools for girls were thwarted by lack of support from the state (Braun, 1901: 102–8). If schools provided some kind of education for girls, it remained far behind what was offered to boys. The systematization and rationalization of the educational system during the nineteenth century at first also worked in favour of the boys (Müller et al., 1987). High-schools were intended to prepare boys for careers, while the education of girls in most European countries was meant to prepare them primarily for the role of wives and mothers, a role that many of them would never be permitted to play. This exclusion of women from the social rights of citizenship, combined with the lack of civil rights, proved to be an important basis for the rise of a feminist movement from the middle of the nineteenth century.

Freedom, equality and solidarity

Seen in terms of economic and social developments, modernization can be understood to have created for women precisely the conditions against which feminists have rebelled. Yet it is too hasty to judge modernity as having been wholly negative for women. Certainly modernity is not the great liberator of women it is sometimes supposed to be. In many respects the immediate results of modernization continued and aggravated conditions that already existed in pre-modern society. On the other hand, the ideological and cognitive offspring of modernization (in particular the ideology of the Enlightenment with its *Projekt der Moderne*) provided the women who wanted to free themselves from the bonds of the female existence with the strongest ideological weapons available. This is not to say that the ideal of citizenship, denoting freedom, equality and brotherhood, as it was originally developed by the French philosophers, was meant to include women. Leading 'philosophes' like Voltaire and Diderot did regard their female companions as intellectual equals. Voltaire, for example, thought of his mistress Madame de Chatelet as an excellent scientist and intellectual. Diderot praised the intelligence of Madame d'Epinay, who was the intellectual and emotional companion of his friend Grimm. Voltaire and Diderot encouraged these women actively to participate in the public scientific discussion of their times (Badinter, 1983). Yet, on the whole, they did not favour in their own writings the emancipation of women into full citizens. Diderot could even be regarded as blatantly sexist. To make things worse, Rousseau, the founding father of so many nineteenth-century ideas on women's specific roles, was something of a fallen angel of the Enlightenment.

The only Enlightenment philosopher who explicitly favoured equal rights for men and women was Condorcet. He was the first to demand, in several of his articles and pamphlets, equal political rights for women. He even predicted a time when the heritage of Enlightenment and reason would abolish not only slavery and inhuman work but also the differences between the roles of women and men (Gay, 1968/70). Indeed the *Déclaration des Droits de l'Homme* proved to be for men only. Despite the fact that women had actively participated in revolutionary activities and believed that they could appropriate for themselves the rights for which they had fought, they were quite brutally turned down by the men. In 1792 the French Convention declared that women were not citizens. In the same year all the political clubs women had founded before and during the Revolution were closed. The revolutionary authorities even beheaded a woman called Olympe des Gouge, because, as a critic of the Convention, she had written a declaration of her own: the Declaration of the Rights of Women. Three years later women were prohibited from attending any political meetings (Kandall, 1988: 53). It was not until the beginning of the nineteenth century that the inheritors of the Enlightenment, like the Saint-Simonians, explicitly linked its ideas with the emancipation of women. These philosophers were joined by still more radical thinkers, such as Fourier, who emphasized what we now call the social construction of the so-called nature of women. At the same time, French feminist thinkers like Jenny d'Herincourt and Juliette Lambert used the ideas of the Enlightenment in order to plead for the civic emancipation of woman and for women's right to equal education. Their focus lay not primarily on women's minds but on their bodies. As men were legally still entitled to dispose of their wives' bodies and wages, the drive for universal citizenship strove in the first place for women's rights to dispose of their own bodies and labour.

Long before the Saint-Simonians developed their ideas, the first English woman to formulate a feminist ideology, Mary Wollstonecraft, had been inspired by the Scottish version of the Enlightenment. However, the ideas of the Saint-Simonians or utopian socialists have been of great importance for the English women's movement. Their ideas informed such English male ideologues as Thompson, James Mill and John Stuart Mill. J.S. Mill, under the influence also of his wife Henriëtte, developed even into one of the most vehement and intelligent defenders of equal citizenship rights for men and women. In his famous essay 'The Subjection of Women' he argued that women are intellectually and morally the equals of men and that they are entitled to the same rights as men. At the same time, women can be expected to contribute independently to the development of society and culture. In nineteenth-century Europe, this essay became the focus of many of the debates surrounding feminism.

Postmodernism and the abortion of emancipation

What postmodernism amounts to – an accurate mirroring of our present condition, a new trend in art and literature, or a fruitful critique of the grand narratives of modernity – is not yet clear. However, its core theme is a radical critique of the grand evolutionary and dialectical narratives of modernity. Traditionally, the equality of all people has been part of the grand narrative of the Enlightenment as Progress. Discarding this narrative means discarding the idea of Western (male) rationality as the ultimate standard against which each and everyone should be measured, and opening the way for paying attention to differences as well as to an equal evaluation of all groups and cultures, including female ones. Postmodernism with its indifference to all differences, its abolition of an Archimedean point, as well as its hermeneutic approach, has an elective affinity with the radical trend in feminism, which eschewed gender equality and greeted differences as the main principle of feminism. Representatives of this approach like Firestone want to claim separate fields for women in which they could develop themselves according to their own principles and potentialities without being hindered by men. For that, instead of continuing to protest against the traditional images of women, they deliberately return to the old models. They claim that women are more caring, more intuitive and less competitive than men and that therefore women could play an important role in counter-balancing the one-sided emphasis that men had placed on rationality. Though the French post-structuralists do away with the idea of biologically founded differences between the sexes, they still conceive of the female voice as having to claim specific spaces in discourse; that is to say, the spaces not occupied by the male 'phallocentric' voice. The question is: what would an alliance between postmodernism and these radical feminisms mean for women's quest for equal citizenship rights?

Though history is a great chain of unique events, sometimes we can use it to learn something. In the nineteenth-century German middle-class feminist movement we have a historical example of a feminist movement that used differences between men and women as its main ideological weapon. More-over, round the turn of the century in Germany the theory of gender differences was linked to the forerunners of postmodernism. As with the other European movements, German feminism of the first wave was originally much inspired by the Enlightenment and the ideal of equality. However, probably under the pressure of the massive attack of the German male intelligentsia on the first German translation of John Stuart Mill's essay *The Subjection of Women*, German feminists soon abandoned this idea. In about 1860 the liberal bourgeois union, which dominated the German feminist movement, the *Bund Deutscher Frauenvereine*, changed its radical ideology for a more modest and ambiguous one. Instead of trying to abolish existing inequalities, they attempted to acquire more privileges for women because of their ostensibly unique qualities within the existing system. The core of the ideology that accompanied this turn was the confirmation of the idea that there existed radical differences between men and women, which required different callings for both of them. Of course, women were specialists in the caring task and jobs. However, in the eyes of the leaders of the BDF, women's specific nature did not necessarily confine them to home and children. Women's nurturant skills also enabled them to contribute to culture and society in general. Moreover, they argued that this contribution was an essential one. Against this background the BDF propagated three principles: (1) that a harmonious culture is based on an equal contribution of men and women; (2) that women's activities are a necessary and therefore valuable contribution to culture; and (3) that the content of their contribution should depend on their specific nature. In short, the BDF tried to upgrade the low status of women's roles in society, as well as to widen their field of action in the public domain. That they preferred this strategy over the equality-oriented one does not mean that the role of German women was more advanced than in other European countries. On the contrary, in the middle of the nineteenth century, German girls could already gain access to some education; however female education was restricted to preparation for the traditional female roles – that is, to home economics. Moreover, German girls could attend school up to a maximum of nine years, while boys were entitled to twelve years. Because the institutions for higher education only admitted those with twelve years' education, girls became automatically excluded beforehand. The only form of higher education available to German girls was the teacher's seminar.

With respect to civil and political rights, the situation for German women was as backward as that experienced by women in other European countries, while for women's sexuality the double standard of sexual morality was also the same as elsewhere. Thus German feminists met with as much injustice as other European feminists. Nevertheless, when it came to education and providing jobs, the BDF under the guidance of Helene Lange and Auguste Schmitt sought two quite limited goals: the betterment of education for girls, and permission for women to study medicine. In themselves these goals were quite respectable. Yet these concrete claims fitted all too neatly within their limited conception of women. Instead of demanding equal education for men and women, they pleaded for still better preparation of girls for their tasks as women. Their plans barred girls from all so-called 'male' subjects like mathematics and science, and included instead subjects like German history, religion and ethics. German feminists also insisted that girls would be taught only by women. Their attempts to enable women to penetrate into the medical world were informed by similar motives. The specific qualities of women, they argued, made them better suited for medicine than men. Female patients often only wanted to deal with female doctors.

Apart from medicine, German feminists did not undertake any further action to have women admitted to the universities. With respect to better access to the labour-market, they followed a similar strategy. Instead of fighting for more and better paid jobs, they urged their members (who then

ゝered 11,000) to undertake all kinds of voluntary, charity work. Ultima-
y they did succeed in encouraging a lot of women to participate actively in
public life. In areas like caring for the poor, women were even so successful
that at the end of the century, they could claim it fully as their own.
Participation in public life gave women the self-confidence to demand
membership of schoolboards and voluntary organizations, and in the end to
even demand the vote. Yet, in spite of these small successes achieved
through adopting the ideology of difference and the belonging strategy,
compared to the achievements of the women's movement in other countries
the balance was negative. For example, compared with English, Swiss,
Dutch and French women, German women were very late in gaining access
to fully-fledged higher academic education. With respect to civil rights and
better economic conditions, German women achieved virtually nothing.
Around 1880 the German middle-class feminist movement stagnated. Its
tactic became increasingly timid and conservative. The movement avoided
any public conflict and declared itself a faithful adherent of the traditional
ideology of motherhood.

German feminism had only a short period, between 1890 and 1910, when
equality reigned as its ultimate goal. In this period German feminists
adopted the more politically oriented and aggressive tactics of the English
feminists and the results were dramatic. They succeeded in getting women
admitted to universities and for the first time women were granted the right
to attend political meetings. Within marriage women also gained more
rights, while the provisions for unmarried pregnant women and mothers
with small children were enlarged. The ultimate goals of full civil and
political rights for women, however, were still not realized. Before more
progress could be made, an internal power struggle put an end to the reign of
radicals like Minna Cauer, Hedwig Dohm and Marianne Stritt. These
radicals were replaced by a number of women who resorted to the old idea of
the specific nature of femininity (Evans, 1976). Gertrud Bäumer, who in
1910 became the new president of the BDF, even presented the old model as
a far more refined and modern ideal than the crude type of equality that the
radicals had propagated. As a pupil and friend of Helene Lange, Bäumer
argued again that the fundamental value of women for society lay in their
female nature.

The main goal for the emancipation of women, therefore, could only be
the penetration of female values into general culture: equivalence instead of
equality. According to Bäumer, equal rights were relevant to the extent that
they furthered the development of female properties and capacities. That
was only the case to a limited extent. The German feminist movement
therefore did not try to gain access to all professions, but only to find niches
suited for women's capacities. Ironically, in that quest they were greatly
helped by the development of new industries and trades, which created new
female domains such as saleswoman and typist. In the end their own
contribution came down to a mere legitimation of the ongoing and to some
extent growing segregation of the labour market into male and female

domains, whereas the female spheres remained the underrated and lower-paid ones. The new 'wave' again proclaimed motherhood as the essence of femininity. As a consequence, everything that related to motherhood and family was brought under the title of emancipation and in due time motherhood even became the main goal. Many German women abandoned the battle for equal rights, often with a sigh of relief.

The idea that women have a specific nature of their own was not only held by representatives of the Counter-Enlightenment like Herder and Goethe and around the turn of the nineteenth century by Nietzsche, Simmel and Scheler, but also by German founders of the Enlightenment like Kant and Hegel. On the level of content, there was little difference between the ideas of both groups. Both the representatives of the Enlightenment and of the Counter-Enlightenment conceived of women as emotionally unified, subject-oriented, understanding and caring creatures. However, there was a huge gap between them with respect to the values attached to this loving being. The Enlightenment thinkers considered women to be the second sex that could only flourish in the company of men. Of course, this idea did not meet with the approval of the leaders of the *Bund Deutscher Frauenvereine*. Their ideas rather had an elective affinity with the tradition of Goethe and Herder as it was developed by people like Scheler and especially by Simmel. These authors considered, in contrast to Kant and Hegel, the specific qualities of women as having their autonomous roots in women's nature and moreover as being able to be developed independently of men. These ideas were elaborated in particular by Simmel who broke through the magic circle many philosophers had drawn round the sexes. Simmel allowed women to follow their own destiny apart from men. Yet Marianne Weber, wife of Max Weber, but also one of the leading figures in the German feminist movement at the turn of the century, could not prevent herself from asserting that Simmel's image of women was still based on an unconscious projection on to the female sex of the qualities men did, or could not realize in their own daily lives (Simmel, 1985: 200–24; Marianne Weber, 1919: 95–133).

History is not a teleological process bound to end up with the abolition of the slavery and suppression of women. 'Most events are the vectors of competing, irreconcilable forces which might well have issued in other far different consequence or in no consequences at all. History is the actualization of the potential' (Gay, 1978). In this sense, there is indeed no grand narrative of modernity. What postmodernism has to offer is the idea of difference. If that would result in an alliance between postmodernism and radical feminism, our analysis of the nineteenth-century German feminist movement does not give much reason to be optimistic about the result of such a union. There is a fair chance that it would end up in furthering the structuring of the social world along the lines of gender instead of diminishing the gender division of labour and thought. For future generations of women this could be disastrous.

The power of signs and the signs of power

A positive contribution of postmodernism to women's emancipation can be discovered by pointing again to the resemblance of Lyotard's postmodernism to the Counter-Enlightenment and its offspring. Lyotard is of course not the first author who has criticized modernity. The intellectual strategies of discarding the grand evolutionary or dialectic narratives of progress, reducing all kinds of knowledge to local knowledge, that is time and culture bound, and widening the concept of 'knowledge' to include all forms of lived experiences, including visual and bodily ones, as well as relativizing all scientific knowledge, have been tried before. Representatives of this approach in the nineteenth and early twentieth centuries included Vico, Herder, Nietzsche, Dilthey and Bergson. In contemporary social science, postmodernism is related to (1) social constructivism in the tradition of Berger and Luckmann; (2) the sociology of knowledge as developed by Barnes, Bloor and Latour; and (3) the interpretive anthropology of Geertz. They all share to some extent Lyotard's rejection of the grand narrative of modernity and everything that rejection implies.

At the level of research, these types of theories act as a liberating principle. No longer hindered by the hierarchization of knowledge and civilization into a pyramid crowned by Western science and bourgeois culture, and no longer hampered by the idea of progress as the tread of reason through history, sociologists and anthropologists could begin to compare local cultures on a new base. They would no longer study them in order to determine which one is in some sense superior, with European culture as the ultimate yardstick, but in order to discover what they look like, how they order reality, how they feed on the local context and which system of symbols and practices they contain. Feminist anthropologists in these ways provide us with a great deal of knowledge about women's domains and women's cultures in non-Western societies (for example, Moore, 1988). Why should that type of research be restricted to non-Western societies? Why should it not be extended to Western society?

Socialization theory teaches us that differences between men and women are produced by cultural variation, and not by nature, while conversational analysis shows the differences in male and female patterns of conversational interruptions. However, as analyses of Western female culture, these are still rather superficial. We need a 'thicker description'. Here postmodernism, but this time of Baudrillard's brand, could prove to be significant. Apart from acting as a critic of modernity, postmodernism has a message of its own. The message is that the media are the message. Reality vanishes in an endless spiral of simulacra (Baudrillard, 1981). Landscapes are replaced by mediascapes. The body is invaded by signs written on it by the restless forces of advertising and publicity, which present us with selves we can or cannot present in everyday life. When he died Erving Goffman left an important heritage in *Gender Advertisements* (1979). That analysis revolves around the signs and symbols of (male) dominance and (female) submission.

Goffman showed us how women in relation to men have been depicted in inferior and/or child-like positions. In addition to Baudrillard, Goffman knew and warned us that advertisements are not reality. Nevertheless, he suggested that ads told us something about real life. The presentation of self to a certain extent is always the presentation of gender. This representation can be reduced merely to the use of power, but the implication could also be more subtle. For example, even in organizations where men and women are used to working together, certain power struggles, even when fought out in the presence of female colleagues, specifically belong to male cultures, like the telling of crude jokes or heavy teasing before the start of actual negotiations. Participation in this kind of impression management is taboo for the women. How to deal, for example, with men who show their power by leaning backwards in a chair with their thumbs in their armpit? What should women do if they want or have to portray similar shows of power? And what could be the female equivalent to crude joking or heavy teasing? Thus, women entering a masculine world both suffer from, and cause something of, a culture shock. Although it is less obvious, this discomfort also can be experienced by men when they enter the world of women. When approaching gender differences from this point of view, emancipation means getting to know the other's culture as well as learning how to transgress its borders in a civilized way. Emancipation means communication; it does not necessarily mean identification.

Apart from these interactional transgressions of boundaries, postmodernism teaches us how to play subversive games with traditional codes. In Canada, a perfume factory recently published an ad which showed a woman in her bloomers embracing a man from behind. In the Netherlands, van Gils, a producer of suits, advertises a naked boy in the arms of a fully dressed woman wearing a man's suit. In France, 'little Arthur' shows his knickers while being supported by a tall naked woman. We could regard advertising these disjunctions as sign crimes, namely the endowing of a woman with the attributes of the phallocentric man from the fifties. Should they be forbidden, or are they fun? Forbidden games are surely the most exciting. And which girls in the fifties ever dreamt of being able to adopt the signs and symbols of men?

There are many feminists who are not particularly enthusiastic about the advent of postmodernism, though sometimes for reasons other than mine. For those feminists, feminism is still a serious enterprise that will not tolerate postmodernism interfering with or mocking its goals. However, for the social sciences postmodernism seems to be nothing less or more than a fashionable disguise for good old theories like social constructivism, symbolic interactionism and critical cultural analysis. If this new outfit provides them with a new stimulus with respect to the analysis of gender relations, it has done its job already.

It is often alleged that constructivism, symbolic interactionism, critical cultural analysis and various forms of the sociology of knowledge, both on the level of morality and of political practice, could end in a sterile and passive relativism. Yet these approaches and postmodernism can also prepare the way for going beyond the simple issues of equality or difference. They allow us to replace unitary notions of 'women' and 'gender identity' by plural and complex conceptions of social identity. This is because postmodernism is more than merely a perspective on difference. It is the celebration of playful plurality. Thus, on the level of political practice, it becomes clear that the diversity of women's needs calls for different solutions (Fraser and Nicholson, 1988: 102–3). Being equal instead of being dealt with in a uniform way will then imply that women should be approached in a differentiated way, attuned to their various changing needs and identities. If this kind of alliance between postmodernism and feminism also enables women to replace the idea of a unitary notion of 'man' and 'male gender identity', with the idea of male identities being just as plural and complex as female identities (thus stimulating women to deal in a differentiated way with what once was called 'the opposite sex'), it could be a major step in breaking down the barriers between the sexes and creating a situation in which equality means the possibility of being.

References

Badinter, E. (1983) *Emilie ou l'ambition féminine au XVIIIe siècle*. Paris: Flammarion.

Baudrillard, J. (1981) *Simulacres en simulation*. Paris: Galilée.

Berlin, I. (1980) *Against the Current: Essays in the History of Ideas*. London: Hogarth Press.

Berger, P.L. and Luckmann, T. (1986) *The Social Construction of Reality: A Treatise in the Sociology of Knowledge*. Harmondsworth: Penguin.

Braidotti, R. (1985) 'U-topies: des non-lieux post-modernes', *Cahiers du Griff*, (5): 51–61.

Braun, L. (1901) *Die Frauenfrage: ihre geschichtliche Entwicklung und ihre wirtschaftliche Seite*. Leipzig: Verlag S. Hirzel.

Evans, R.J. (1976) *The Feminist Movement in Germany 1894–1933*. London: Sage.

Featherstone, M. (ed.) (1988) 'Postmodernism', *Theory, Culture and Society*, 5 (2–3).

Flax, J. (1987) 'Postmodernism and gender relations in feminist theory', *Signs: Journal of Women in Culture and Society*, 12 (4): 621–43.

Foster, H. (ed.) (1988) *Postmodern Culture*. London and Sydney: Pluto Press.

Fraisse, G. (1989) *Muse de la Raison: la démocratie exclusive et la différence des sexes*. Aix en Provence: Alinea.

Fraser, N. and Nicholson, L. (1988) 'Social Criticism without philosophy: an encounter between feminism and post-modernism', in A. Ross (ed.) *Universal Abandon? The Politics of Postmodernism*. Minneapolis: University of Minneapolis Press. pp. 82–104.

Frevert, U. (1986) *Frauengeschichte zwischen bürgerlicher Verbesserung und neuer Weiblichkeit*. Frankfurt am Main: Suhrkamp.

Frevert, U. (ed.) (1988) *Bürgerinnen und Bürger*. Göttingen: van den Hoeck & Ruprecht.

Gay, P. (1968–70) *The Enlightenment, vol. 2: The Science of Freedom*. New York: Random House.

Gay, P. (1978) *Freud, Jews and Other Germans: Masters and Victims in Modernist Culture*. Oxford/New York: Oxford University Press.

Geertz, C. (1973) *The Interpretation of Cultures*. New York: Basic Books.

Goffman, E. (1972) *The Presentation of Self in Everyday Life*. Harmondsworth: Penguin.

Goffman, E. (1979) *Gender Advertisements*. Cambridge, Mass.: Harvard University Press.

Kandall, T.R. (1988) *The Woman Question in Classical Sociological Theory*. Miami: Florida International University Press.

Knipnis, L. (1988) 'Feminism: the political conscience of postmodernism', in A. Ross (ed.), *Universal Abandon? The Politics of Postmodernism*. Minneapolis: University of Minnesota Press. pp. 149–67.

Lepenies, W. (1985) *Die drei Kulturen: Soziologie zwischen Literatur und Wissenschaft*. München/Wien, Hanser Verlag.

Lyotard, J.-F. (1979) *La condition post-moderne: rapport sur le savoir*. Paris: Editions Minuit.

Moore, H.L. (1988) *Feminism and Anthropology*. Oxford: Basil Blackwell.

Müller, D., Ringer, F. and Simon, B. (1987) *The Rise of the Educational System: Structural Change and Social Reproduction 1870–1920*. London/Paris: Cambridge University Press/Editions de la Maison des Sciences de l'Homme.

Owens, C. (1988) 'The discourse of others: feminism and postmodernism' in Foster, H. (ed.) *Postmodern Culture*. London and Sydney: Pluto Press. pp. 57–83.

Reijen, W. van and Kamper, D. (eds) (1987) *Die unvollendete Vernunft: Moderne versus Postmoderne*. Frankfurt am Main: Suhrkamp.

Ross, A. (ed.) (1988) *Universal Abandon? The Politics of Postmodernism*. Minneapolis: University of Minnesota Press.

Rowbotham, S. (1973) *Hidden from History: 300 Years of Women's Oppression and the Fight Against It*. London: Pluto Press.

Simmel, G. (1985) *Schriften zur Philosophie der Geslechten*. Frankfurt am Main: Suhrkamp.

van Vucht Tijssen, Lieteke (1989) *Auf dem Weg zur Relativierung der Vernunft*. Berlin: Duncker und Humblot.

van Vucht Tijssen, B.E. (1988) 'De vrouw en de moderne cultuur: Marianne Weber contra Georg Simmel', *Sociale Wetenschappen*, 31 (2) 83–103.

Weber, M. (1921) *Gesammelte Aufsätze zur Religionssoziologie*. Tübingen: J.C.B. Mohr.

Weber, Marianne (1919) 'Die Frau und die objektive Kultur', *Frauenfragen und Frauengedanken*. Tübingen: J.C.B. Mohr. pp. 95–133.

Wilson, E. (1977) *Women and the Welfare State*. London: Tavistock.

12

CITIZENSHIP IN THE SEMIOTIC SOCIETY

Philip Wexler

Citizenship

In this society, citizenship is an archaic term. It is not part of the language of everyday life. Its value for understanding this life is not evident either. Of course, political scientists and educators write about citizenship and citizenship education. Does citizenship have meaning outside of such an expert culture? Or, is citizenship a linguistic residue of the modern era that has passed?

Citizenship has a long cultural history. But its best hour was the eighteenth century, the Enlightenment. It was an emblem of modernity. The individual emerges from the hierarchical particularisms of collective status to the equal freedom of civil contract. Political freedom extends civil rights to a new, more autonomous reinsertion of the individual into collective membership. Citizenship requires a sovereign individual with the right and capacity to choose on abstract and universal rather than particularist grounds. It requires a 'bond' as T.H. Marshall wrote (1965: 101), 'a direct sense of community membership based on loyalty to a civilization which is a common possession.' Citizenship is built on rationality and solidarity.

Despite the extrication of the individual from traditional social status, then, citizenship has social requirements. Marshall describes the continuing socialness of citizenship by intertwining its evolution with capitalism's. The civil, political and social aspects of citizenship have evolved separately since the middle ages. 'For civil rights,' according to Marshall (1965: 103), 'were in origin intensely individual and that is why they harmonized with the individualistic phase of capitalism.' 'And civil rights were indispensable to a competitive market economy' (ibid.: 96). The twentieth century promises a fusion of these historically separate spheres, and an extension of citizenship to social rights and social equality. The social character of citizenship – its relation to capitalism and equality – is contradictory, however. Social citizenship is a vehicle for the 'modern drive towards social equality' (1965: 78). Yet, 'citizenship operates as an instrument of social stratification' (ibid.: 121). The principle of equality of opportunity can secure the legitimacy of inequality of result. In Marshall's words (1965: 127): 'Status differences can receive the stamp of legitimacy in terms of democratic citizenship provided they do not cut too deep . . .'

Citizenship is an archaic term because social evolution has not only gone beyond the social context of its origin, but also beyond the welfare industrial society in which Marshall placed it in dialectical relation to equality. Society has changed so much that the social prerequisites for citizenship – rationality and solidarity – seem to have disappeared. Simultaneously, the type of sociological analysis that Marshall practiced has faded; its place has been retaken by philosophy and cultural criticism.

I set out to show how citizenship is an ideology, a term left over from the past; even its prerequisites no longer exist. Contemporary society killed the Enlightenment's modern individual, first by commodification, then by communication. The death of the individual is the cornerstone of the poststructuralist philosophy that superseded liberal humanism. How can we think about citizenship when the autonomous individual has been decomposed into a network of non-synchronous signs? How can we talk about social belonging or solidarity when society is not being produced, but only simulated, when the social itself is seen as an ideology of the modern era?

Citizenship is a term in a much broader discourse of modernity, that even its staunchest defenders acknowledge has failed (Habermas, 1981). The conquerors on the academic and cultural fields are poststructuralism and postmodernism. As a practice, citizenship means autonomy, participation, influence (Thompson, 1970). These are all means of an individual/society relation that is dissipated on both sides; no individual, no society. Instead: semiosis, the structural law of value, the free play of signifiers without references (Baudrillard, 1984). The language and constituent practices, the social organization and values that made citizenship such an historically important sign have, by this account, all been replaced by a new culture, a new person, a new society (if I may use the old terms). Not only citizenship, but everything that made it possible to talk about and practice it are absorbed and disintegrated in a new social formation. It belongs to a bygone era.

I set out, in true postmodernist fashion, to underline this death of citizenship (Jameson, 1984b). But, I want to do more than that. I want to work through a poststructuralist, postmodern or semiotic vision to an analysis of the future of what were once the social bases of citizenship; I want to see what has happened to rationality and to solidarity.

I survey the semiotic society which has, I think, pushed sociological analysis into the language of culture. Yet, the cultural debates are about politics. The culture of postmodernism, in everyday practice and in academic theory, conceals practical action. By reifying culture, attention is diverted from institutional change and class dynamics. I explore these dynamics to show that what is missing for both Marshall and the postmodernists lies beyond the economic and the cultural. Rather than accept the 'end of the social,' I cut still deeper into the social. An everyday psychology of social classes opens the way to understand the meaning of inequality and of citizenship in a new age.

Semiotic society

In the future, language and practice may not have to be put in any context. A purely compositional ethic will demand attention only to the local, immediate process. I call this future a semiotic society because both the social organization of life and its representation are emerging together: postindustrial and poststructural. The term provides at least a condensation of the context that we still need because we are living in the operational, but decadent, period of modern society.

The change in social organization is what we know as postindustrialism or, more recently, informationalism (Luke, 1988). But the change is more than a shift in the basic energy of production, although it certainly includes that (Wexler, 1987: 153–63). It is a change in organizational forms, in modes of communication as well as in distribution and production. But it may be a change so dramatic that the very order of causal relation between energy and product is different. The product or artifact is quickly coded as a sign or image that gives it distributional value. This value is what energizes the investment of resources for re-production. Signs and symbols are the necessary value added to any traditional production process (Luke, 1988: 13).

The integration of signification and production may seem less far-fetched if we recognize that the major transformation of the production process earlier in this century was through the development of new means of distribution. Advanced industrialism is characterized by the integration of production and distribution. As Chandler demonstrated (1977: 376): 'Changes in transportation, communication and demand brought a revolution in the processes of distribution. And where the new mass marketers had difficulty in handling the output of the new processes of production, the manufacturers integrated mass production with mass distribution.' Metaphors of society as a cybernetic code driven by images (Baudrillard, 1984) represent an evolutionary leap in the production process. The regulation of consumption and production of demand have become so systemically important that their production system – advertising and the image – is transvalued from a derivative to primary condition of societal maintenance. If by 'real' we mean production, and if by 'hyperreal' we mean distribution, consumption and demand, then the power of signs is not a revolution in theory, structuralist or otherwise. It is a representation of an historic shift in the weighting of the internal elements in the means of production.

The semiotic society of course carries with it elements of the 'old,' modern society. Chief among these is modernity's insistence on differentiation. The rise of culturalism – the importance of cultural studies for critical social theorists and the more general success of literary over all kinds of social theory in the academy – is, in this sense, entirely modern. My view, expressed differently also by Finlay-Pelinski (1982), Jameson (1984a) and

Baudrillard (1984) among others, is to emphasize not the differentiation, but the integration, of society and culture. Poststructuralism in philosophy and literary theory, postmodernism in art and architecture, and the electronic revitalization of capital's motors via informationalism that simultaneously elevates distributional imaging are all part of the same emergent society of signs: the semiotic.

This new era is not just a great leap for advertising. Aside from the sectoral reallocation of capital investment, energy and labor, the traditional workplace site of production is reordered according to the flow capacities of electronic communication. Luke writes about an 'information society' (1988: 13): 'Data-intensive management techniques, robotized materials processing, numerically controlled tools, aesthetically intensified marketing tactics, and the telecommunication of images all now are used to add value in the production process.' Integration occurs within production as well as between production and sign-distribution.

Military research and practice is the most explicit example that production integration requires surrender of an earlier vision of the autonomous individual who chooses to act on the assumption of group membership or solidarity. In his research on the role of the military in technologizing education, Douglas Noble (1988) describes the integration of both human capacities and their conventional discipline representation in psychology into weapons systems. Weapons systems simulation not only becomes a model for educational systems, but effects the same primacy of the image that we ordinarily ascribe to advertising (Ewen and Ewen, 1982). Noble writes (1988: 16–17): 'Simulations in computer education are not simply instances of "spinoffs" of a military technology. They carry within them the military's preoccupation with the formalizable and fantastical, and they encourage a confusion of the real and the unreal.' Noble's description of the air weapons systems as 'cockpit cognition' presages a full integration, a 'comprehensive symbiosis of mind and machine' (1988: 25). Poststructuralism's 'death of man' is not imaginary.

Every separate domain of institutional society that was homogenized by a process of commodification (that now seems only the preparatory phase for a new kind of society) is integrated into the same structural logic of the relational value of signs. Baudrillard's (1984) new order of simulation, where (1984: 60) 'referential value is nullified, giving the advantage to the structural play of value,' the hyperreal simulacrum of the code, is sighted by specialized observers in literature, science, organizations, and politics.

Newman (1985) describes literary production and distribution as part of a market-dominated commodification which is precisely post-modern in the extent to which it is driven by and feeds on the 'inflation of discourse.' The meaning of literature changes. In science, the end of the grand metanarratives, according to Lyotard (1984), are part of a redefinition of the meaning of knowledge and the practice of science. Postmodern science is dissensual, temporary, destabilizing. As 'paralogy,' it looks toward the unknown rather than the performance-based efficacy of earlier narrativized science.

The typical form in which social practices are now organized has evolved from earlier technical, bureaucratic or professional systems of control. Beverly Burris writes (1988a: 1) that 'a new type of organizational control structure, technocracy, is emergent.'

> Technocratic organizations are characterized by a flattening of bureaucratic hierarchies, a polarization into 'expert' and 'non-expert' sectors, a substitution of expertise for rank position as the primary basis of authority, a de-emphasis on internal job ladders in favor of external credentialing and credential barriers, flexible configurations of centralization/decentralization, and other organizational changes.

She notes the analogue between technocratic organizational form and poststructuralist philosophy (1988b: 32): 'Technocratic systems increasingly assume a form of domination similar to that described by Foucault: a diffuse political technology of knowledge/power deeply embedded in institutions, technology, and the form of knowledge itself.'

Luke (1986–87: 62) adumbrated his more recent and extensive analysis of 'informational politics' by placing electoral politics within a 'spectacular' system of 'a society based on sign-circulation ... Elections, in fact,' he wrote, 'are now commodified and packaged modes of democracy; the exclusive signifier of democratic practice. Their forms and appearances, so closely monitored in all details on the news media, represent democracy, because that is all that is remembered from traditional democratic activity.' Further, 'Citizenship is now like being a fan, who votes favorably for media products by purchasing them, extolling their virtues, or wearing their iconic packaging on one's bill cap or tee shirt' (1986–87: 72).

I have emphasized the integration of institutional spheres in a semiotic society partly because analysis and debate about what I have called the social bases of citizenship can no longer envision, the way that Marshall did, interweaving the possibilities of citizenship with the evolution of society. Even social analysts who see development to the present as a social process, project the future culturally, cognitively, personally. Reflexive critics of modernity accept modernity's ethos of differentiation. Society and culture are divided. How can the social bases of citizenship be understood if the social has been sublimated by culture?

Cultural politics

Modernity is the era of differentiation. Postmodernity is typified by dedifferentiation, blurring of boundaries and disintegration of separate domains. Postmodernism and what it may mean for the lives of individuals in society is not ordinarily described as an aspect of the societal, institutional transformation that I have indicated as 'semiotic society.'

Postmodernism is seen first as a cultural tendency. Huyssen, for example, asserts (1981: 25) that 'the notion of postmodernism has become key to almost any attempt to capture the specific and unique qualities of contemporary activities in art and architecture, in dance and music, in literature and theory.' In modernity, high culture is separate from mass culture, and culture is separate from everyday social life. The Enlightenment establishes autonomous spheres of science, morality and art as institutionally independent activities (Habermas, 1981). The autonomous individual citizen belongs to the pattern of separation of activity domains, exemplified by institutional subdivisions of culture.

Contemporary postmodernism, on the other hand, is foreshadowed by the cultural avant-garde's attempts to 'subvert art's autonomy' and to *reintegrate* 'art and life' (Huyssen, 1981: 27). Fusion of spheres, domains and practices creates a world lacking independent, universal standards of judgment in morality, aesthetics, and science. Full contextualization dissolves the object, the subject, and therefore, any possibility of relation between them – no less one with the tension that motivates change. Without such a relational possibility, the concept of citizenship is meaningless.

Postmodernism is not a culture that creates a political individual characterized by critical distance, alienation, and reflexive rationality. Rather, the individual subject is decentered, diffused and fragmented. The absence of structural differentiation and relational tension results in a culture of flat, surface, ahistorical, eclectic textualism. Baudrillard understands what this means for the possibility of politics (1983: 19): 'Quite simply, there is no longer any social signified to give force to a political signifier.' The end of the social as a productive force leaves the sign world commodified and preeminent. Culture is the medium of social analysis because the postmodern world incorporates social relations and structure into the circulatory dynamic of the images that it created.

The importance of consumption for production leads to a new exaltation of the production of consumption itself (Baudrillard, 1983: 35): 'And it is the production of demand which has become crucial for the system.' The effect of this reversal is that the medium of its realization, 'mass media,' creates the culture of postmodernism on a scale far beyond the elite audience of any artistic avant-garde. Society becomes (1983: 83) 'a random gravitational field, magnetised by the constant circulation and the thousands of tactical combinations which electrify them.' In this view, 'The rational sociality of the contract ... gives way to the sociality of contact.' Culture absorbs society. The medium is the message. The simulacrum – signs and images, culture commodified – takes over social life (1983: 84): 'The hyperreal is the abolition of the real not by violent destruction, but by its assumption, elevation to the strength of the model. Anticipation, deterrence, preventive transfiguration, etc: the model acts as a sphere of absorption of the real.'

Television is the exemplar of postmodernism. Kroker and Cook argue that television is 'the real world of postmodernism':

> Our general theorisation is, therefore, that TV is the real world of postmodern culture which has *entertainment* as its ideology, the *spectacle* as the emblematic sign of the commodity-form, *lifestyle advertising* as its popular psychology, pure, empty *seriality* as the bond which unites the simulacrum of the audience, *electro-*

nic images as its most dynamic, and only, form of social cohesion, *elite media politics* as its ideological formula, the buying and selling of *abstracted attention* as the locus of its marketplace rationale, *cynicism* as its dominant cultural sign, and the diffusion of a *network of relational power* as its real product. (1986: 270)

There is a sense of matter of fact, taken-for-granted perpetual present in these accounts of postmodernism. But, for critical theorists like Habermas and Jameson, postmodernism is a political movement that occurs in the context of social history. Habermas (1981; 1985: 79–94) criticizes postmodernism as an element of contemporary neoconservative cultural criticism. Neoconservatives fault the individualization and specialization of the modern era for the absence of social cohesion, for the (Habermas, 1981: 7): 'hedonism, the lack of social identification, the lack of obedience, narcissism, the withdrawal from status and achievement competition . . .' While it condemns cultural modernity, this postmodernist conservatism ignores that a 'more or less successful capitalist modernization' is the result of social modernity. It rejects the culture of modernity, but denies that the society of modernity is the basis of the capitalist world they want to preserve.

More importantly, for Habermas, by negating the modernist, specialized culture of autonomous domains, by opposing the abstractness of modern art, architecture, and independence of aesthetics, all the various forms of postmodernism ultimately support social conservatism. For modernism, unlike both avant-garde and neoconservative postmodernism, fostered the autonomy of universal moral and aesthetic principles which provided a point of judgment of, or a standard of criticism against, the present.

Habermas wants to redeem the universal Enlightenment criteria, and to recast universal reason as 'communicative rationality,' in opposition both to cultural reactions against modernity and its dialectical negation by the administered society of instrumental reason. His criticism of the neoconservatives is that they (1981: 8) 'turn our attention away from such *societal processes*' (emphasis added). The alternative to both reified reason and postmodern conservatism is to establish social conditions for a practically embodied universal reason in everyday communication.

Jameson goes further toward recontextualizing postmodernism in society. On the one hand, he seems to accept the sublimation of the social by the cultural (1984a: 87): 'we must go on to affirm that the dissolution of an autonomous sphere of culture is rather to be imagined in terms of an explosion: a prodigious expansion of culture throughout the social realm, to the point at which everything in our social life . . . can be said to have become "cultural" . . .' But, on the other side, Jameson places postmodernism within a 'whole new type of society,' as a 'distorted figuration of something even deeper, namely the whole world-system of present-day multinational capitalism.' While it does have 'positive' aspects, postmodern culture finally so fragments the subject, breaks the chains of signification, transforms the world into 'sheer images,' supplants time and movement by the hyperspace of postmodernist anti-urban architecture, that the capacity of the individual mind to locate itself in social history is lost. The antidote for Jameson is a

(1984a: 92) 'pedagogical political culture which seeks to endow the individual subject with some new heightened sense of its place in the global system . . .' Socially recontextualizing postmodernist culture leads him to call for – as a political practice – an 'aesthetic of cognitive mapping.'

Habermas and Jameson do not overcome culture's sublimation of society. They bring cultural debates only part of the way back to social life and social practice. Habermas's communicative solution to the dilemmas of autonomy and integration understates the causal importance of current institutional changes in society. While he chastises postmodernism for culturalism, he underplays the institutional bases of contemporary boundary politics. Just as the autonomy of modernism is the effect of a societal process, so too is the cultural integration of postmodernism The fusion of separate spheres is a basic element in the current *corporatist* reorganization of society, an institutional change of scene from which postmodernism speaks (Wexler, 1988). Jameson's allusion to postmodernism as a (distorted) figure for multinational capitalism – even as part of capitalism's third stage – remains silent about contemporary *social class* relations.

In a recent paper, I have explored how corporatist driven processes of *deinstitutionalization* are changing the character of social knowledge, and what that may mean for social practice (Wexler, 1988). Here, I want to explore what the semiotic society implies for the changing character of individual identity, when set in the context of continuing differences between antagonistic social classes. Identity dynamics, like knowledge, are different in the semiotic society. If citizenship is to be a meaningful term again – to be expanded along with social evolution, as Marshall attempted – it will have to be recreated within this new social, class, and psychological reality.

Identity dynamics

The fissionary fragmentation of the self attributed to postmodernism is dealt with differently, depending on where the self is located in socially structured 'space.' While I know that we can say that there are more than two classes in society, and also that identity dynamics are overlapping rather than isomorphic, I think that there is a dichotomously bifurcating class difference in adaptations to semiotic society.

The first adaptation is that of the 'first' class, the so-called new middle class; the second is of that 'other' class comprised of youth, poor and unemployed people, minorities, domestically laboring women and the aged. The first class is engaged primarily in the identity work of ego bolstering; the other class works at ego binding. Neither class has any longer the motivation of libidinal 'desire' to act. But, in both cases, the character of relation to the semiotic apparatus of production/consumption creates needs.

The dichotomy is that in the emergent society, the older attributes of rationality and solidarity are recast and divided between the two classes.

Rationality now appears in the guise of a program of identity work centered on activities of strategic self-reconstruction. The earlier historical practice of reflexive rationality now appears as meaning-drudgery, and self-narratology. Under this heading fall all the activities of subjective gentrification: 'retro' cycling, narcissism so-called, restoration of temporal construction, activation of autobiographical memory (Barclay and Hodges, 1988). In the absence of collective memory of traditions, in conditions of simultaneous demand for orderly, serial practice – the administered world of modern corporatism – and flexible response to destabilizing sign circulation, the burden of identity labor falls toward the personal, narrative construction of a fictitious self order. Socialization is desocialized, deregulated, and like the more visible institutional apparatuses of the phase of industrial welfarism in decline, self-constructive practices are reprivatized. Absent desire is replaced by immediate, personal rational reconstitutive activities – self stories. Instead of libido, activity is motivated by the need for orienting thinking.

From this vantage-point, Jameson's 'cognitive mapping' is the quintessential practice of the first, new middle, class. Its version of rationality is a 'retro-reflection' or self-centered narrative reconstitution. All elements of the new middle class, cultural creators as well as rationalizers, work to draw cultural resources from the environment in the service of their restorative activity of constructing an orderly life, a life as a secure sequence or even, as a 'work of art.' Habermas's communicative rationality, despite its universal aspirations, reflects the same cultural capital dexterity that Gouldner vaunted in the new class. Reason is severed from solidarity as a class specific practice and reconfigured as the auto-reason of identity work.

The new middle class watches television, but television is not its first life. The 'other' class lives from television, which it repays by surrendering the capacity for attention that it produces. Here, the ego is more splattered than bolstered, drawing its strength not only from a direct dynamic relation to television, but through videated binding with its commodified television family of stars. This is citizenship's other basic ingredient, semiotic society's example of solidarity in a new key.

Television, as a class practice, is deadening and enlivening at the same time. On the one side, it works as a soporific, narcotizing to restfulness any vestige of instrumental thought or collective memory. Yet, it also injects a rush of visual inspiration. Image-energy, in the very fragmentation of its fractured juxtapositions, works as an awakening stimulus. It induces a discomforting tension that substitutes for the internally elaborated libido of desire. Tension 'escalators,' going in both directions, are the 'other class' parallel to orienting thought as the postmodern substitute for energizing desire. This is the class practice class and this the form of solidarity that Baudrillard and the epigoni of postmodernism conflate with all culture and society itself. If Habermas and Jameson willy-nilly choose the historical rationality of the new class, Baudrillard chooses this mediated, image-bound solidarity of the other class, which is a reciprocal absorption of energy between medium and audience.

The imaginary solidarity of the other class is itself a product of electronic communication devices that require the work of attending to realize their productive cycle. Attention becomes, under these conditions, a class resource activity or practice. The other class gives its attention in exchange for solidarity, while the first class collects and rationalizes communicative artifacts – 'signs' – in narrative self-reconstruction. Without attention, however, the communicative apparatus which produces artifacts for privatized, rationally-oriented self-collection is deprived of its energy. The class dichotomy of identity work is, by this account, not simply different and complementary, but mutually exclusive and antagonistic. The first self lives off the doubly-mediated attention of the other class.

Citizenship again

If we follow the social evolutionary logic of Marshall's argument, citizenship can be again expanded in this new social formation. To realize a 'semiotic citizenship,' the appropriation of the social ought not to be retrenched to the purely cultural or economic spheres. Rather, a new social psychology of identity work would become the socially deeper cut in which a new phase of citizenship might develop.

The real analytical problem of culturalist postmodernism – in whichever form – severed from semiotic society, is that it closes the door on societal evolution. Social recontextualization, however different the social may now appear, establishes a plane of dynamic possibility. What is the path from such a semiotic society toward a new model of citizenship that takes account of class psychology and identity work?

The simplest solution, but one that underestimates, I think, the tenacity of antagonist class difference, proposes the restoration of collective memory as part of a project of collective emancipation. Narration does not serve individual self-order, but the realization of new collective identities. The most historically viable current example is the women's movement. Collective reconstruction of shared individual life histories is the best example of expanding social rights to the level of identity work. How much postmodern collective identity projects touch the structurally reproductive energies fed by class division is not clear to me. Nor is it evident how feasible is the combinatory possibility of overcoming continuing class processes by unifying capacities for semiotic rationality and solidarity that now stand divided. Such an easy combination is precluded by the hypothesis of antagonistic, exploitative relations between classes. Of course, the old cry goes up for a revolutionary solution that would, at this level too, abolish classes, or short of that, urge an 'attention strike' of cultural insularity and obfuscation, a withholding of modern forms of labor by the other class.

All of these solutions imply for me a collective practice for new citizenship, an education to citizenship that goes beyond the divided paths of cognitive mapping and fantastic mesmerism. What education can this be is the next question. For now, citizenship will remain the appropriate sign of postmodernism and semiotic society – a restored sign artifact that may be recycled and used so long as it does not disturb contemporary society's profound need for superficiality.

A recent reportage (*New York Times*, September 30, 1988: B6) registers this condition succinctly:

> Mr Dukakis had a flat tire.
> Television camera crews scurried to the car. Dukakis aides were angry and flustered, mindful of the possible symbolism, nervous that the evening news would turn the right front flat tire into an Event . . .
> All was not lost. At a rally several hours later at Rutgers University, Mr Dukakis was introduced by a surprise guest.
> 'Hello, I'm Dan Quayle,' said Robert Redford.

References

Barclay, C.R. and Hodges, R.M. (1988) 'Content and structure in autobiographical memory: an essay on composing and recomposing of one's self,' paper presented at the Colloque Européen sur l'Identite: Construction et Functionnement, University of Provence, Aix-en-Provence, France.

Baudrillard, J. (1983) *In the Shadow of the Silent Majorities . . . or the End of the Social, and Other Essays*. New York: Semiotext(e), Inc.

Baudrillard, J. (1984) 'The structural law of value and the order of simulacra,' in J. Fekete (ed.), *The Structural Allegory: Reconstructive Encounters with the new French Thought*. Minneapolis: University of Minnesota Press. pp. 54–73.

Burris, B.H. (1988a) 'Technocratic organization and control,' unpublished.

Burris, B.H. (1988b) 'The transformation of organizational control and the emergence of technocracy,' unpublished.

Chandler, A.D. (1977) *The Visible Hand: The Managerial Revolution in American Business*. Cambridge, Mass.: Harvard University Press.

Ewen, S. and Ewen, E. (1982) *Channels of Desire*. New York: McGraw-Hill.

Finlay-Pelinski, M. (1982) 'Semiotics or history: from content analysis to contextualized discursive praxis,' *Semiotica*, 40(314): 229–66.

Foster, H. (1984) '(Post)modern polemics,' *New German Critique*, 33(Fall): 67–78.

Habermas, J. (1981) 'Modernity versus postmodernity,' *New German Critique*, 22(Winter): 3–14.

Habermas, J. (1985) 'Neoconservative culture criticism in the United States and West Germany: an intellectual movement in two political cultures,' in R.J. Bernstein (ed.), *Habermas and Modernity*. Cambridge, Mass.: MIT Press. pp. 78–94.

Huyssen, A. (1981) 'The search for tradition: avante-garde and postmodernism in the 1970s,' *New German Critique*, 22(Winter): 23–40.

Ingram, D. (1987) *Habermas and the Dialectic of Reason*. New Haven: Yale University Press.

Jameson, F. (1984a) 'Postmodernism, or the cultural logic of late capitalism,' *New Left Review*, 146 (July/August): 53–92.

Jameson, F. (1984b) 'The politics of theory: ideological positions in the postmodern debate', *New German Critique*, 33(Fall): 55–65.

Kroker, A. and Cook, D. (1986) *The Postmodern Scene: Excremental Culture and Hyperaesthetics*. New York: St. Martin's Press.

Luke, T. (1986–87) 'Televisual democracy and the politics of democracy,' *Telos*, 70(Winter): 59–79.

Luke, T.W. (1988) 'Screens of power: ideology, domination and resistance in informational society,' University of Illinois, in press.

Lyotard, J. (1984) *The Postmodern Condition: A Report on Knowledge*. Minneapolis: University of Minnesota Press.

Marshall, T.H. (1965) 'Citizenship and social class', in *Class, Citizenship, and Social Development*. New York: Anchor Books. pp. 71–134.

Newman, C. (1985) *The Post-modern Aura: The Act of Fiction in an Age of Inflation*. Evanston: Northwestern University Press.

Noble, D.D. (1988) 'Intelligence at the interface: American education and military man-machine technology,' unpublished.

Thompson, D.F. (1970) *The Democratic Citizen: Social Science and Democratic Theory in the Twentieth Century*. Cambridge: Cambridge University Press.

Wexler, P. (1987) *Social Analysis of Education: After the New Sociology*. New York, Routledge & Kegan Paul.

Wexler, P. (1988) 'Social knowledge as practice,' unpublished.

INDEX

Index compiled by Meg Davies (Society of Indexers)